ELEPHANT
-The Lady Boss

ECOLOGY AND MANAGEMENT

Dr. C.H. Basappanavar

INDIA • SINGAPORE • MALAYSIA

Notion Press

No.8, 3rd Cross Street,
CIT Colony, Mylapore,
Chennai, Tamil Nadu – 600004

First Published by Notion Press 2021
Copyright © Dr. C.H. Basappanavar 2021
All Rights Reserved.

ISBN

Hardcase 978-1-63781-619-6

Paperback 978-1-63806-676-7

Contents

Preface

Lord "Ganesha", the elephant headed God, perhaps came into being (created) since Vedic times- between fifth and second century A.D. to bring about cohesive understanding between two most powerful living species on earth-human *Homo sapiens* and the elephant *Elephas maximus*. Because of many a human like qualities in elephant, an excellent human-elephant relationship existed, since the human history. Elephant, the animal of fertility and good fortune required to be understood and loved by generations to come. The conservation of elephant, the "Flagship species" is synonym to biodiversity conservation, the most essential for human survival. The elephant conservation has, therefore assumed global significance.

The captivating experiences in the company of wild elephants in their natural domain, while working as field Director, Project Tiger, Bandipur Reserve and with the background knowledge of wildlife management, I found myself excited in writing the book, "Elephant-The Lady Boss", breathtakingly intelligent, noble and gentle giant of the Indian jungles, no matter what role she played or how man treated her, the 'Lady Boss' is truly a mirror of nature's heart. She is the gentler side of all forest gods- the beasts, I came across during my tenure there!

While I wrote the book, Elephant-The Lady Boss, I had not taken any partisan stand, nor was there activism but actively considerate to educate the readers about elephantine problems- "human-elephant conflicts". I have attempted to unearth causes and concerns about conflicting factors and chisel-out practical solutions against potential problems faced by elephant tribe, using results of my research work, more than a well wisher talking with authority on the subject.

The situation of elephant population in India was very critical, when the book, Elephant -The Lady Boss was written and published, as the first edition in 1998. With the judicial activism to rescue forests, wildlife and environment in the country, by preventing de-notifications of forests, deforestation and release of forests for non-forestry purposes and above all, throwing spanner into spokes of converting the country's forests into concrete and glass jungles, I now feel optimistic that the Indian elephant-the gentle giant, may well see through next millennium. The book, Elephant-The Lady Boss-Ecology and Management, is aimed to help Foresters, Wildlife Managers, Scientists, Judiciary and environmentalists, the world over to render service in favour conservation of elephant-race and to regain the lost glory. In view of the decision of the Government of India, declaring Indian elephant as, "The National Heritage Animal", the population gradually increased to 6000 in Southern India.

Simultaneously, timely action by the Government of India constituting the "Project Elephant", in conjunction with the "Project Tiger", country's elephant populations are found gradually on the increase @2.4% each year, over a period between 1998 and 2018, accounting for 8000 elephants in the forests of Southern India, while there are 30,000 elephants, spread over the forests of Indian subcontinent.

Apart from wild pachyderms, about 3,500 captive elephants that are managed by Zoological parks, temples and private organisations and individuals need to be protected, under the law.

Depletion of prime forests and disappearance of pasturelands around buffer zones along the boundaries of the elephant reserves, increased problems in elephant conservation have surfaced in recent years: Ever increasing human-elephant conflicts leading to more cases of crop damages, human deaths and consequent killing of elephants needed to be addressed. Impact of human killings is evidenced by granting of compensation to the tune of Rs.5.0 lakhs in each case, by the Government of Karnataka, in consultation of the Government of India, helped reduce confrontation to a considerable extent. Confrontations are also decreasing trend by effective protection providing Elephant-Proof-Trenches, Solar fencing and Steel-rail-barricades.

In view of country's increasing trend in elephant populations there is urgent need for extending number of elephant reserves, possibly by interconnecting island like forests by insulated corridors, to enable existing elephant populations interact in exchange of genes with distant populations, thus help improve the progeny. These essentially, require constant monitoring of elephant populations, through scientific management, followed by technological inputs. The crux of elephant management needed to be addressed are: Habitat management, rainwater harvesting, mitigating human-elephant conflicts, curbing poaching, and regulating livestock grazing. Relocating of tribal and rural populations outside the reserves, where necessary, is essential part of development of ecology by rewilding and restoration. It may be recalled here that "The Federal Government of United States (U.S. federal government) had expressed their concern about dwindling elephant populations of India on account of increased human-elephant confrontations and passed resolution to rescue them along with their habitats".

Chapter I

Bandipur Reserve - The Temple of Elephants

The richly varied Kaleidoscope of Bandipur Reserve is complemented by magnificent elephants, while gaur, sambar, chital, barking deer and four-horned antelopes are hunted by tiger, leopard and dholes (wild dogs). With its rich tropical mixed deciduous vegetation, the biodiversity of the reserve makes it a veritable paradise on earth. In such an ecosystem, inhabits the largest terrestrial animal, the elephant. It requires much larger space to range about, apart from huge quantities of fodder and drinking water for survival than any other large ungulates. The elephant is, usually, one of the first species to suffer the consequences of habitat fragmentation or destruction. Protecting our elephant, the "National Heritage Animal" with its rich habitat is asprecious as preserving our 'Tajmahal', the National Cultural Heritage of India.

Once, during her visit to Bandipur reserve, I asked my seven year – old daughter, Aarti, to list out her favourite animals. The immediate response, showing a high degree of imagination and deep interest concerning the vision of the animal kingdom; she came out instant answer – "the elephant, the giraffe, the camel, the horse". The younger the child, the larger are the animals selected as her/his favourites. Why did younger girls and boys express such a clear preference for animals, so much larger than themselves? Sub-consciously, no doubt, larger animals are the symbols of power of strength and to some extent they appear to possess human-like qualities of sociability and intelligence. The elephant, in particular, is known for its giant size, gentleness, far reaching memory and by nature, is a graceful and peace loving beast. It is eminently social, living in a kinship group, known as "matriarchal society". The animal of fertility and good fortune, it is gracefully, termed by the nick name, "the gentle giant of the Asian jungles".

My experience, while in the jungle is that those who respect the 'law of nature' always remain safe, of course, safer than our concrete jungles. In many parts of the country, *adivasis*, the aboriginal tribes are still living in the heart of the jungle, inhabited by wild animals, in particular, wild elephants. They have been living there, since the times of human history. But elephants and other wild animals rarely enter their hutments/ habitations. Animals will be moving around, but are rarely found raiding their *haadi*, the hamlet or cluster with huts. The elephants seem to have accepted local tribes as parts of denizens of the jungle and learned to coexist with them, as long as they didn't compete for their food While tribes have learnt to live with elephants. But the same elephants take every available opportunity to raid kitchen gardens and crops, if any, grown by tribes within the range of their distribution. Why?

The answer could be that elephants, being intelligent animals, do not like their food resources are robbed by growing crops on wild land or grass to be cut and removed. There are innumerable examples of farmers/grass cutters having been attacked and killed.

My association with nature and natural history of Bandipur reserve is a long standing one. Ever since, I joined the Forestry Service in the erstwhile Mysore State (now Karnataka), bought some leisurely time and visited Bandipur reserve. I was always fascinated by grace and nobility of the elephant moving majestically, like a tiny hill in those pristine and dynastic jungles. I, rather, fell in love with elephants; must have definitely been their body language that I was drawn toward them. It is a pleasure to see them in the wild, what a graceful gait and beautiful body language speak! It is the finest form of body language, associated with the body structure and gait that make the animal alluring. It was Kalidasa, who lyrically described graceful walk of a beautiful woman, as *Gajagamini*, relating to the description and admiration of elephant's graceful gait that is simply out of the world.

Straddling the south-west part of the Deccan plateau, the Bandipur Reserve is described as the "Temple of elephants". For me, it is a romance with the nature and an adventure to move in the company of elephants, but rarely with tigers. Tigers in Bandipur tiger reserve mostly eluded me. It is even today it's rarely I meet a tiger eye-ball to eye-ball. During my morning trekking in the jungle, I followed herds of elephants and found myself excited in watching their tender movements and playful activities. They tolerated my presence at reasonably safe distance, but never crossing line of critical (LoC) danger, may be due to the relationship having been intertwined between man and the beasts, since the dawn of human history. The Bandipur reserve, I describe as a paradise on earth for elephants, as much as, the hunters and the hunted. The reserve is also described as the level hunting ground for powerful predators, such as tiger, leopard and wild dogs and lesser known carnivores that prey on herbivores like gaur, sambar, chital and four horned antelopes. I soon realised, the specific role of the elephants in the reserve, as top order users of the habitat, but not included in the menu of big cats, like tiger and leopards. The presence of elephants in the reserve is described in ecological terms, as "Keystone species" that plays a critical role in maintaining the 'balance of nature', by way of regeneration and an indicator of health of the habitat.

1.1 Tropical Paradise

The Bandipur Reserve was constituted as the 'National Park' in the year 1974 by an act of legislation. In the meantime, 'Project Tiger' that was launched in the year 1973.

The Project Tiger envisages preserving wildlife right from autotrophs to heterotrophs, in fact, the whole of biotope/biome with the tiger placed at the top. Concurrently, the reserve also boasted of its large elephant population, in addition to large herds of gaur among the big herbivores. In fact, Bandipur is known for elephants, though it is managed under Project Tiger. One can't miss an elephant at any point of time.

1.2 Operation Elephant

The geographical area of the reserve was, subsequently, increased to 880 sq km after a decade of success story. The achievement of success came to be known as the "crowning glory" of the dying species, the elephant. The Project Elephant was undertaken by the government of Karnataka with the financial support of Indian Government. The eco-restoration was the topmost objective in the priority list of the planning process under the Operation Elephant.

The Bandipur reserve has since, been managed both under 'Operation Elephant' and 'Operation Tiger' on sound principles scientific wildlife management techniques and demonstrated to the world, the important achievements – bio-ecological recovery, environment educational recognition, technological realisation and cultural values. Improved biodiversity, assured water supply for a longer period of summer season and afforded security, were mainly responsible in the increased elephant population along with other herbivores.

The gradual recovery in elephant population, evidently, helped in providing safe habitat for elephants, as much as to the potential prey population of tigers. The unique feature of the management of Bandipur reserve, under the 'Project Elephant', is that the tigers are managed in association with the elephants, since neither of them could be managed in isolation.

1.3 My Maiden Visit to the Reserve

On that wintry morning, I set out into the elephants' own country of Bandipur, at the first call of the *koel*, in order to introduce myself to "Forest Gods" – the wild animals and birds. I was also keen in visiting some of the landscapes and features, such as distribution of ponds, tanks, streams, grasslands and salt-licks. I was accompanied by Kala, an experienced tribal tracker. A Jungle fowl started calling intermittently with its guttural notes somewhere from the nearby bush, perhaps, to express its happiness over the dawning of yet another new day. I was, as a matter of fact, a hunter without a gun; a hunter of peace and harmony in that pristine jungle. A camera with tele-lens and a pair of binoculars were my weaponry.. These were my usual armoury, when I was amidst the denizens of the jungle. While, I gazed and learnt about wonders of nature, I zoomed in my camera to shoot and express my feelings. I was fascinated indeed to spend much of my time with the nature than the natural history.

The first rays of the morning sun, as I kept watching, kissed the dew covered tree canopy. Oh! Yet another day had just begun in the jungle, I called out!! Eventually, every moment in the jungle surprises with many wonders to tell their stories. It was a misty morning though, the pencil beam of the young sun pierced through the thick green foliage. The warmth of the sun fuelled in me and spelled hopes of good luck for the day.

Rays of tender sun piercing through the jungle canopy, kissing the forest floor to rejuvenate activities of all life forms)

"Look here, *Saar*", Kala who accompanied me invited my attention, as he bumped over a heaps of defecation, accompanied by urination at a tri-junction point of jungle roads. The place overlooked vast expanse of grass land with the backdrop of bamboo brakes. The scat marks were freshly dropped, as I could see them still steaming. Obviously they were dropped by a pack of wild dogs, just few moments prior to our arrival. Such heaps of defecation at a common place by wild dogs are called, "community lavatory". Wild dogs select such vantage spots to defecate, so that the scat marks stand out as their territory markings. I asked Kala to count them. He could count nine droppings that gave me the clue of their total number in the pack. On examination of a shit, it was revealed that their previous kill was of sambar doe. Wild dogs may have been waiting there for their next quarry. Our approach seemed to have disturbed their strategy of potential hunt, forcing them to move away. Asking Kala to collect sample of faeces for laboratory examination, I treaded fast along freshly beaten elephant path, meandering through the bush jungle. I waited for a while at the edge of the bush jungle for Kala to join me.

"Which of those wild animals, men and women of tribal communities fear the most"? I asked Kala on his joining me.

Kala politely and resolutely declared, "It is *Kadaane*", the wild elephant.

"Why do you say only the wild elephant?" I questioned him inquisitively, "While there are, in the forests, other beasts such as tiger, leopard and sloth bear which are believed to be fearsome?"

Kala, an old forest guard of Betta Kuruba tribe quipped, "It is the fear created in the minds of forest dwelling tribes and its nature of steadfastness against threat and so also impending danger from man". He added, "The elephant, has been able to hold on to its grounds, since the dawn of human history". He went on to add, "Even forest guards, who are on a routine forest protection job, including lumbering men, bamboo-cutters in the forests are very much scared of elephants;but encounters and proximity of tiger and leopard, Kala asserted, "did not pose much of an anxiety and danger, as those of pachyderms".

His statement, as a forest guard, was based on his long association with elephants and experiences in the jungle craft.

1.4 Architectural Genius

As I was recovering from the awe-inspiring sight of the morning sun that brightly illuminated the forest canopy, Kala escorted me through a thick bush. He slowed down and pointed at a cob-web, architecturally woven across our path. The spider was sitting pretty, ready in its colourful dress at its breakfast table, as if to announce, "don't be afraid of my charm! Don't get alarmed of my colours!! Crawl into my beauty parlour!!!". The web was an unique architectural marvel, the strategy of its survival.

I explained to Kala, "Copulation in spider is a complicated politics of her own. The male does not have any special anatomical apparatus for introducing his sperm directly into the female. Instead, he spins a small silken napkin. On this he deposits a drop of sperms from the genital pore on the underside of his abdomen and sucks it up with his palps, feeler-like organs on either side of his head. He must then thrust one of these into the female's genital pore and squirt out the sperm, like liquid being expelled from a pipette. His main problem, however, is not how to transfer the sperm, but how to get close enough to do so without losing his life. His mate, after all, is armed with murderous poison-laden fangs, how can he let her know that he wishes to be a mate and not a meal? One must watch the entire drama of hide and seek of female and male spiders in most complicated system of copulation".

My explanation seemed to have no impact on Kala; it was like Greek and Latin to him, as he simply nodded his head in utter confusion attempted to distance from me. "Since how long are you working in these forests?" I asked Kala, to confide him.

"Since my boyhood *Saar*", came the quick answer. "I was born and grew up in these forests. My father worked here as *mahout* in charge of an elephant. I used to assist him in the upkeep of the elephant and its feeding. He died during widespread plague, while still in service. I was given a job of grass-cutter/*kawadies*. on compassion grounds. I know nook and corner of these forests. Later, I was given a job as forest guard", Kala narrated his brief resume.

For me he became moving book of jungle crafts, since then.

1.5 Elephants' Own Country

The landscape of Bandipur national park, the paradise on earth, serves as haven for herds of elephants and forms part of the Nilgiri Biosphere Reserve. The NBR is spread over an area of 5,520 sq km and is one of the largest conservation expanses of India. Bandipur reserve also forms a corridor link amidst adjoining protected areas(PAs), such as, Madumalai national park and Tiger Reserve of Tamilnadu state, Wayanad (north & south) Wildlife sanctuaries of Kerala state and Nagarahole national park and Tiger Reserve and Biligirirangan Hills Tiger Reserve of Karnataka. The rugged and beautiful landscape of Bandipur reserve is an eco-biological refuge and the most conducive home for elephants. This biodiversity retreat provides them, undoubtedly, the best habitat with its tropical mixed deciduous forest types interspersed by grasslands and bamboo glades. The quality of vegetation and its regeneration potential is marvellous and provides boundless opportunities in the reproduction of various ungulate spp. Elephants and tigers, though almost equal in strength and born adversaries, are able to share the common landscape of Bandipur. There is no conflict between them, concerning niche, food and water. While the tigers hunt on their potential prey base, the elephants feed on vegetation, such as grass, browse, bamboo and tree bark of selected species*.

Though elephants are not a potential prey species in the menu of tiger, occasionally, attempts are made to kill elephant babies, just to exhibit his/

her brutal superiority. Elephants have, as their survival strategy, developed a fighting spirit against tigers and tend to keep them at bay. Similarly, tigers' survival strategy is that in order to keep their cubs safe from possible attack by elephants have developed a power of counter attack.

While, wild animals enjoyed their share of earth planet at Bandipur reserve, I did observing them closely, during inspections and zoomed in my camera to capture every movement of their activities in their natural set up.

1.6   Pristine Nature's Bounty

Bandipur National Park, being dynamic in its floral and faunal composition, lies between North latitudes 12°3'30" and 12°54'17" and East longitudes 76°7' and 76° 52' 40". The terrain is undulating and broken by chains of rolling hills with vast stretches of valleys that are sprinkled with tiny meadows and seasonal water courses. The highest point, the "Gopalswamy Hills", also described as Kamaladri is at a height of 1,454.5 m. It is aptly, called mountain of clouds (also called Venugopala or Govardhanagiri of the South), always sucking biting winds from the funnel like the sun kissed valley below. The place commands panoramic bird's eye view of vast stretch of green valley. One can also have from the same point a contrasting picturesque overview of the grey valley of cultivated fields of the civilised world in the opposite direction. Nearby the temple is the Forest Guest House built during the time of Maharajahs. The hill is shrouded by thick fog for most part of the year and hence, the name 'Himavat Gopalswamy Hills'.

The place is regularly haunted by herds of elephants, which some times enter temple premises for some tit-bits left behind by devotees. The hill had fortifications all round and was called Bettada Kote, but alas, only traces of ruins are seen now. Bettada Kote was ascribed to one "Somana Dandanayaka" *Palegar*, the chieftain of the region. The Bettada Kote *Palegar*s were said to be related to Mysore Royal dynasty and Katti Gopalraje Urs was the father-in-law of "Krishnaraja Wadiyar II". Atop the hill, another tall rocky hillock to the west of the temple, at a distance are the holy ponds, like Gopala tirtha, Shankha tirtha, Chakra tirtha, and Gadha tirtha; while in the lower valley of the reserve, Hamsa tirtha, Tottilu tirtha, Panakada kola, Saranga tirtha and Padma tirtha are reported to have been located. Nearby Hamsa tirtha is a small cave called Sadhu gavi – the cave, where this author had once seen a tiger resting during a trekking expedition.

An aerial view from Chamnahalla Forest Lodge, atop the hill, a few km away from Gopalswamy hills, commands a breath taking scenic beauty of vast expanse of green canopy, as far as one can see. It is nothing but the "Green Ocean" spread over from horizon to horizon.

The river Moyar, at the eastern edge of the reserve, cuts into a grand picturesque gorge with vertical fall of 260 m presenting the second deepest and the most beautiful landscape in the whole of India with the famous Nilgiris – the blue Mountains as the back drop. The rain water from Nilgiris cascades down the Moyar River. The seasonal Kekknahalla forming the frontier line between Bandipur reserve and Madumalai reserve flows down the Rolling-rock falls before joining the slow flowing Moyar River, down below.

While in the western edge of the reserve, a view across the Kabini reservoir, at the site of erstwhile Mastigudi, the Goddess that was worshipped in invoking the blessings, before the commencement of erstwhile *Khedda* operations, presents the most beautiful, pristine and an unique scenic spot in the whole of the country!

An ancient type *anicut* – the stone barrage, locally known as Sulekatte, said to have been constructed across the river Nugu, near Lakshmanapura during the time of Heggadadeva, *Palegar*, the chieftain. The river Nugu, the tributary of Kabini River, flows down from South to North and divides the Bandipur reserve into almost equal halves. The *anicut* is located inside the Reserve, providing perennial supply of drinking water for elephants and other wildlife.

There are good number of tanks and ponds, some of them perennial provide drinking water for the resident animals and birds. There are also seasonal water bodies that go dry in the height of summer. The elephants in the reserve keep drifting from place to place within their home range in order to introduce these water bodies to their toddlers. Being a rain-shadow area, the Bandipur reserve gets scanty rains from both the monsoons; the south-west monsoon from June to September with fairly heavy precipitation in July and the north-east monsoon, comparatively, with light rains in October-November that help the park to remain green for a longer time. The clouds suck dry, as they move towards the eastern parts of the reserve reducing the quantum of rain fall during south-west monsoon. The rain-fall varies from 1200 mm in the western parts to 900 mm in the eastern parts of the reserve.

The climate is equable, with mean temperature of about 24°C (75.2°F) and even during the cold weather the days are sunny, except when they are windy and rainy; the nights are cool. The maximum temperature is around 29.5°C (85°F) and the minimum of about 18.5°C (65.5°F). The sun is strong in the height of summer and the forests dry up, turning dusty from February to April. If the reserve receives some stray heavy showers during December-January, the reserve remains green, preventing possible mishaps from wild fires in hot season. The relative humidity drops down to 42% from that of 70% during November-February. With two to three good pre-monsoon showers during April-May, the park would come alive again. Gathering monsoon clouds during June would eventually end the desiccation.

Yes, continuing the day's trekking, accompanied by Kala, I realised the tender morning sun had brought hopes of next meal for all the diurnal creatures – the small and the mighty. The continuous wild piercing shrieks, "brain-fever, brain-fever" raising from low to high pitch of the Brain fever bird from a distant tree attracted my attention; continuous and reverberating harsh calls kept pestering me. Meanwhile, there emerged a herd of gaur from their morning siesta at the distant meadow. Experiencing ebony beauty of those beasts, we waited for a while, enjoying the warmth of the rising sun.

"A perfect harmony between the beasts and the green meadow was well established", I announced, while clicking my camera.

"Of late, an arrogant assumption of human superiority has led to destruction of biodiversity – both plant and animals from their habitats. It is really shocking to see people sneaking into the reserve and carry out unlawful activities like smuggling timber, bamboos, fire wood and poaching elephants for ivory and other herbivores for meat. We better rescue these natural wealth for the future; rescue from threshold of extinction. While attempting to rescue natural resources, we must understand that extinction is not an event, but a process; we can't stop it. We can, however, slow down the process by effective protection and scientific management. They are within our reach; not until we are lost do we begin to understand ourselves?" I declared.

Kala simply nodded his head in affirmative.

1.7 Forest Fantasy

The gaur herd on seeing us waiting, they entered thicket, as if to make way for us. Thanking them to have obliged us we crossed their way silently. As the day unwound itself and wintry mist started melting fast, the bright hues of the Glory lily *Gloriosa superba*, came alive on our way. My eyes could not be trusted for the splash of vivid colours in that golden light, spreading fast the forest valley. The most beautiful flowers of the Indian jungles were bracing the sun to outdo him in the rich interplay of colours. It was truly, a "Forest fantasy" – a feast for the eyes and a treat for the soul.

In all its glory, the nature often gets a chance to show off her grandeur with marvels of beauty and intelligent activities that go on every moment of which we have no knowledge. A melodious song, "One more bottle-one more bottle", of Racket-tailed drongo from a tall rosewood tree standing in the valley attracted my attention. By the time I raised my binoculars to focus on that incredible bird, it glided away like waves, this time uttering different musical notes.

Mid-morning turned the golden light in to light warm when the mist over the forest valley had thinned out. "A perfect day indeed", I admired. There it was, the 'Coffee locust grasshopper', in his brilliant coat of many hues, collecting his thoughts for the day, as if to say, "be quick with your click!" And before I could say, "thank you", off he was.

As we kept ambling towards a nearby water body, sweet fragrance of the forest caught my olfactory sense and led me to a blazing tree, called 'Flame of the forest'. At the edge of the water hole, a carpet of flowers splashed the floor and the tree with bright orange colour, impregnated with nectar attracted my attention. The ground underneath that short tree was also sticky, as nectar droplets from the flowers still continued. Amidst flowers that carpeted the forest floor, to our utter surprise, fresh foot-prints of a sloth bear drew our attention. Obviously, it was the business of a sloth bear that had climbed up the tree of Flame of the Forest *Butea monosperma* and shaken the branches to feed on flowers. The hairy unpredictable omnivore, perhaps, took to heel on seeing our approach.

You will never miss a Flame of the Forest tree in full bloom, brightly-lit orange coloured flowers of tiger-claw shaped, clinging to the bare tree was a feast to the eye. The tree provided a dramatic relief to the lush green canopy of the forest. I plucked a flower and chewed it. Yes, it tasted like "kissing the first woman I loved!"

Super elephant that acts as the 'Keystone Species' of the Indian jungles.

By then, the enchanted world unfolded the most elegant of all land creatures. A master of fascinating world of web artist – the Cat-leg spider was almost missed from my sight. Kala called out pointing at banded pattern of creature on a tree-trunk. The tiny creature was found clung and perfectly camouflaged against the tree-bark. I identified it, 'Cat-leg spider', dressed in his formal black and white and perfect in table manners, he was all set for his brunch.

"It is a delightful and an exciting world of flora and fauna, one could experience in the jungle-trails of good and bad overnight events. The drama of ever changing life on earth in that complex forest ecosystem revealed every action and reaction that goes on every moment" I declared.

Talking about the biological classification of vegetation types of Bandipur reserve, it has been designated as "Southern Tropical Mixed Deciduous Forest Type", featuring a varied ground flora, including glades of short grass and belts of bamboos. Satellite imagery analysis has revealed occurrence of accurate extents of vegetation ranging from Moist deciduous, Dry deciduous, Semi-evergreen sholas with grassy blanks, scrub jungle, grasslands and Bamboo brakes including riverine gallery forests.

Elephant Habitat –managed by elephants themselves by seed dispersal.

While we continued our brisk walk, Kala came to a jerking halt and called out, pointed at a trail of fresh pug marks of a leopard that were left behind the previous night. The trail of leopard pug marks had served Kala as a visiting card. He identified them belonging to the territorial male. As I started making notes, as to their size, shape and stride of pug marks, I had a strange feeling of being watched by some third eye! I looked around. There he was on the tree top, the 'queen of the swingers' – the Bonnet monkey. He blushed, for he was caught spying on us, while other members of the troupe were busy in feeding on wild fruits, as part of menu in their breakfast.

"Wild animals are the best teachers of the natural law. They simply obey the natural law, lest their death is imminent. We, humans have to learn the law of jungle from wild animals, before venturing into the jungle. Drama of biological survival is staged in nature every minute; in the process, fights and deaths are inevitable; butSurvival is not guaranteed in the wild. It is guaranteed only by tactful living", Kala advocated.

As I was about to endorsing his wisdom backed by experience, the calm of the mid-morning was shattered by an alarm call of a peacock. The flamboyant and self-appointed sentry of the forest had warned against the lurking danger around to the denizens of the jungle. I paused…! The atmosphere was charged!! I had one sweeping glance of the horizon. Then I spotted the peacock sitting over an ant-hill. It got panic and disturbed. The law of the jungle prevailed. For me, it meant, perform or face a comprehensive wipe out. I prepared myself mentally and physically to expect the unexpected. I could raise my body temperature through a process of meditation while standing still. One would never know what was in store in that lonely jungle. Kala also stood firm, tensed up, listening to jungle language.

1.8 The Signal

Catching the signal in the direction of excited peacock's gaze, slowly and deliberately, I fixed my sight on catchy glimpses, silhouetted against the horizon. Yes, confirmed as it was, the predator on its morning prowl. I stood transfixed as I spotted, rosette 'sphinx' – the leopard! "Oh, there he was, queen of cats", I exclaimed! Kala reconfirmed my identification of that big cat.

It was, as though, I had an appointment with the leopard on that wintry morning. Asking Kala to keep an eye on the movements of the big cat, I crawled and hid myself behind a bamboo bush. The leopard snarled at me staring in my direction, as if to say, "You are an uninvited guest at my breakfast table". Unmindful of his disliking of my presence,

I stayed put and looked through the binoculars. There laid a kill, proudly guarded by the owner beneath the leafless Teak tree; the victim seemed to be Sambar doe. Broken evidences around scene were corroborated and led me to arrive at a conclusion that the kill was made just before dawn. The scene had justified the jungle law, "beauty and cruelty are part of the nature". After all predation is a way of life and a survival strategy for these carnivores. I soon realized that he was oblivious of my presence. I relaxed and gazed in wonder at the rich rosette coat of the magnificent feline. Though it was not possible for me to shoot with my camera, I felt satisfied that I had undertaken a stunning journey in the world of hunters and the hunted.

Forest pool under total control of elephant herd; until elaborate of rituals, like drinking, dip-shower, mudsling followed by body dusting are complete.

The very sight reminded me of slogan, "the wildlife reserves may hold no gold, but they are loaded with riches just the same, if they are left alone". This was literally true in respect of Bandipur National Park, which lived on its own songs and sounds.

It was a perfect sunny day indeed. "Eerie-hoo; Eerie-hoo", shrill cry of the avian predator, the Crested hawk eagle, broke the stillness of the jungle air. The eagle was attracted by the unexpected bounty of the remains of the leopard's kill. But the carnivore lifted the kill, almost his body weight and climbed up the tree to protect its hard earned meal. Among the eyes in wait was the pair of jackals to arrive for "scrap business" with 'swift fox leap'. Leftover fortunes of the kill served as next meal for them. It is said, in nature, those who eat survive, but not necessarily who kill. As the air borne vultures started descending one by one, it was time for me to leave the scene.

Raised trunk in elephants is said to shower fortune and wisdom.

Makhana-tuskless male elephant with large head and powerful trunk to compensate absence of tusks in combat. Compare it with tusked males the Bachelor group.

1.9 Bandipur Sanctuary with Glorious Past

A journey back in time, as revealed by historical records is that the need to conserve wildlife was realized in the princely state of Mysore, right at the commencement of the 20th century. The Mysore Game and Forest Preservation Regulations were enacted in the year 1931, when 90 sq km of game sanctuary was set up. Subsequently, Venugopala wildlife park was constituted in the year 1941, extending the area over 800 sq km. The park was named after the deity of the shrine, atop the hill, Venugopala, worshipped by the former Maharajahs of Mysore. The 'sanctum sanctorum' over 60 sq km of the wildlife park had long been famed for its faunal richness and in it, no commercial forestry was permitted. Despite its dominantly deciduous complexion the park still holds many magnificent tree species. Sculptured relics and idols, existence of domesticated trees like Ficus, Tamarind and abandoned paddy fields seen all over the park, indicated that the aboriginal clans lived in these forests hundreds of years ago. They prayed fire-god, rain-god and earth-god to keep them safe from harmful creatures and epidemics that haunted them periodically. But still, there existed a powerful partnership between the aboriginal races and the nature.

As we wade back into the history of Bandipur forests, hunting of elephants, Gaur and large predators had played its own setback, during the princely regime. Erstwhile Maharajahs of Mysore and their royal guests used Bandipur forests as their potential *shikar* ground for large tuskers, magnificent gaur and record size tigers. Even after the Venugopala wildlife sanctuary was established Maharajahs shot many tigers and tuskers. A 'Tiger Block', comprising of eight sq km was reserved for this purpose, at the eastern sector of the sanctuary. No reliable figures, however, are available as to number of tuskers, tigers and gaur shot during the times of erstwhile Maharajahs.

"We the present generation feel betrayed as our forefathers failed to realise the values of natural resources. They did many things without the forethought before they realised, what was in store for the future. Let's learn from their mistakes and do the right things at the right time by exploring the past, experiencing the present and visualising the future. We have the driving force in planning for the future, backed by scientific and technological innovations. Let us put them to proper use in the conservation of biodiversity – the flora and fauna. Conservation, however, must become more participative", I recounted.

The rising sun had burnt away the mist. My eyes had often feasted on the riot of colours, the many-hued flowers of the Indian jungles. Hardly ten cm tall, ground orchid proudly presented a dazzling spectacle lending its own grace and charm, which alas, only few eyes could enjoy! Enchanted nature, by now, had unfolded most elegant of its biodiversity. The dynamic nature frequently gets chance to show off with its vivid colours, cascades, waterfalls, heavenly songs of birds and the like. The fine tuned ecosystems of Bandipur reserve – a paradise on earth, are a living museum. Strikingly, with its most captivating landscapes, the reserve is, described as a "Jewel" in the national parks system. Impressed by the grandeur of the unspoiled terrain, I could find the relationship between man and the nature was indivisible.

1.10   Living in the World of Hunters and the Hunted

With all the antecedents since morning, evidently, I felt one with the nature, loving and caring. There came "Ghoo-goo-goo; Ghoo-goo-goo", calls of the Crow-pheasant from a nearby bamboo glade, perhaps, inviting his mate. The call of this attractive and shy bird was an indication of rising heat in the jungle. A nearby chital herd intently watched a pack of *dholes* (Asiatic wild dogs) that emerged from a bamboo brake. The body language of the pack had given chital an indication that they did have their meal and not in a mood to hunt around that time. Looking at their belly, I also could judge, they were returning to their den after a successful hunt. They were nine in the pack,. It is perhaps, the same pack whose community lavatory was spotted in the morning. The chital stag followed by its harem challenging the pack by shrieking calls in synchronization of its stamping front foot, disappeared in the thicket.

"The strategy of the hunt by the pack of *dholes* is remarkably tactful, but ruthless. They are most efficient in bringing down their quarry. Using a high-pitched whistling calls, the pack (comprising as many as 9-15) will isolate an animal from a herd and pursue it relentlessly until it is over powered. At this point, an all-out assault will be launched by the dogs on hapless victim from all sides, one hanging on to the muzzle, another its hind quarters, while others attempting to rip open the soft underbelly to disembowel, so that each of them gets its pound of flesh. Their attack, though looks inhumane to watch, there is no element of cruelty attached to it under the law of nature. After all, the food will be shared among all the members of the pack, even among pups, including the Alfa female, for whom food will be regurgitated, when the pack returns to their den. In nature, the wild dogs play a critical role in weeding out diseased, weak or ailing individuals from a herd ungulates, thus furthering natural selection. In the economy of killing and deaths of ungulates nothing goes waste under the jungle law. While wild dogs work for the welfare of prey animals, as prey animals for the welfare of dogs", narrated Kala.

"One of the most endearing sights in the Indian jungles is the Chital, an inimitable combination of grace and beauty, prancing around sheer poetry in motion. Razor-edged sharp sight is the best means of defence in chital. Always alert, the chital herd bounds off to safety in a blink of an eye. Predators and prey animals have evolved indigenous disguise in nature over millions of years of evolution. But in the end, the most proficient only survives in the deadly game of prey and predator", Kala disclosed continuing his narration as a tribesman.

Alerted by the sudden disappearance of the chital herd from the scene, wondered I looked in the opposite direction. There, we sighted a twosome of Betta Kuruba trackers on their daily perambulation in the forest. They were approaching a strategic point to place a green twig – an evidence for having gone round a block of the park allocated to them to check movements of poachers/smugglers.

"Men of Betta Kuruba tribes of Bandipur reserve are a 'walking encyclopaedias' of the jungle. Some of them whose ancestors were hunters and food gatherers are a good trackers even today. Highly experienced tribesmen can do tracking of wild animals in the jungle, as it is highly specialized job. I am of the strong opinion that traditional tracking should continue regularly, so as to gain more and more field knowledge on secrets hidden in the depth of the jungle. An important and valuable information about wildlife could be gathered by tracking regularly in the jungle. Of course, tracking involves ability to protect oneself apart from courage. Tourists rely on efficient tracking, while trackers provide them the safety and the satisfaction. Tracking is also a critical tool in the conservation of wildlife. Many trackers risk their life in wildlife protection against poachers. Traditional knowledge in tracking should be passed on to the future generations", I suggested to Kala.

The day was already heating up. "Elephants might be beginning to move for a drink", suggested Kala.

"Kala could make a good guess of elephants' possible intension of paying a visit for water at this hour of the day. Yes, let's move to a nearby waterhole and wait for their arrival. We must take our position before the arrival of elephants", I declared.

While we walked briskly, Kala cautioned me stating that in a jungle, especially, inhabited by elephants, one must be constantly on the look out for spying eyes to protect self. It is said, 'in a jungle, if you see one animal, hundred animals will have seen you'. Elephants, particularly, sub-adult males are cantankerous and mischief mongers. Unprovoked, they might emerge from unknown bush and charge from behind, sensing danger from intruders like humans. But for elephants, one could be safe from other animals, like tiger or leopard, as long as they are not provoked. The presence of elephants in the jungle could be detected from the sounds of breaking twigs, branches and bamboos, apart from their growls, grumbles or trumpets of members of the herd.

"Eventually one should never venture into the jungle after consuming alcohol. After all, 'drinking provokes in him devilish level of courage'. While he chases that courage, he is likely to become a victim of circumstances", I warned.

It was high noon, when we arrived at Hulikatte waterhole. Weather was humid and sultry. Movements of a herd of elephants were heard at a distance. So, asking Kala to stay back, I crawled through bamboo brook and landed at the edge of the forest pool before the herd arrived. "Life here in the jungle always revolves around the water source", it is said.

I found a peacock doing a graceful sun dance with a perfect choreography before his harem. The fantastic display of courtship thrilled me with its dazzling colours. There was stillness and lethargy in the air. The water hole provided clues of movements of the king and the commoner, all of whom shared it. It was unexpectedly, a long wait for me. Elephants seemed, as though, they were not in a hurry to drink water or was it due to my body smell, they had delayed their arrival, I did not really know the reason. The place, however, looked beautiful and wild. I never felt lonely amidst such a natural set up. Listening to the calls of birds and watching through binoculars and making notes kept me busy. The surrounding plants with colourful foliage also inspired me. My basic ability to communicate with birds and animals was developed over the years. Year after year, I got closer and closer to them.

After testing my patience the herd found ambling towards water hole. Kala's guesswork proved right. The herd led by matriarch, the oldest and the wisest female, entered the edge of the water without the slightest sound.

I remembered Kala telling me that elephants walk on tip-toes and the legs are provided with pads which help them walk without the slightest sound. The herd consisted of nine cows accompanied by calves at their heels and half-a-dozen sub-adults. Here matriarch, the lady, was the boss. The elephant family is a female dominant society. But the absence of a breeding bull was noted, except two sub-adult males.

The arrival of these heavy-weights abruptly ended the nuptial dance of the peacock. The thirsty elephants drove them away before getting into water for a drink. Elephant herd exhibited great affinity for water. Though they wander great distances in search of greener pastures, they choose their grazing grounds, as far as possible, closer to a water source. Their powerful olfactory sense could help detect presence of water even at great distance, say 10-15 km. An elephant normally drinks 90-100 litres of water per visit, while it requires 150-200 kg vegetation per day.

It was fun time for the herd. Cleansing their massive bodies is no small a task. The trunk provided them an effective shower. The simple bath turned soon into an elaborate ritual of a mud spray. The mud bath cools the body and protects the skin against insect bites. The above rituals of elephants appeared strictly a private affair.

The retreat from the water was a grand finale. They looked as if they were carved in ebony. Each mother accompanied by its calf at heel, the single file march-fast was rhythmic.

The elephant's instinctive desire for mineral-salt led them to a nearby salt-lick to satiate the hearty appetite for mineral salts that dictates all herbivores to frequent salt licks-both natural and man-made.

It was late afternoon. We slowly made our way back to camp. A solitary tusker towering above the roof of plant canopy peeped out, as if to say, "Hello, who's there"? My camera turned out to be too much of a temptation even for this recluse. He came out of the bush and presented his best profile. I wanted to be gentle, affectionate and communicative with this gentle giant. He was a photographer's delight. Anxious as I was, his face be properly captured in my camera, he obligingly placed his trunk on the tree canopy. His shining tusks turned out to be "crowning glory". The afternoon light enhanced the personality of that large tusked male, the regal majesty. The body structure and body language of that magnificent male was attractive. I clicked and clicked and again clicked. Before I could express my gratitude, he wheeled around and vanished into the depth of the bush.

The mighty pachyderm slowly made his way in the direction of the herd. The tusker was winding its way in a snaky movement through a thick thorny bush to reach the herd. I followed the magnificent bull at a comfortably safe distance. When the bull joined the herd, the matriarch greeted him with respect. Other females in the herd followed suit, in the way to please their lover while pleasing themselves. He watched them as the females seductively made their way towards him and planted nasal kiss in his mouth. I could recollect an adult school rhyme summing up "A kiss is not a kiss without some tongue in it". The world proved wrong in case of elephants. In elephants, a kiss may be termed as 'nasal caresses'. The youngsters and kids too approached individually and greeted him with a nasal caress by placing their tip of trunk in his mouth. The male in return blessed them by caressing their head with tender movements of his trunk. The object of their affection stood tantalisingly silhouetted against the blazing sun – there could not have been a better ambience to induce in me the tender loving words. In keeping with the magic of the moment, I whispered my self, "I love natural history sharing love with the nature". The matriarch slowly led the clan into the thicket, keeping all the members in a close-knit herd. Herding in elephants is not just for convenience, it is a strategy of survival. It was time for me to retreat. I signalled Kala to follow me.

Tuskers are kept at trunk's distance by Matriarch. She permits a tusker to join the herd to sample any female in heat.

Contemplating on the events of the long and tiring day, we walked hurriedly, as the night falls quickly in winter. I was looking forward for an enchanting evening and to give some rest to my tired limbs. It was impossible for me to retire for the day until I finished my notes on the day's events of that captivating journey in the reserve – "the temple of elephants".

To sum up, "No university could have taught me scores of secrets of the jungle, than did tribal Kala, the moving encyclopaedia".

For more details on elephants and their social structure please read the following chapters:

Chapter II

Profile of Elephant

Man has always been fascinated by the elephant's remarkable ultrasound communication capability and high degree of intelligence; its massive body moving like a small hill with graceful gait, its enormous power, keen sense of smell, steadfastness against threats from enemies are the survival strategies adopted by this sure footed animal. The matriarch, her regal majesty, with social life system, needs human compassion, so that her tribe will survive for posterity to enjoy the share of the earth planet and contribute for the wellbeing of humanity. Elephant, the flagship species and tiger, the charismatic species live side by side as adversaries of the Bandipur national park.

2.1 Close-Ups of Elephant

The elephant legs are described to be columnar. It is known to walk on tips of its toes. The four feet together cover an area of more than 1 sq m. The skin on the soles is flexible and contains irregular or triangular or quadrangular horny pieces measuring about 5 cm^2. What looks like its knee, actually, corresponds to the hand bones in humans. The soles of the feet act as horny cushion to bear enormous body weight. The sole expands beneath the weight of the animal as it walks, taking some of the burden from the leg bones. Column like legs are superbly adapted to move a massive body weight. The bones are large but lack bone-marrow. Females have two nipples, called breasts as in humans between their fore legs. The calves suckle with their mouth like other mammals, coiling their trunk in

'S' shape and taking support of their mothers' body. The skin being 2-4 cm thick is very sensitive. Large folds in the skin often form towards the hind portion of the body, where skin is the thickest.

New born have a sparse brown hair gradually increasing dense-bristle-like dark hair, during its babyhood. The dense brush like hair, largely disappear in juveniles and sub-adults. Adults do possess sparse growth of hair around the head. The only prominent, thick wiry hair in adults is found at the tip of the tail. They form a brush like with specific function to perform. Halfway between the eyes and ears, there are cheek glands on either side with definite function, known to secrete *musth* fluid only in adults. These are found both in males and females.

A cow elephant with her calf. Mother allows her calf to breast feed till about two years, sometimes even elder calf also continues to feed along with younger one.

2.2   Caste System in Elephants

The old Indian *shikar* and faunal literatures exhibit a tendency to be conservative in estimating the height of an elephant in the field. The build of the animal is such that the height at the shoulder is more reliable indicator of the size than with most other animals; the length and circumference of the body, the thickness of limbs, the trunk and the relative size of the head vary so much with individuals that the indigenous system of classifying elephants into the *Koomeriah*, the *Meerga* and the *Dwasala* types, recognizes that animals of all three types may be seen in the same herd. In a large herd of over 22 elephants at a forest pool of Bandipur reserve, when I closely observed, there were striking variations in individuals in their build and conformity. It was, however, difficult for me to categorise the elephants according to the above classification.

Eventually, the Asian elephants were also classified into three categories by Valmiki. They are as under:

1. *Bhadra* – **dwarfish in size but proportionate in shape.**

2. *Mandra* – **with large limbs, but somewhat sluggish.**

3. *Mriga* – **slim and strong.**

Elephant herd: where one finds different age groups-Matriarch, her sisters, their offspring making the family unit.

1. Gaur bull:

There seem to be numerous hybrid progenies developed from cross-breeding among the above categories, as the time passed by.

2.3 Elephant – the Keystone Species

Asian elephant, *Elephas maximus* L., is considered as the 'Keystone species', because of its overall influence over other animals, including the ecosystem. As a general concept, a keystone species is one that contributes more than other species to the overall integrity of a habitat; within that habitat, each species interacts and depends on other species and each species contributes to the overall habitat functioning. But the keystone species contributes significantly, so much so without them, the overall habitat would change markedly. A keystone species is a pivotal mammalian species of the forest ecosystem. The elephant is an indicator of eco-biological health; it fosters the ecosystem as a whole. Adequate protection of habitat is, therefore, crucial for the survival of Asian elephant, as well as survival of all other animals including carnivores. Similar considerations hold good for African elephant *Loxodonta africana* B. as well.

Considering overall performance of the Indian elephant, it has however, managed to hold its ground with the present population of about 28,000-30,000, an increase by about 40% over the past 25 years. This is contrary to what has been happening in most other Asian countries, where elephants have declined during the above period. This increase, we can infer has offset the decline elsewhere. With about 3,500 captive elephants, India is home to more than 50% of the Asian elephant populations.

The Asian elephants are now found in 59 distinct ranges across 13 Asian countries and foresters are unanimous in their agreement that the species is under grave threat across South-East-Asian continent. Today the Asian elephant, as a whole, is declared as an endangered species. But the overall distribution of Indian elephant is limited to four widely separated geographical regions of the subcontinent. In peninsular India, it ranges in the forests of Tamilnadu, Kerala and Karnataka, including certain parts of Andhra Pradesh, Goa and Maharashtra.

It is home in mixed deciduous forests with scrub type vegetation of Kalakkadu-Mundanthurai at the southern most parts, Periyar, Parambikulam-Anamalai and the Silent Valley tiger reserve of Western Ghats. Further north elephants in splinter groups range in the forests of Brahmagiri hills of Kodagu, Doddabetta forests of Hassan district, *Bhadra* tiger reserve and Kuduremukh tiger reserve of Chikkamagalur district and Dandeli-Anshi tiger reserve of Uttara Kannada districts. A smaller herd of elephants from Ansi-Dandeli tiger reserve is moved over to Maharashtra and operates in the forests of Goa as well. Connecting the Western Ghats with the Eastern Ghats is the Nilgiri Biosphere Reserve, comprising, Madumalai and Mukurti national parks of Tamilnadu; Nagarahole-Bandipur, Biligirirangan Hills tiger reserves and Kaveri Elephant Sanctuary of Karnataka, and Wayanad north and south of Kerala, where large concentration of elephant herds occur. Elephants also range extending over to the Eastern Ghats, comprising the forests of Sathyamangalam, Dharmapuri and Vellore districts of Tamilnadu. Some elephants migrated from Tamilnadu into Andhra Pradesh some 35 years ago, have successfully established their home range in Koundinya Elephant Sanctuary in Andhra Pradesh.

In central India, elephants are distributed in the mixed deciduous forests of Chhattisgarh, Orissa, Jharkhand and extending their range of distribution up to southern parts of West Bengal. In the north-west of India, elephants are found in sub-Himalayan forests of Uttarakhand and Uttar Pradesh. In the north-east of India, large herds of elephants range in the forests of West Bengal, Assam, Meghalaya, Karbi Anglong, Mizoram, Manipur, Tripura, Nagaland and Kameng valley of the sub-Himalayan range of Arunachal Pradesh. The elephants are also found in Nepal, southern most parts of Bhutan. In Sri Lanka the elephants are found to occur in Yala, Wasgomuwa, and Minneriya and Udawalwe national parks.

While the grim news on the status of tiger in India is a cause of concern, the total population for the entire country stands between 32,284 and 32,334, as per 2007-08 survey. In North-East India, the population accounts for 13,620. The previous survey conducted in 2002, had pitched the figure for the country excluding the population of East of Chicken Neck at 17,170. The total population of elephants including that of North-Eastern states was 26,413. The big jump seems to have come from the southern elephant populations, where critical and small but nebulously surviving land corridors for movements of the jumbo between the Eastern and the Western Ghats has helped ensure large contiguous range of distribution for the gentle giant. The southern elephant population has risen from 12,814 to 14,005. The population in the Eastern region has remained stable recording a population of 2,633 against 2,649 in 2002. In Northern India there has been a marginal jump from 1,667 to 1726 in half a decade, which considering the low natural population growth rates, seems to be very healthy sign. Chhattisgarh has 100 plus as compared to 20 and odd earlier

The level of poaching as well as retaliatory killings across the country had hit a high around 2001-02. Poaching seems to have come down and added to healthy growth in the elephant population. But this increase also has seen a continuation of human-elephant conflict across the country. Almost 300 people die each year in conflict with the pachyderm. Traditional migratory routes are being cut off from encroachments and the habitats are also getting fragmented in addition to migratory corridors being wiped out. The fragmentation of their ranges of distribution is the principal causes for increased conflict. The elephant's tryst with urbanized areas as well as thickly populated villages is well documented all over the country. Elephants from Utharakhand are reported migrating to as far as Himachal Pradesh and Haryana, which had not seen elephants earlier. Elephants from Tamilnadu and Orissa are moving into the state territories of northern Andhra Pradesh. Unless we have a rational policy of creating insulated corridors connecting present elephant reserves with isolated and island like forests, region wise, we will continue to see elephants increasingly in conflict with humans. In addition, in *situ* conservation of elephants helps mitigate human-elephant conflict by increasing the extents of areas of isolated or island like habitats, through a process of acquiring adjoining lands where possible, rather than attempting ex *situ* protection by shifting out genetically isolated populations and relocate them at distant habitats.

2.4 The Size

In the book 'Big Game Shooting' (London 1895), the following interesting information is provided: The skeleton of the well known "Arcot rogue elephant", now in the Madras Museum, measures 10 ft. 6 in. at the shoulder. Mr. Rowland Ward considered that when alive it must have stood 10 ft. 10 in.

A bull elephant over 10 ft 6" and a cow elephant over 9 ft are so exceptional among Indian elephants that must be left out of consideration in judging adult sizes in modern times. Though, I have never seen a tusker of ten feet tall in the wild, it does not mean that such massive giants never existed in the past. The height of Drona which carried golden *howdah* weighing 800 kilograms during *Dashara* procession taped 9 ft 3 in. This was the tallest among the living elephants of 1990s. The sad demise of Drona, the 67 year old majestic tusker occurred, in Kakankote forest on 4ᵗʰDecember 1997, when he came in contact with high tension electric wire that passed through Nagarahole forest. Drona with his cool temperament had the distinction of carrying golden *howdah* 18 times during the world famous Mysore *Dashara* celebrations. While, former palace male tuskers – Biligiriranga and Rajendra, which also carried the same golden *howdah* with the Maharajahs astride in it were considered the largest in the days of bygone era and measured 9 ft 9 inch and 9 ft 6 inch, respectively. The tusker, Balarama at the age of about 40 years, which was named a successor to Drona, taped 9 ft tall, when I measured in 2003. Balarama having participated 16 times in *Dashara* festivity carried golden *howdah* 12 times till the age of 52 years by 2010. This 400ᵗʰ year of *Dashara* festivity was said to be Balarama's last participation, on account of his aging. But, there is no other tusker with demanding qualities, such as "*Gaja Gambhirya*", the elephant's stately gait, as required to carry golden *howdah* during coming *Dashara* festivities. It is advisable to continue Balarama till he attained the age of retirement at 55. All these male elephants had the required characteristics of Royalty – sober, majestic with steady walk and balanced mind, never going astray, especially during procession carrying golden *howdah*.

2.5 Field Measurement of Elephant's Height

Among the Asian elephants the average height of a bull is between eight and nine feet and that of a cow between seven and eight feet. Tuskers more than 10 ft 7.5 inch in height are rare, though one may occasionally come across in literature, quoting bulls up to eleven feet in height and cows up to 9 ft. Such quotes may be considered as exaggerated. To ascertain the exact height the animal should be made to stand erect on a level ground, with all four legs close together and the height measured like that of a horse, at the shoulder by using a device called, standard cross bar and not by means of a piece of string over the rounded muscles of the shoulder.

Those well versed in elephant lore; believe that wild ones are usually taller than domestic ones. As a matter of fact, this has no corollary. The length of the body, however, varies considerably in big bulls, as also its body size. A massive bull, 6 inches shorter than a leggy and thin animal may easily defeat the latter in a combat.

Very few people agree with regard to a method of height estimation of wild elephants in their natural surroundings. The differences in field measurements of shoulder heights of wild elephants are wide and confusing as in case of measuring the size (length) of tigers. Field assessment of shoulder height of wild elephants is done by applying a "thumb rule" – twice the circumference of a front foot print (CFFP). This is among the first few lessons to be learnt by a Forester/Wild-lifer during his/her field training. While recording measurements, at no time, diameter of a front foot print of an elephant is considered. It is for two reasons: firstly, the fore foot-imprint of an elephant is not perfectly circular and therefore, the circumference of an elephant footprint cannot be calculated by multiplying the diameter by the factor, $22/7(=3\ 1/7)$. Secondly, even a small error gets magnified in such a calculation, because by the time the height of the elephant is computed based on the diameter, the error could have been multiplied by $6\ 2/7$ times. This is what happened when heights of one or two tuskers of Bardia national park in Nepal were estimated based on diameters by Adrian and others.

Here, care and accuracy in measuring the circumference are essential for reliability. It is the clear (not defaced) print of the forefoot that must be selected and measured. The print must be on hard dry dusty ground and not on moist soil, because in soft soil the foot print tends to splay. The sole of elephant's foot does not splay in the manner of the pug mark of a tiger or even the slots of a sambar on wet soil. Of course, in loose sand, the imprint is not clear and the sand pushed out at the periphery leads to errors and in mire (when the foot is pulled out of the mire at each step) there is never a clean imprint. But it is on moist earth, as on the edges of paddy fields or on bare ground after a rain that the clear imprints could be found. I have measured the foot print of the same elephant on such moist muddy ground and also on firm dusty ground, a few metres away and it was the print on hard dry dusty ground that gave the circumference greater by an inch. This is because with slightly yielding soil, it is the cushioned sole of the animal that yields beneath its great weight.

A well-formed footprint on a hard surface is selected for tracing. The outline of the impression is traced out on a piece of glass measuring 1.5 sq ft with a free flowing pen taking care to avoid the parallax error by moving the eyes with the pen so as to keep always the line of sight vertically above the segment under tracing. Simultaneously, a thread is laid along the edge of the footprint taking care of the concave curve at the heel and notches between toes. The circumference of the foot print is measured and shoulder height is estimated in the field by doubling the length of the thread.

The tracing on the glass plate is transferred to a sheet of paper on reaching office. The plate over-laid with the sheet of paper (held firmly to the plate with the help of clips) is held against the light and the tracing copied on the paper taking care to avoid the parallax error. The perimeter is then measured with the help of measuring equipment called, plannimeter. The circumference so obtained, is then multiplied by 2 to estimate the shoulder height (h = 2C) of the elephant.

2.6 Field Device for Height Measurement

Iain Douglas-Hamilton was able to measure the heights of African elephants by adopting the principle of stereo photography. He eventually evolved a machine, called 'Bubble Chamber Track Analysis Measuring Machine'. He was able to enlarge his negatives twenty five times by projecting them on a screen with micro-manipulating servo-mechanism. He could, thus, record heights to the nearest two microns on paper tape, which was then fed into a computer that computed elephant's height and age.

The most sophisticated measurements that were subsequently recorded by him, often, did no more than confirm the age estimates he had already made in the field by 'rule of thumb', comparing the heights of young against old and by recording a hierarchy of size within each family unit.

His final height-measuring instrument was made of light weight aluminium and was carried in a foam-filled box. Great care was needed to avoid jogging the mirrors which were calibrated carefully. The slightest displacement would throw out the accuracy of the calculations. Nevertheless, he found on trials that range at which he used was accurate within two cm.

2.7 Weight

Weight is a much more reliable indication of size in an elephant than body measurements, but eventually, it is very seldom possible to weigh such a huge beast. Of course, newly captured animals and camp elephants could be weighed and recorded. However, the weight of a *kumki*, the tamed working elephant is no guide, for, it is seldom that an elephant in captivity attains the mass and musculature of wild elephants. A very big bull in the wild may probably weigh between 4 and 5 tonnes. The weight of new born calf varies from 90-100 kilograms, while its height varies between 90 cm to 1 metre.

2.8 Heavy Weight Champions

The weight of well grown elephant may be anything between 5,000 to 7,500 kilograms. The Mysore Palace elephants – Biligiriranga and Rajendra weighed 7,632 and 7,315 kilograms respectively. Drona, the successor to above two successive palace elephants, weighed 6,712 kilograms, while Balarama, who was picked up after the death of Drona, weighed 5,620 kilos at the age of 40 years. The Asian elephant, owing to its bulkier body and shorter legs, as compared to African elephant, is almost steady even in 'quick march'.

"Why do we take so much trouble to take all these body measurements and other details"? One may ask.

A clear cut objective of assessment of body growth is much more important than just an academic exercise. For example, it is possible that body growth rates slow down in over-utilized habitats, where food becomes scarce and this in turn could reduce the birth-rate in a population. If this can be determined and measured then it could be possible for a biologist to make more realistic population projections. Growth studies are also essential in the estimation of ungulate population and consequent herbivore biomass estimation on a sustained yield basis. Last, but by no means the least, information on growth with age is of great significance in taxonomic studies and of vital importance in the preparation of age determination techniques in the field.

2.9 Colour

The body colour of an adult elephant largely relates to the colour of its skin, for when full grown, the hair on the body is too sparse to influence colour. Some animals have a lighter coloured skin and some others much darker. In lighter grey animals there is often a pink tinge mixed. However, the colour of a wild elephant is exceedingly difficult to judge, because the colour of the animal is often that of the earth, it has been throwing over itself; occasionally, even a bright red body colour may be seen due to red earth smeared. Fresh from a bath or after swimming across the lake and before they have mud-plastered or dusted themselves, elephants appear gleaming black, as if carved in ebony. The lighter coloured animal, if any, in the herd is then easily noticed. Some animals are definitely and noticeably light grey in colour. During bath the tips of ears, trunk and forehead in most of the adult elephants look pinkish with blotches. Apparently, this is an ageing factor.

Calves up to the age of first 6 months may be covered with thick brown hair, not in regular coat but in a loose tomentum. The colour of the hair may be quite light at times a warm yellowish grey may give the calf a light coloured appearance. However, this hair is not retained permanently and such calves usually grow up into dark grey animals.

The reports of 'white elephants' heard, occasionally, are based on people seeing such calves with light coloured mud application or dusting. No authentic white elephant (i.e. a notably light skinned animal, a creamy grey in colour with some pink in places) has been recorded in peninsular India.

2.10 Senses in Elephant

Elephants' bodies are engaged in a kind of evolutionary mating dance with steps that were genetically choreographed long before humans discovered fire. The way elephant smells, the way its body is shaped, the sounds of its communication and the touch of its trunk are all designed to send out coded messages, that have but one purpose, i.e. to entice a healthy and compatible mate and lead a successful social life system, in order to pass on the genes to the next generation. Reflexes in elephant are quite fast; all elephants except bulls in *musth*, react spontaneously to an impending danger. *Panchendriyas*, the five senses in elephants in order of their excellence are graded as under:

    i.   **Smell – excellent; love at the first sniff.**

    ii.   **Hearing – acute; forest sounds are not a music to his ears.**

    iii.   **Touch – very good; the evolutionary ice-breaker.**

    iv.   **Taste – better; the spice of desire.**

    v.   **Sight – good in dull light; the look of love.**

2.10.1 Sense of Smell

The sense of smell in elephants, of course, is paramount. Of its five senses, smell may be one of the most emotionally important and that goes in spades where romance in elephants is concerned. Each animal has an odour – a unique chemical signature – as individual as his or her personality, especially, for elephants who have much more highly developed olfactory functions. It may want to make sure to get a good whiff and see if love is in the air. Even the presence of water and female in oestrus or bull in *musth* at far off distances, specially fancied by the animal seems to be by smell; a near blind riding elephant was still able to know that tree, the foliage of which she liked the most was some 15 feet away on one side of the elephant path, she was treading, altered her course to eat the foliage. The presence of men nearby is often revealed to an elephant by smell, when it instantly, pinpoints the direction of smell with raised tip of its trunk; it also looks hard in that direction to ascertain. On two occasions, when I provoked young tuskers to charge in my direction, the animals instantly charged, the moment, I gave them my location, sitting inside the hide. Even the reverse of the seeking of visual confirmation of the proximity of men perceived, initially, through smell was observed; olfactory confirmation sought by the trunk pointing in the direction of the men seen, when the animal could not possibly smell them, the wind blowing from it. When an airborne scent is above the level of the elephant's head the trunk is raised like radar to heavens to investigate.

Elephants are well able to follow ground scents, like hounds. On two occasions, wild tuskers followed the trails of the *kumki*, I was riding by ground scent; another wild tusker was observed sedulously following a ground scent, probably the track of a wild cow.

G.P.Sanderson says that when there is an alarm, the big bull of a herd runs away on his own and does not cover retreat of the herd. This is generally not true. Invariably, a breeding bull does cover the retreat of the herd. Once, I was following a herd along with Keechanna, a tribal tracker at Bandipur. We were halted by a singularly burly and powerful tusker which stayed behind, while the rest of the herd vanished into the thicket and staged the most impressive demonstration after return and pushing over a stout sapling and then kicking it between his legs; later we retraced our steps, while he moved off in the wake of the herd. Frequently, such demonstrations to intimidate and halt men take the form of pushing over trees or gorging small clumps of bamboos or bushes. A cow may demonstrate at a man following her by turning round and rushing towards the intruder in a short, formal charge. Sometimes, an elephant resenting the presence of a man may graze gradually towards him at a tangent and then turn in sharply for a charge when near enough. A cow that demonstrated her charge, while we waited deliberately and barely at a distance of about fifty feet from the matriarch of the herd that was to cross forest road near a puddle on our way to Kalkere, during our five day-trekking from Bandipur to Nagarahole, was a typical of elephants' charge to drive away intruders. Members of the trekking party ran for life helter-skelter amidst thick jungle. It was a razor-edge escape for all of us from the charge.

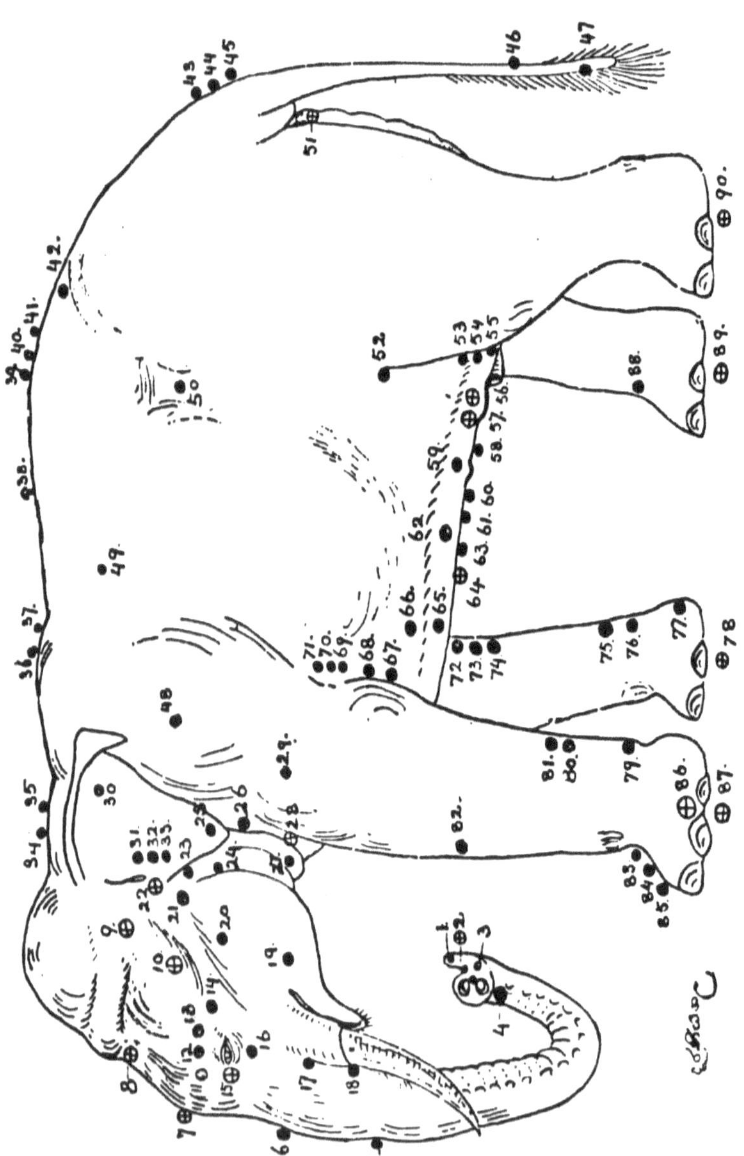

Figure 1. Nerve centers or nīla goaded by mahouts in controlling elephants. Hard prodding at ⊕ results in death (after Deraniyagala, 1955, see text).

2.10.1.1 Sense of Smell in Elephant, Superior Than in Hounds

The largest of our terrestrial mammals, known by the long trunk, at the end of which the nostrils are placed with a finger – like pointed tip dorsally and a lip-like feature ventrally, are used as finger and thumb as in humans, while the whole trunk serves as an arm. Lower lip spout-like and upper tip pointed, can seal the nostril air-tight. The nostrils do not have the same size throughout, but the difference is very small. This author measured the nostrils of a dead female elephant; it recorded 4 cm at the tip and 5 cm close to the cranium. An elephant can squeeze using individual nostril at different lengths along the trunk. Elephants have an acute sense of smell, manifested by 7 turbinals (scrolls of bones with tissue sensitized for olfaction); but hounds have 5 such turbinals. Interestingly, Hyrax (a small mammalian spp. found in parts of African countries), a little brother of elephant has nine turbinals. In hyrax, the sense of smell is highly evolved, since its body hair and footpads also assist in grasping.

Incidentally, receiving cue from the above facts, as to acute sense of smell in elephants, it is important for the forest/wildlife officials to harness the captive elephants in 'tracking down poachers and smugglers using elephants'. Elephants having seven turbinals are better equipped in grasping the sense of smell, as compared to hounds (dogs) with five such turbinals. Elephants are also intelligent and have better memory power than dogs. These qualities in elephants help retain the smell of criminal acts grasped for longer time than dogs. Elephants could, therefore, be a better option in detection of poachers and other criminals involved in such offences. Elephants being forest dwelling animals, with their powerful sense of smell and good memory, are better suited to track down poachers by following their spoors. They may be well suited in detection of criminals involved in robbery cases as well, provided their giant size could be compromised. Trained 'anti-poaching elephant squads' including their keepers are a better bet. Once the elephants pick up smell left behind by ivory poachers and the carcass from which tusks are removed, tracking down poachers by following spoors along their escape routes becomes easy to locate offenders. Elephants need to be taken to the place of occurrence of offence before evidences are erased or obliterated or washed off by torrential rains. Both elephants and their *mahouts*, however should undergo intensive training in detection techniques before they are put on the job, just as in case of police dog squads. Such anti-poaching elephant squads can well be used for regular perambulation in the reserve forests and along interstate or international frontiers.

2.10.2   Ears and Their Functions

The powerful skull bears huge ears. The skull contains sponge like material inside, which makes it weigh less than if it were to be a solid bone. Some of the pores in these spongy regions can contain 0.25 l. They are lined with mucus membranes, like those found in the nose. The sponge like system reduces the massiveness of the skull in favour of increased mobility, reported to be an important compromise with increasing age and the large tusks in male would become useless, if the skull found to be extremely heavy.

Large pinnae (the external ears) provide a large surface area to trap greater number of sound waves than smaller pinnae would. This is imperative since elephants depend greatly on their sense of hearing, always alert, filtering 'sounds of the forests' for their survival. The extremely keen hearing of elephants has long been able to impress hunters and *mahouts*, but it was not scientifically studied until 1951. A particular elephant could distinguish one specific tone from six pairs of pure tones. The elephants also learned simple melodies and rhythms that could be recognized independent of the instrument creating the music (i.e. whether the music was performed on violin, piano, organ or xylophone).

Anyone who has seen elephants in zoological parks or circuses can immediately identify the Asian or African species by the size and shape of their ears. There are, of course, many other differences between them – the trunk tip, the head and its shape, the shape of the body are the more obvious popular diagnostic features known to most people. Both species of elephants have very good hearing, which suggests that each has ears of the size and shape well suited to its particular needs. It may be tempting to assume that the African elephant with much larger ears give it a better hearing, but this is not true. The discrepancy indicates an alternative explanation that certain organs have more than one function. In this respect, the larger ears of the African elephant have several important roles to fulfil.

The basic role of the ear is to detect sounds and convey them to the brain. The external portion of the ear, the pinna, receives sound waves which are then passed over as vibrations, through the bones of the inner ear. Messages are sent to the brain where they are interpreted accordingly. The discrepancies between the two species arise only, among others, is in respect of external sections of the ear. In case of African elephant's ear, apart from being bigger, the shape resembles somewhat African continent, while in case of Asian elephant's ear, being smaller, the shape of the ear resembles somewhat Indian sub-continent. Why should the ear agree on internal structure and disagree so remarkably on external proportions? The answer must have something to do with the terrain/habitat where and how they live.

There is another African elephant *Loxodonta cyclotis*, essentially a forest dweller, occupying the regions with fairly a well defined seasonal climate somewhere north of the equator. Its ears are smaller compared to the large-eared African savannah elephant *Loxodonta africana*, by contrast, lives on the equator over parts of its range and country. The smaller, forest bound species of African elephant, have proportionally smaller ears than its large Savannah cousin. Thus, there seems to be some correlation between ear size and exposure to the environment, more so to the sun. The elephant of the savannah naturally has less shelter from the constant heat of the equator than does its cousin of the forest. For this reason savannah species must make every effort to keep its body cool. So, keeping cool their huge body is higher in the priority list of elephants.

Indian Tusker (top) and

African tusker to project comparative shapes and size.

Until recently, African elephants were considered to be two sub-species or populations of the same species of *Loxodonta*. However, today they are specifically considered to be two distinct looking pachyderms. Using gene sequencing tools, research teams from Harward, Illinois and York Universities have shown that instead of being the same species-as scientists long believed – the African savannah elephant and the smaller African forest elephant are distinct cousins, as that of Asian elephants, having been largely separated for over 2 to 7 million years ago.

2.10.2.1   Keeping the Body Cool

Generally speaking, land animals that live in cold regions of the earth planet possess some extremities, such as ears, tails, bills and appendages, in order to reduce heat loss. Conversely, animals that live in warmer parts of the globe have large and longer extremities. This natural phenomenon is a well established ecological maxim and is known as 'Allen's Rule'.

Allen's rule is only part of the answer, though; the large ears in elephants serve as built in fans. It is observed that under natural conditions, as the temperature increases, so does the flapping of the ears, per unit of time. The ear flapping not only creates air currents to blow on the body, but also exposes the ventral (back) side of the ear, where large blood vessels are concentrated close to the surface, allowing for increase of heat loss in hot weather. The large surface area of the ears acts as the most important external organ of the body heat control. In each ear, there is an extensive fan-like network of blood vessels running just below the under surface. During the hot time of the day these vessels are fully extended as warm blood from the depths of the elephant's body flows through them. The blood quickly looses its heat to the air around it and then returns to the body where it will collect more unwanted warmth for transportation to the ear. The whole process is accelerated by the elephant flapping its ears forward and back, so that the undersides are continually exposed to open air. Without this cooling mechanism, the elephant would run the risk of over heating internally, possibly, with fatal results. Iain-Douglas-Hamilton recorded a drop of more than 16 degrees Fahrenheit in the temperature of blood that had just passed through the ears of an African elephant. Such an experiment in Asian elephant is yet to be carried out to have a comparative data.

There is an evidence to suggest that if an elephant loses the ability to move back and forth its ears due to injury, it may suffer cooling problems for the rest of its life. Eventually, it has to find shade all through in the forest, even at the expense of other animals. It has to invest plenty of time in cooling its body at forest pools.

Like any other mammal, the elephant must keep its body temperature within a limited range, if it is not to die. Cold is rarely a problem within the geographical range of wild elephants, but heat is another matter. The elephant's slow metabolism means that its body does not gain heat quickly and the thick skin acts as an insulator to maintain an even internal temperature. There is also evidence to suggest that an elephant can permit a much higher body temperature than any other mammal, without apparent ill effects. As there are no sweat glands on the body surface to aid heat loss, the most important thermo-regulatory device, however, is the elephant's ear. In the absence of sweat glands on the body, the sweat is collected in "pharyngeal pouch", located at the gullet, where from it is drawn by its trunk and sprayed over the ears and the body, when needed.

The captive elephants that are used for riding on long distances or hauling of timber logs, the tropical sun push up the body temperature, when flapping of ears increases. Simultaneously sucking out the sweat collected (some writers have erroneously, called it as saliva and others have gone to the extent of describing it as regurgitated water from the stomach) from the gullet and sprays alternatively to ears and body to keep itself cool. The sweat so sucked from the gullet and sprayed to body and years acts as a coolant.

During the course of its life, an elephant may lose certain part or parts out of its large ears, either through fights or by mishaps. Although these may leave them ragged and torn, the damage will not affect the heat regulation process as long as the muscles controlling the movement of the whole ear are not impaired. The ears, whose basic function is to detect sounds have therefore, evolved to provide a vital survival appendages.

Besides this, the ears have another use of paramount importance. One of the ways in which many animals can increase their apparent size, particularly during threat displays, is to make use of their body size or appendages in such a way that they appear more formidable than they actually are. This type of display, which has evolved because animals that save energy by not fighting tend to outlive their more aggressive fellows, depends upon the external feature of the animal and the ways in which they can best be used to intimidate a potential enemy or a potential rival. Typically, a bird will increase its body size by raising its feathers, a lizard may erect a large, brightly coloured frills around its head and a frog may gulp down air to swell the size of its body, human may expand his chest and raise arms sideways; in the same manner the elephants, both Asian and African extend their ears.

From a distance these ears may not seem so very large, especially, as seen in relation to the body size of the elephant. When seen close to and head on with the body largely obscured, they can be used to a devastating effect. When they are held forward at an angle of 90O to the head, they are seen in their full enormity. They may treble the width of the elephant's head, framing and exaggerating the power of the gleaming, forward-pointing tusks. Each ear may be more than three feet long and two feet wide – enough to wrap itself quite comfortably around an average human being. When the dust beneath the agitated feet is pounded into a frenzied cloud, the vision of towering strength, is truly awe inspiring, if not, the most terrifying of the animal's spectacles.

2.10.3 Touch

Elephants begin with most casual gesture about the intended cues. A flirtatious female nonchalantly touches male's temporal glands to test, if he is in *musth*. When both male and female meet they greet each other, touch the temporal region, where cheek glands are located, followed by mouth and then genital regions, exhibiting oral-sex. The oral-sex is not a sex-theory, but triviality the real issue about sexual intimacy between two animals. The bull sub-consciously responds to such cues by allowing caresses or by mirroring her preening behaviour, thereby signalling his mutual attraction in agreement. Once the initial contact has been made, touch evokes a host of other roles to follow. The touch can put prospective mates into the proper mood for sex. The touch can certainly be used to arouse and excite, but it can also be soothing, calming and reassuring to young calves. When animals caress and groom each other, they are basically putting each other into a relaxed state. The mouth is also sensitive to touch and the bristles around the mouth region may likewise have a tactile function.

2.10.4   Sight

When we consider the eye of an elephant, it cannot see very clearly the objects at long distances. So if one quickly hides himself behind a tree, an ant-hill or a rock at some distance, he is not detected by the elephant. The elephant is described as 'poor-sighted' rather than as 'short-sighted'. The elephant can, no doubt, see as far as man could, but its small eyes as compared to the body size cannot focus themselves on the objects very accurately. It requires a little longer time to adjust its vision. In view of this, elephants tend to approach closer to humans or a vehicle to investigate and make sure, who the intruder is. To make up its short-comings, elephant largely depends on trunk and ears, which are sensitive and highly developed.

It is true that the elephant is not good at picking out stationary human being, inconspicuously clad in dark colours. Elephants are said to be colour blind. At the same time the pachyderm can easily spot white objects with ease. It doesn't, however, tolerate white colour; any thing that is white in the jungle, is simply smashed outright. Even it doesn't spare km/mile stones painted white on road side, passing through forests. Another peculiarity in elephants is that the field of vision is oriented downward and to the side in the normal head position, causing the elephant to lift its head to have frontal view. Elephant's inability to see what is right in front, such as a man crouching under a bush, is no doubt partly due to the bulge of its cheeks and the base of its trunk, the fact that a great many intra-specific signals are usually sensed visually must offset. The elephant also is unable to see a person sitting up on a tree, above its eye level. However, experiments have shown that the elephant's vision is as good as that in man. It is less able to adapt to changing illumination than humans are. Powerful torch light and or beaming head lights blindfold the elephants in the wild; they get panic or get flabbergasted when poachers take advantage of this weakness to shoot at close range.

Investigations have shown that good visions are supported by the ability of elephants to recognise objects they have seen after a long period of time. A seven year old female juvenile could distinguish one figure from thirteen figure pairs. Later experiments showed that this animal could recognise twenty six individual figures with an accuracy of 73-100 percent. After twelve months the same animal correctly identified twenty four figures.

2.10.5 Taste

In elephant society there is no ritual called licking or grooming each other; hence it is difficult to judge the taste. The male can insert the tip of his trunk in the mouth of female partner. But there is something about the natural taste of her mouth that the bull loves. Taste in elephant, therefore, can't be described, since they don't even offer or exchange food to each other. However, elephants persistently visit crops, such as rice, millets, pulses, banana, sugarcane, fruits, vegetables, including salt that are consumed by humans. Taking the cue of raiding food crops an inference can thus be drawn the taste in elephants is next to humans.

2.11 Trunk – The Survival Tool

The most striking feature of present day elephants – both Asian and African – besides their mighty size, is their trunk. The trunk not only substitutes for a hand in human as a grasping instrument, but also used for touching objects, for smelling and many other important purposes. The trunk of an elephant is a prehensile elongation of the upper lip and the nose. It is a very complex organ, believed to be manipulated by a complexity of about 150,000 muscle-tissues. It contains no bones. The trunk is also a highly sensitive organ innervated primarily by the maxillary division of the trigeminal nerve. The trunk being telescopic, reaches as high as 20 feet and incredibly sensitive. The trunk is as sensitive as human hand in touch. A variety of functions are performed by the trunk, such as feeding, drinking, spraying, dusting, smelling, touching, picking, lifting, sound production, communication, weapon of defence and offence, punishing and protecting the young and so on. These are some of the basic functions of elephant's trunk and an important survival tool. It is indeed an indispensable and probably, the elephant's single most important organ in every day living. In view of the paramount importance, the trunk in elephants, justifiably, is described as the 'survival tool'!

The ability of the elephant to perform so many functions with its trunk is, undoubtedly, related directly to the remarkable structure of this appendage, which involves no rigid tissues, and yet contains a musculature construction, so as to provide the most amazing strength, mobility and control. It is seen that a tusker can lift objects 37% of its own weight with its trunk. How exactly the trunk functions and the mechanism involved in operating this extraordinary function remains an obscure. A tusker weighing about 6 tonnes, I have photographed, could easily lift a timber log weighing more than 1000 kg.

I have seen young elephants having been trained to write with chalk on the black board at an elephant camp in Kerala state.

Elephants have been observed carrying their new born calves that were too young to walk. A similar eye-witness was reported that a mother was observed carrying her dead and rotting calf with which she was unwilling to part with. New born babies can not use their trunk in the first few months of their life; they attempt to drink water with their mouth. These young calves seem to be inept with their trunks. They have been seen to suck their trunk (much as human babies sucking their thumbs) and inadvertently, step over their trunk while walking or playing.

The trunk in elephant is an exceptionally vulnerable organ. Severe injuries to the trunk may cause elephant's death. Injuries or accidents can be inflicted by sharp twigs and bamboo spikes, by disturbing an occasional resting snake in the grass or by man made devices like a snare or a trap or electrocution. There are also authentic reports of elephant's calves losing their trunks to crocodiles. Crocodiles, the aquatic master predators very often pull such victims into the depths of waters and make big meal.

In both Asian and African elephants, the trunk is animated and is covered with sensory hair. The trunk of the Asian species differs from that of the African, in having one dorsal finger-like process at its extremity. The African elephant has two-a dorsal and a ventral finger like processes at its extremity. Water holding capacity of the trunk is about one and a half gallons. A trained circus elephant can hold a trunk full of water for a long time for certain performances. At this time the elephant breathes through her mouth. It is also known that some elephants sleep with the mouth partly open and some times actually snore; this stertorous breathing can be heard for long distances.

Interestingly enough, the Asian elephant is found to have a curious valve-like canal communicating between the right and the left nasal passages of the trunk, about 5.5 inches from its tip. Trunk is used in reassuring babies and even disciplining them by punishing when they go wrong. The spring loaded trunk may even unleash the opponent wildly. Another notable thing about trunk is that while gathering grass the trunk moves in anti-clock direction and mows in tufts. Strangely enough, part of the grass gathered is held in position ventrally without being dropped while more grass is collected before the entire tuft is neatly packaged and pushed into the mouth. Trunk is not only used to produce affectionate and greeting sounds but also known to be an important organ during courtship. On such occasions, the trunk caresses, slaps, explores by sampling a female in heat and tickles by touching the clitoris. It is even inserted periodically into the mouth of the partner in a manner logically suggestive of an elephantine form of 'kissing'!

Once, I witnessed a young female inquisitively exploring the pendulous penis of a bull which was sampling another female in the herd. The male suddenly felt tickled and squeaked with a shudder. The trembled female's trunk then smothered his belly and chest with kisses, as if to say, "will you play love-game with me'? The bull moaned with both pleasure and surprise with the raw ache in his voice. He felt, perhaps, a growing sense of sexual power in him. The bull then took control of her and his explorative move in touching her clitoris excited the female. When she finally straddled him, he was also aroused as she was. The bull had, by then, surrendered to her and perhaps, she knew how to respond to his submission. It appeared she was determined to make the situation an overwhelming experience. The young female being a virtuous animal, the bull appeared almost seduced. While the female was very enduring and arousing, the bull proved to be a dynamo on the forest floor. The combination of both could produce rapturous results. As the herd continued to feed in the meadow these ravished couple vanished into the thicket with a 'French-kiss'.

The trunk in elephant quite literally serves as a fifth limb and its degree of flexibility is apparently at odds with the rest of the elephant's massive inflexibility. Such a solid heavy body would hardly survive unless it was equipped with some efficient means of satisfying its daily needs of food and water intake. The trunk fulfills the need admirably. It plucks leaves and branches growing high up on trees and grasses from the ground and stuffs them all into its small, fleshy mouth below the base of the trunk. A gallon or more water is sucked up at a time and then squirted into its throat.

The sense of touch is important in maintaining the proverbial 'steady footing' of elephants; the trunk is used to test unfamiliar terrain, touching and tapping each spot where the foot will be placed. It is likewise, the trunk a highly sensitive tactile appendage, as we see an elephant picking up a coin from the floor or tugging a great load about. Large motor-nerve fibres extend up and down the trunk, corresponding to the pyramidal tracts in humans. Considering some of these important factors, no doubt, the trunk is essentially, the "survival tool" in elephant.

There are many other functions for which the trunk is employed. One must not loose sight of the fact, whatever its shape and the most obvious uses it is put to, it is still basically the nose. The nostrils are located at the very tip, as much as 7-8 feet from the head and run the entire length of the trunk. They are divided along their length by a fleshy partition, the septum. The thousands of separate muscles that are woven around these internal tubes allow the trunk to be twisted and turned through any number of contortions to test the air for scents of neighbouring elephants or potential predators/enemies. This is an invaluable asset to the animal, because its eye-sight is not particularly sharp enough. The length of the trunk enables it, not only, to be cast around through a wide arc in search of air borne messages, but also to be held high above thick vegetation where the passage of the wind is neither interrupted nor strongly infused with smells from lower levels.

Blowing may also be expelled forcibly from the trunk to produce noises of varying pitch and intensity and becomes an organ of communication. Soft, pleasurable squeaks of greeting are used between individuals and harsh and high pitched trumpets are blasted out as warning signals to an enemy or a man approaching beyond the line of critical(LoC) danger. It is a warning to be heeded for; once committed to its charge, an adult elephant with its sensitive trunk curled up for protection, can out run a man on a forest floor. It can vent its fury on a large vehicle, reducing it to scrap metal in a matter of minutes.

In the heat of the tropical day most animals are driven to a shade under trees. The elephant is no exception to this rule, but its trunk acts as an extra cooling device. It can loose heat through the large surface area of the trunk's skin and can also use the trunk to spray showers of water over its body. It may stand for hours in water, alternately, squirting water into its mouth or over its rough hide. An elephant in deep waters may even use its trunk as a snorkel occasionally, breathing air with just the last few inches projecting above the surface. Trunk also is used to help the baby in swimming across rivers and reservoirs by lifting lightly. The trunk may also be used to spray mud-slurry or blowing over clouds of dust over the body when flies, mosquitoes and other external irritants are proving troublesome.

Perhaps to the human observer at least, the most remarkable attribute of the trunk is its combination of brutal strength and finger tip sensitivity. It is awe inspiring to watch the same organ that wraps itself around a fallen tree and hauls it roughly out of the way, then turns its attention toward a single, delicate leaf/flower on another tree and plucks it without causing more than a ripple of agitation across the rest of the branch. It is this same delicate touch which elephants employ when they caress each other. Their relationship is strong and when two individuals meet, their trunks feel each other, before intertwining in a display of mutual affection. The trunk is also described as incredibly 'sensitive instrument' in elephant.

Sub-adult males sparring with their trunks coiled each other. Such frolicking in young age help win serious clashes in adults to win over females in heat.

2.11.1   Raised Trunk – The Benefactor of Fortune?

A belief in the orient holds, "raised elephant trunk relates to showering of riches and wisdom". When an elephant's trunk is held up, it is an indication of good luck (just as holding precious liquid or fortune), while the trunk is down, its contents drained off or lost.

The trunk is reported to be made up of eight major muscles on each side (total 16, as the trunk is bilateral like most organs in the body) and a total of about 1,50,000 fascicles (portions of muscles) for the entire trunk. Without its trunk the elephant cannot survive any longer. Usually, Asian elephants pick up objects with their trunk by the "grasp" and "pinch" methods, while African elephants by the "pinch" method only. Under captive situations, when both species of elephant are together, African elephant may soon learn that the grasp method enables to collect food faster and it employs that method as well. The trunk of an adult elephant can hold 8.5 litres of water at a time and can drink between 90-100 litres per day. It eats between 150-240 kg of food per day. Elephant's digestive system is not that efficient, as it could be made out from the dung. The study has revealed that only about 44% of the food is digested and rest is passed through as partially digested roughage. Elephant may consume browse anywhere from 100-200 plant species, depending the locality and vegetation types it can access within its home range.

Raised trunk in elephants is said to shower fortune and wisdom.

2.11.2   Trunk – The Food Processing Device

The sheaf of grass is neatly packed before it is cropped by the trunk or pulled out by their roots in marshy lands, it is then dusted against raised wrist by slapping sharply with whirl of turns and placed into its mouth. Especially, when the bunch of fodder consists of long grasses with stocks or sedges, the trunk is formed into a double twist near its tip and then violently spins in the air. This whirling movement generates considerable centrifugal force and the adherent mud and debris; even insects are sent flying away from the sheaf. When feeding in tall grass/thick cover, what is held in the trunk cannot be easily dusted against the foreleg, then the trunk is raised high above the head and the fodder swiftly twirled aloft to clean it. No doubt, in addition to clinging mud and dust and debris, the sheaf is freed of snails and slugs by these manoeuvres.

The sheaf of grass is placed crosswise in the mouth, with the basal roots projecting from the edge of the lips-line on one side and the tips of the blades on the other; then at a bite, the projected parts of the sheaf are trimmed that fall off to the ground, before it is masticated and swallowed. When the grass is tender, the blades are consumed and it will be found that the rejected parts of sheaves (which mark the passage of the animal in the course of its grazing) consist largely of the basal stalks and roots; when the blades of grass are mature and hard, but basal shoots are succulent, the apical part of the sheaf is trimmed and rejected and the shoots (with only the roots bitten off) consumed. The placing of the sheaf in the mouth and the consumption of a part of it is biologically selective action and not purely mechanical, indicating clearly that the taste in elephant is good. When the elephants feed on the grass grown at the edge of lake waters or swamps the mud attached to roots is washed in water by rigorous churning action and put into the mouth. Roots are then trimmed off holding sheaf cross wise in the mouth; succulent sheaf are then consumed. It is indeed, 'an art of food processing', which only elephants can perform.

the tusker collecting bark from Teak tree and processing it before feeding. Tree bark of different species forms @5-12% of food intake in elephants.

Bamboos (*Bambusa arundinasea* and *Dendrocalamus strictus*) and *Ochlandra travancorica*, sugar cane and standing crops in the fields are among other grasses much fancied as food. In feeding on the giant bamboo, the entire clump is not pushed down; individual bamboo is selected and pulled out. It is not only the foliage and tender shoots that are eaten, but also the green bamboo. Elephants on occasions, I have observed eat even dry bamboo pushed down or fallen on the forest floor, during prolonged summer, when scarcity of food raises its dirty head. Rattan cane is also much fancied and eaten by elephants. Banana plants are pulled down, the stem splits open by the trunk with the assistance of forefoot and the pith eaten greedily – a noticeable preponderance to banana fibre in the dung betrays over night raids on garden crops and plantations. Occasionally, young coconut trees up to the age of ten are pushed down and tender shoots including nuts are eaten by crop raiding elephants.

I have seen elephants feeding on exotic weed, the water hyacinth (*Eiechornia crassipes*), while wild buffaloes and rhinos frequently by invading the *bheels* of Kaziranga national park. It is known that this plant has a considerable iodine content; in fact, in an emergency it is utilized for the commercial manufacture of iodine. How far and in what ways the sustained intake (even in small quantities) of this iodine-rich plant will influence elephants and other animals is a matter which needs investigation.

Among the succulents eaten by elephants may be mentioned are: *Pandanus odoratissimus* (Screw Pine) and *Ardisia solanacea*, both growing amidst bamboo brakes along forest streams and banks of marshes: these provide a source of water even when the streams are dry in summer. An exotic plant that seems to be more freely eaten now than some 50 years ago is the *Lantana camara*. This exotic plant is also eaten by chital and sambar during the pinch period of summer.

The barks of certain trees such as *Kydia calycina, Grewia tiliaefolia* and *Tectona grandis* are skillfully stripped off and eaten. It is not the dry bark that is eaten, but barks that are sappy. The elephant applies the ventral surface of the base of the trunk to the tree with a firm pressure and then jerks its head laterally; this causes the bark to split open and gets detached from the stem into a strip of some 4 to 6 inches wide; the lower broken edge of the strip is then gently lifted up with the tip of the trunk till the bark is stripped as high as the trunk can go and hangs from the bole/stem; then this strip of bark is held lax in the trunk and given two or three preliminary oscillations and then one quick upward flick that detaches it for another 2 or three ft up the trunk. After eating this, another strip of bark; next to the peeled strip, is similarly peeled off and consumed. *Kydia calycina*, being soft and sappy, is the most favoured plant, the bark of which is largely stripped open, especially in summer; by coming year new bark may have covered the bole/stem. On many occasions, another favourite tree, namely, Teak including plantation poles are pushed down to feed on bark and twigs. Yet other favoured species, whose bark frequently eaten are, *Terminelia tomentosa* and *T. belerica*. The barks and twigs are found to form at about 5% of elephant diet, according to my own study. All these intricacies involved in functioning of the trunk, as a survival strategy of the elephant, strongly support the theory, "Elephant –The Technical Animal".

2.12   Elephant – The Technical Animal

The Asian elephant is unique in its survival strategy: its trunk is the most versatile instrument; it possesses thousands of muscles, each of which needs appropriate orders from the central nervous system to function. No wonder, it takes a long time for a youngster to master its intricate functions. When it itches inside it could roll it under a forefoot and rub. At its tip are tiny hair which are probably useful for feeling the shape, texture and temperature of objects or perhaps in locating the precise bearing of a scent marks in the wind.

I have seen a cow using her trunk to scoop out sand which she had loosened with her toes, while digging for water. Same cow was found to pluck grass by holding it in place by her trunk, while her toes cut across the stems in a sweep. If the roots came up with full of dirt, she beat them against her shins until they were clean. When stripping a tree, her trunk would be used to grab the shreds of bark and exert a steady pull. If one of her eyes needed massaging she would rub it in a sinuous rolling motion. Her tip of the trunk also anointed her leg-pits, neck and wounds, if any, with mud-pack and blew them with slurry followed by dust. Even she could wrap up encircling her free end and slid it to get rid off insects stinging at the base the trunk.

TRUNK IS A SURVIVAL TOOL IN ELEPHANT

Trunk in elephant is an all purpose device like hand in humans.

The elephant could, therefore, be described, as the "Technical Animal" and accordingly, be presented in the book, the Animal World. And while classifying the Asian elephant – in the Animal Kingdom, necessary addendum needs insertion, as the "Technical Animal".

In addition to the above narrations, the following facts also justify to support the above theory:

i. Elephants cover themselves with broad green leaves or grass to protect their head from the scorching sun, just as man wears a solar-hat or a headgear to protect scalp from the sun.

ii. The trunk in elephants is used as a survival tool; it is used, among others, as a food processing device and all other activities.

iii. The finger like tip of the trunk is used in applying mud-pack at pits and in sealing or covering the wounds against flies. It is also used in removing and collecting bark from tree-trunks.

iv. The trunk is used to hold a stick that is used to scratch the portion of the body that can't be reached easily by its trunk.

v. By holding green twig with leaves the elephant engages itself in driving away the "daily monsters" like flies and mosquitoes to escape from their menace.

vi. As a nature's "water diviner", the elephant digs water holes in dried up river/*nalla*/tank bed to draw water for a drink during prolonged summer or drought.

vii. The elephant pushes logs, and pulls down trees or branches using its trunk, simultaneously using its tremendous power, like that of mechanised crane or bulldozer to feed on leaves, bark and twigs.

viii. Soft stones or some times cement platforms on either side of culverts are used by elephants to file their nails as a process of pedicure.

ix. Above all, trunk is skilful, powerful and a wise work force; a living crane in logging operation in addition to obedient and disciplined armoury on command, as a captive elephant.

    x. **The use of the trunk as a tool and its application in various skills is nothing but a "survival strategy". These amazing adaptations, therefore, justify in reckoning the Asian elephant as the "technical animal".**

    xi. **In all its glory, the elephant's higher level of intelligence, fantastic memory, highly emotional (by grief, joy, anger, threat, fear) and highly social (like extended human family) and human like qualities also support the theory of "technical animal".**

2.13 Foods-Cape and Feeding

Food habits in elephants are very diverse, ranging from grass to bamboo, foliage to bark, flowers to fruits and sugarcane to millets. Elephants feed at different levels of vegetation in woodland habitats. While feeding, the trunk is used to detach food and convey it to the mouth, the fore feet are also used as adventitious aids, to crush and break up large fruits and small branches or bamboo shoots and scraping short grass and dusting it to remove mud sticking to roots and finally trimming the root portion or over-matured blades of grasses, before it is pushed into the mouth. Watching the elephants feed, one is impressed by their elaborate process, such as, the care with which they select and prepare each mouthful for ingestion. Though elephants are choosy feeders, they eat a lot. They have to keep feeding not by choice, but by necessity for nearly 18 hours a day with 4 hours sleep and two hours to play and drink. They must eat to survive, but not survive to eat. The matriarch knows where to take her family, the exact locations of availability of food, water and mineral salt. Her fantastic memory and long standing experience are aptly used in sourcing her needs, in times of drought other critical situations. They always go in search of greener pastures within their home range, ranging 80 to 150 sq km.

The fodder naturally varies with locality and season and what follows is merely indicative of the many kinds of plant food they eat. They are entirely vegetarian. Feeding by elephants and other ungulates help keep the grass healthy; otherwise, it becomes woody and unpalatable. Elephants and other ungulates depend on grasses, as much as grasses on elephants and ungulates in a healthy ecosystem.

Foliage and twigs of many shrubs and herbs are also eaten. Among these may be mentioned: *Helicteres Isora, Grewia aspera; Hibiscus lampas, Acaciaconcinna, A. Intsia, A. ferruginea, A. Catechu, Cordia myxa and Zizyphus Xylopyrus, Phoenix humilis* are much liked; Some of the wild flowers and the fruits are avidly consumed.

In south Indian forests, it is not rare to come across *Buchanania latifolia* saplings that look as if they had been pollarded; wild elephants eat the crown of this tree when it is in new leaf to give it this appearance. *Emblicaofficinalis, Ficus mysorensis, F. bengalensis, Premna tomentosa, Elaeodendron glaucum, Albizzia odoratissima, Diospyros* spp. and *Bauhinia racemosa* areamong the trees whose flowers and fruits are regularly eaten.

Many kinds of tall grasses (all those appropriately and loosely termed 'elephant grass') are eaten, as also some short grasses and herbaceous plants. Among the grasses commonly eaten may be mentioned: *Saccharumspontaneum, Ischaemum pilosum, Panicum oreades, Sorghum* and *Themeda cymbaria, Apluda mutica, Arundinella lolocoides, Eragrostis gangetica, Hackelochloa granularis* and *Paspalum scrobiculatum.*

Grass may look to be a simple almost primitive plant, little more than leaves with roots. In fact, it is highly advanced species, bearing tiny, unobtrusive flowers which rely not on insects to disseminate their pollen grains, but the wind that blows so freely and widely across the open expanses, where it grows. It produces horizontal stems running close to the earth surface or just below it. Fire acts as a great leveller and serves as an agent to improve fertility. When fire sweeps across the meadows, consuming the old dried blades of grass, the flames run over quickly, so that the root stocks remain unharmed and they produce new sprouts almost immediately. They can do this because grass blades grow, not from the tip, as do those of bushes and trees, but from the base. This also enormously benefits the grazing animals, for it means that even though the blades have been cropped, they will continue to grow unchecked and very soon produce another meal.

Some sedges of *Zingiberaceae,* such as, *Costus* and *Alpinia* species are also commonly eaten by elephants.

The aerial roots of Banyan tree are much fancied and regularly broken off at the level of the elephant's reach, as they grow again. During prolonged drought period elephants forage on Ficus bark, wood, twigs and leaves. Camp elephants when marched to towns and cities for procession and celebrations of festivities, Banyan tree branches serve as a staple food; these are easily available around the suburbs.

I have seen elephants laboriously gathering and consuming flower heads including shoots of *Mimosa pudica*, especially when it is tender. However, wild flowers do not form any significant part of their diet, but they painstakingly collect tiny morsels that they especially fancy. A variety of forest fruits are eaten, among them are: *Aegle marmelos, Artocarpus integrifolia, A. hirsuta, Careya arborea, Cordia Myxa, Emblica officinalis, Feronia Elephantum,* Figs, *Pandanus odoratissimus* and *Randia uliginosa.* The grains of seeding bamboo and the seeds of *Cycas* are also eaten. I have seen a tusker rising to reach Jackfruits attached to the tree with his hind legs resting on the ground and plucking raw fruits in front of Keshve Forest Lodge at Bhadra Tiger Reserve.

An average bull elephant weighing 4000 kilograms would require about 200 kilograms of food in a day of 24 hours. A cow elephant requires correspondingly a smaller amount. Studies, such as, those have demonstrated the very pronounced seasonal variations in the elephant's diet; after the onset of the rains the grass intake increases significantly falling down to a low level as the dry season wears on.

Eating plants is no easy business for elephants. It demands particular skills and structures just like any other specialist diet. For one thing, unlike cultivated varieties, wild vegetative matter is not very nutritious. An animal has to eat great deal of quantities in order to extract enough calories for its sustenance. Dedicated vegetarians like elephants have to spend three-quarters of their waking hours, solidly gathering, preparing and chewing grasses, foliage, bark and twigs. That process, in itself requires the creature to stand out in the open exposed to dangers, not only from predators, but also dreaded poachers. Because of its huge size, the elephant can not avoid from exposing itself and herding will provide added safety. But the smaller herbivores, in order to minimise that risk of attack by enemies, grab as much as possible, as quickly as possible and run off to safety, where they masticate before digesting.

Plant eaters have to have, particularly, good teeth. Not only do they use them for a very long period but the material they have to deal with is often very tough. Once gnawed, ground and pulped, the food has to be digested. Elephants have, particularly acute problems, for they eat in addition to grass and leaves, a great deal of fibrous bark, twigs and woody material. Their only teeth-molars at the back of the mouth form massive grinders. As they wear down, they are replaced every few years by new ones erupting from behind and migrating forward along the jaw.

The molars pulp and crush with enormous power, but even so, the elephant's food is so woody that it requires a very long period of digestion to extract anything of nutritive value from it. Surprisingly, digestive system in elephants is very poor; digestion of food depends on thin microbes found in alimentary canal. The elephant's stomach, however, is big enough to provide for the same. An elephant's meal takes about two and a half days (almost 60 hours) to make the journey passing through the body and for most of that time it is kept stewing in the digestive juices and bacterial broth of the stomach. Wade back in history, some dinosaurs eating ferns and cycads, had encountered similar problem and could solve it in similar way – by increasing giants' size.

Elephant dung, even after all this protracted treatment, still contains a great deal of twigs, fibres and seeds that have remained virtually untouched. Once during my morning trail at Bandipur, a partially digested bark of

Bende *Kydia calycina* that was retrieved from the dung, taped as much as nine feet. Some plants that have been stripped by elephants for millennia have reacted to the treatment by coating their seeds with rinds thick enough to withstand a prolonged soaking in digestive juices. The paradoxical consequence has been that unless the hard coat is softened by passing through the stomach of an elephant, the seeds do not germinate. Elephants and gaur are usually found in the same forests and it has been said that they feed amicably. This has been my experience as well. No doubt, gaur benefit by following in the wake of elephants and consuming the bamboo and other tree foliage pulled down by the latter, but elephants do not tolerate gaur to feed along with them. They may use the same habitat for feeding one after the other. But they never feed together. Because elephants being dominant species, they don't tolerate the presence of any other beasts or birds either at grazing grounds or at forest pools. They are mercilessly driven away by members of the herd of elephants.

Elephants, while feeding in a group or feeding singly are strangely unsociable or partial with other grazers. Elephants are also found to be partial in scooping or digging fresh water-holes for themselves with their feet, where the water is tainted by other animals having drunk at the same pool earlier.

2.14 Brain and Intelligence

Encephalopathy Quotient (EQ) is the relative size of the brain compared to the body size; elephants have large EQ value (about 2, similar to some higher primates). The elephant's brain, when considered in relation to its body size is conspicuously small. When compared to man, the elephant's intelligence potential is less, since man's brain to body ratio is much larger than that of the elephant (by about 20-25 times). The presence of large number of temporal lobes in elephant's brain indicates the increased capacity to remember and recognise objects/places/humans. Why do the elephants need good memory for? Unlike other ungulates, elephants live longer, as much as humans. As humans need good memory for long living, so also the elephants need good memory. Matriarchs are the store-house of such knowledge for the benefit of their families/clan. With all their better level of intelligence and long memory, they are still at the mercy of man – the farmers and poachers for survival.

Whether an elephant has the capacity to acquire and apply the knowledge and has highly developed reasoning powers of its own, is rather a debatable point. We all know, the elephants have, undoubtedly an exceptional aptitude for absorbing instructions and their ability to learn and perform, is an established fact in captive elephants. A well trained elephant can recognize 60-100 words and phrases. Elephants have exhibited a long memory and extraordinary docility; the rate of learning varies with each elephant, but once it has mastered a trick, it will repeat it faultlessly, as often as, the trainer wishes to, even after a lapse of time. Some of these training achievements by elephants exhibit the highest degree of virtuosity.

2.14.1 Elephant Never Forgets

Long memory in elephant is a survival tool, especially in scanning water source in that vast expanse of home range, spread over more than hundred of sq km. An elephant does have a remarkable ability to remember places of activities, so that it can lead the herd where food, water and safety matter the most for their day to day survival. The size and structure of the elephant's brain suggest a considerable potential for information storage and retrieval. An adult elephant's brain weighs about 5 kg, as against an adult human's brain of about 1.6 kg. But in terms of ratio, that of the elephant is 1:500 of its body weight, where as that of human is 1:50 of the body weight. An old proverbial saying goes, "elephant never forgets" is nearer to truth. A majority of elephants migrate or travel considerable distances to source their food and water. They undoubtedly, have good memory that allows them to remember locations of water supplies many years later. The capacity of the elephant brain to store information is said to be next to human and better developed among all other terrestrial mammals. An elephant can differentiate up to 200 individuals. Elephants have a growing/developing intelligence, as they grow up to maturity, just as in humans.

Bernhard Gizimech's studies have shown how well an elephant's memory is adapted to its needs in the wild. Gizimech placed food in one of five boxes in sight of elephant cows. Initially, the animals chose boxes randomly, when they sought to get the food. After being trained, the elephants waited no more than fifteen seconds and chose the correct box in seventy six percent of all trials.

"Food never disappears in nature before the elephant's eyes/nose", it is said. Of course, experiments revealed, how well elephants make use of previous experience, once they have found food. Innumerable incidents with captive elephants have an impressive record of the proverbial "elephant memory". Many years of my observations of elephants in the wild indicated that the members of herds numbering 9 to 22 individuals recognized each other individually. They also knew the exact route of their movements even though many of these paths are used only every few months. They also knew exact location of forest pools, salt-licks and natural springs alike.

A story at the beginning of the century tells of an elephant that was ordered by his master to stay under a tree until his return. That elephant broke twigs from the tree and placed them under his feet in order to prevent himself from sinking in the wet and muddy ground.

Some conservationists advocate talking for themselves, while in the company of wild elephants. I could not understand whether talking has any effect on the animals. But, it is true; the elephants might become familiar to the person, by constantly, listening to his or her voice.

The above information and those uncanny tales described had, undoubtedly led to the belief that elephants are intelligent animals, having their own reasoning powers. Presently, there is insufficient data to prove or disprove such statements. However, the elephant's survival strategies also lead us to justify it as the "Technical Animal".

2.14.2 Calf Brain – Human Baby Like

The calf is a long term investment in elephant's society. Its level of brain development is human like; at birth the level is said to be at 35% and would attain full development at adulthood. Calf's brain grows gradually, because of prolonged immaturity, during which learning plays a crucial role, its eventual development is all the greater. The same is true of human beings, where lengthening of childhood and delaying the age of puberty are the factors associated with the evolution of intelligence. Most other mammals, however are born with the brain nearer to their adults.

Young calves subsist on their mothers' milk up to the age of about 6 months, and then they begin to feed on succulent grasses and herbs. They may be suckled occasionally till they are 3 years old. A young calf is singularly clumsy with its small, undeveloped trunk, which it rests against the axial of its mother in 'S' shape, while suckling milk and it is only as it grows up that the trunk develops and it acquires skill in the use of the appendage. The breasts of cow elephants have a slight outward lean, towards the flank and this facilitates suckling the calf.

2.14.3 Brain Maturity in Elephant, Just as Human

In its period of infancy and growth to adolescence and maturity including its longevity, the elephant bears striking points of resemblance, totally related to human being. Females in their teenage reach their sexual prime at the age of 13-15, while their male peers are beginning to wind down at 18-25 years, when they are more fertile –'riding high'. These age structures match the attainment of adulthood in humans. The bull gains in height and especially in orgasmic bounty at 30. At these ages both take time to give and receive pleasure, exploring fantasies. The male is in his prime from 30 to 50; the age of enlightenment – middle-aged from 45 to 55, and definitely aged at 60 years, though he may still be often quite robust. Cow elephants continue to breed till the age of about 55 years, as from sexual and sensual stand point; the fifth decade of life could qualify as the richest, as far as wisdom and experiences are concerned. An older cow probably, has a better idea of what she does and does not want. For, her sex is like a Hot-Fudge sundae and seeks the association of bulls even when past 60 years, no matter how far the female has come on the amazing journey of female sexuality; it has got plenty to anticipate. As the female ages, she tends to grow more conscious of her mortality and limitations.

In recent years, doubts have been raised by some foreign writers on the Asian elephant, really being a long-lived one and it has been said that it does not live beyond 70 years. No doubt, it exceeds this classical span of three score – and ten on occasion, even as men do, when free and wild. Anyone who has some knowledge of wild elephants in India will appreciate how better conditioned they are than the captive ones and how much less subject to wearing down.

2.15 Communication System in Elephant

2.15.1 Vocalization

Elephant cows communicate with their young by slapping their ears against the head. When companions meet, they softly "peep", followed by "rumbling".. Elephant's growl and trumpet when they are surprised by predators or humans. The shrill tones of trumpets often initiate either flight or attack by the elephants. When they threaten predators/eneimies, they often beat their trunks against the trunk of other animal, producing a sound like that of automobile tyres, striking against a hard surface. Vocalization either originate in the larynx (as in rumbling and roaring sounds) and are then amplified in the air columns of the trunk or they are created in the trunk itself. When in distress cows moan, when bogged down into mud-flats; they also groan as in case of agonising babies, when they are separated from their mothers.

2.15.2 Infrasonic Sound Mechanism

In recent years, we have learnt the elephants can produce and hear calls below the range of human reflexes. The low frequency calls of the Asian and African elephants can be perceived by other elephants within a distance of five to ten km. Mechanism of elephants' communication system through "infrasonic calls" is well documented. Evidence also suggests that Mammoths and American mastodons were also able to communicate with infrasonic sound frequencies below the range of human reflexes.

Among elephants, it is the females who are born politicians, cultivating robust and lifelong social ties with at least 100 other elephants, a task made easier by their infrasonic power of communication miles across the forest floor. Elephant society is organized as a matriarchal system. They are, it is reported, constantly making decisions, debating among themselves, over food, water and security. One can observe their behaviour in the wild, you can hear them disagree, see them fight among youngsters. Typically, the matriarch intervenes and has a final say and all others abide by her decision. If a faction of the herd/clan disagrees strongly and wants to try a different approach, the group will split temporarily and reunite again later.

2.16 Marvel of Elephant's Walk

We have been acquainted with the stealthy tread of cats, both big and small. They walk on their tiptoes. But those who have seen elephant walking in the jungle cannot but marvel at the smooth, noiseless ease with which he/she moves despite cumbrous bulk. The leg-bones are so arranged that the elephant virtually walks on tiptoes: hence it's described as delicate movement. The foot is cushioned and the elephant's weight distributed by a thick fatty pad inside the sole of the foot. Its thick soles are liable to get worn off by constant walking, particularly on macadamized roads and they may bleed in severe cases. For this reason the mahout, generally chooses the sides or road covered with sand or mud.

The average walking speed of an elephant is about 5 km an hour, while running it can attain a maximum speed of 15-18 km an hour. Elephant herds, while feeding in the jungle maintain a snail speed of half a km to a km per hour. Their maximum speed some times surprises an athlete, especially when they attempt to chase away enemies like tigers and human intruders. In Bandipur Tiger Reserve, once I had to drive the Waggoner out of its reach of a charging young bull, when I clocked a speed @20 km as he pursued for a short distance of about half a km or so.

Elephant being a quadruped, even if slips down by putting leg in a burrow or a pit or tumbles against a dry stump, while running or charging human being or a vehicle, it can still balance itself on three legs. Whereas, man has only two legs; he would easily slip or tumble down while trying to escape on the forest floor and is likely to get killed. One must choose his escape route only along beaten track or a forest road.

Tusker walking gracefully – *Gajagambhirya,* **and poetically described as** *Gajagamini,* **in Sanskrit language by none other than Kalidasa, the priest of all poets.**

2.17 Gajagamini – the Graceful Gait of the Elephant

People are always fascinated by elephants, moving with grace like a small hill with its massive body. The gait of its leisurely walk is graceful with expressive body language and attracts one's attention on the jungle track. When you intently watch the elephant's gait from behind, its gait is comparable to the gait of a graceful woman with impressive body language. It is this gait of the elephant, lyrically described by Kalidasa (about 400 A.D), the greatest poet of the Golden or Classical age of the Imperial Guptas, as "*Gajagamini*". Some romantic observers opine that elephant's gait has the effect of aphrodisiac. I discovered such a lyrical gait with wonderful body language in Madhuri Dixit, the most sought after film actress of the silver screen of Bollywood. She is vividly associated with *Gajagamini,* the elephant gait and is romantically known by the nick name – *Gajagamini.* In real life too, she is the same as she is in the movies. The beauty may not necessarily be in the face and body curves, it is in her graceful movements as well. One is indeed deeply fascinated by her 'Mona Lisa' smile.

I have been the great admirer of elephant gait – *Gajagamini*, in a natural set up. To appreciate the grace of an elephant's walk, one need to observe it from behind. It is a great feeling! It could be more appropriate for our organisers of 'Fashion Models' and 'Man Hunts' competitions to adapt the theme of *Gajagamini*, the graceful gait of the elephant. It is immensely impressive and romantic than popular "Cat Walk".

But riding an elephant on wildlife safari teaches you patience. Long riding is strenuous; one needs to withstand swinging and swaying with forward and backward jerks. The elephant's legs of a flank move forward at a time during its stride. Sometimes, patience in riding the elephant runs out, as much as to the animal. Though they are much more nimble in their feet, while walking long distances in the sun, they may break out suddenly,. in search of shade of a nearby tree, amidst thorny bushes and creating panic among the safari riders. In extreme hot sun an elephant may refuse to obey the commands of the mahout. In such an eventuality keep pouring water over its head and ears to cool the temperament.

Now a day, taking visiting tourists on elephant back in wildlife reserves for viewing wild animals and birds is a common practice. Once a couple from North India, who visited Bandipur reserve with their children refused to sit on the captive elephant, leave alone riding by saying, "We offer fruits and flowers with reverence, when elephants pay visit our home; we worship elephant-god, the Ganesha. Why on earth, should we ride the godly vehicle and the jewel of the natural world?"

I admired her true sense of respect towards the elephant and informed wisdom and declared, my eyes filled with *Ananda bashpa*, the tears of joy, "You are the green warrior to be remembered"!

2.18 Leg Work

It is not surprising that an animal which has evolved to such a massive size had to equip itself with anatomical peculiarities: feet, legs, nose, ears and teeth all operate in a peculiarly 'elephantine' way to ease the tasks of walking, feeding, drinking, keeping the body cool and protective against pests and enemies.

The whole foreleg from shoulder to nail is an amazing infrastructure! It was, perhaps held, in ancient times, as straight as a column of steel to give long and vertical support. Before the elephant was held and kept in captivity and observed at close quarters for any length of time, it was reported to have been accepted that the straight and powerful limbs were totally devoid of joints. There seemed to be a certain stiff-legged, which accompanied the normal, ambling gait of the elephant and the idea of one bone running the entire length of the leg, had caught on to such an extent that Shakespeare alluded to it in his play, Troileus and Cressida. Ulysses remarked, "The elephant hath joints, but none for courtesy, while commenting on Ajax's, rather, inflexible attitude towards Achilles. His legs are legs for necessity, not for flexor". Yet the limbs are also oddly flexible appearing at times to possess an extra joint. Thus, the elephant has four knees. There is a shoulder, knee in each leg (or elbow), an ankle (or wrist) and digits comparable to those of cat and dog families. The peculiarity concerns the ankle, which is set much further down along the length of the limb. Thus it takes the position of a joint almost halfway between the knee and a place where one might expect the ankle to be.

There is a second feature of the elephant limb which demands special attention. It is elephant's walk virtually on tiptoes. However contradictory to their weight this may seem, it is not only true but also an ingenious means of enabling the foot to act as a cushion softening the blow of every step. The bones of the toe actually point toward the ground, but their position is not outwardly visible. They are embedded in elastic fibres which are themselves held fast within large quantity of fatty tissues. The whole collections of bones, fibres and fat are held in shape by the thick outer covering of the elephant's pad and externally represented by nails, equivalent to hoof in ungulates. Their position corresponds approximately to the position of the fingers in humans, although they are not attached to them. These nails may be very small and may sometimes, worn/torn off during the normal passage of life. The number present on each foot should not, as has previously happened, be used as a means of identifying different subspecies of elephants (in rare/abnormal cases some Asian elephants are reported to possess 16 nails-four in each foot as against 18 and as in case of normal Asian elephants). Thus, at the end of each of the elephant's legs there is a compressible, shock-absorbing pad which, because of its sponge-like qualities, is able to expand and contract, when the weight of its owner is alternately lowered or raised upon it. Its stabilizing qualities also render it highly adaptable to any unevenness on the ground. Steep inclines and rocky terrain or strewn with boulders can be negotiated with silent ease, because each pad adjusts itself independently (like the car with a system of independent suspension) to the immediate requirements of a 'sure foot hold'.

2.19 Elephant – the Sure-Footed Animal

Elephants act like sort of bulldozers in the forests; they perform yet another significant function of enriching forest soils. There is no other animal in Asian jungles that uses specific paths as regularly as elephants. These elephant paths help human expeditions, such adventure tourism and trekking and to move through the jungles quickly and effortlessly by forest protection staff. Many of these paths have been used for generations and are so wide that they could be used by jeeps even. Elephants skillfully make use of the surroundings of such paths for their benefits. They follow contours and terraces to climb mountain slopes as high as possible, without loosing balance/equilibrium. They reach the valley floor by following narrow zigzag paths or by following natural steps deliberately and steadily. Many other animals such as rhinoceros, tiger, deer and gaur, use elephant paths, during their daily and seasonal movements. Foresters and Forest Engineers in India, Sri Lanka and Malaysia build forest roads taking alignment along the elephant-paths. Elephants are excellent at ambling along at a moderate speed; they have a fine sense of balancing, in treacherous and mountainous terrain. One could be more secure in riding an elephant than a horse/ mule in such terrains. Elephant is, proverbially, termed as the "sure-footed" animal of the jungle terrains.

Elephants do not normally crash through the jungle; they move very quietly. They walk with a very light step, unbelievable as it may seem, a bull weighing 4-5 tonnes, its feet distribute the body weight, such that only 600 grams of pressure act on each square cm of sole. In the light of this, it is perhaps, somewhat less surprising to learn that entire herd of elephants is often unnoticed until they actually show up.

Chapter III

Myths, Art and Culture

"A long tail in the front, a short tail in the rear", what a manifestation of that giant creature oh? "Do you know, where it puts all that stuff gathered by its long tail...?" came a phone call to the local police, by dumbfound old lady complaining, what she had witnessed in her back yard, at the crack of dawn! Yes, that creature happened to be an elephant. Elephants have always been so much a part of India's myth, history and cultural heritage; protecting and ensuring the survival of this noble animal means much more to an Indian than protecting just another historical monument, like the Tajmahal. It is more of a saving the magnificent and incredible animal, the elephant which has come to be known to symbolise India. Realising the urgent need to conserve the Indian elephant the Government of India have since, declared it as the "National Heritage Animal". The government's action comes as a bid to give elephant conservation, under "Project Elephant", the same momentum of national pride that 'save the tiger' campaign evokes.

I arrived at my HQ office in Mysore from Bandipur and opened my morning mail to find that I had been invited to deliver a lecture on "Ecology and Management of Indian Elephant" to the Probationers of Indian Forest Service (IFS), by the Director, The Indira Gandhi National Forest Academy, Dehradun. I didn't waste my time to reply, accepted the invitation and accordingly, confirmed my programme to the Director, IGNFA, Dehradun.

On the schedule date and time I arrived at the New Forest campus, Dehradun, duly prepared for a talk over slides presentation on Elephant-Its Ecology and Management. The programme started, as usual, with an introduction by the Director, about me and my contribution in the field of elephant conservation in Bandipur national park.

While I was in the midst of introductory part of my lecture on "A Strategy to Mitigate Human-Elephant Conflict" (Controversy on Human Rights versus Elephant Rights), a series of questions were hurled by inquisitive young minds from among audience comprising of probationers and members of teaching faculty. They are:

* **Do we find white elephants in our forests?**

* **Does elephant possess four knees?**

* **Does elephant take revenge against killing its relatives?**

* **Do elephants have secret burial grounds?**

* **Do elephants mourn the death of a fellow animal?**

* **Is the elephant a good soldier?**

* **Do you find** *chela* **among bulls in the wild?**

* **Will the Indian elephant join the fate of dinosaurs? And**

* **Why tigers are smaller than elephants?**

Deviating from the main topic of my talk, I attempted briefly to clarify misgivings in the minds of young audience present there. They are reproduced here as under:

"That the white elephants are regarded as sacred animals in the East, especially in Thailand, where they enjoy immense symbolic importance even today. The law of the land there specifies that all white elephants are the property of the King. They are only used in special ceremonies, national festivities and as royal parades. White elephant is a freak of nature, in the same way as white deer, white crows and white python are. White elephants are a rarity. In ancient India, elephant breeders treated white elephant with great veneration. The white elephants are not generally found to survive in the forests. Any thing that is white in the wilderness is easily spotted by enemies and killed sooner or later".

"Contrary to the belief, no animal on the earth has four knees. These so called knees in elephant are nothing but the elbows and wrists. They are situated, relatively speaking high above the ground and therefore, mistakenly referred to as 'knees'. However, the elephant's front legs and hind legs function just as hands and legs in human respectively, while sitting or sleeping. While the hind legs fold backward, the front legs bend forward".

"Man is the only enemy of the elephant. He is the greatest threat for the existence of the elephant and hopes of its survival. Occasionally, tigers do kill calves, but elephants do not form a potential prey base in their menu. Elephants dramatically react to the presence of tigers in the vicinity. Mating tigers are a potential threat to baby elephants. The elephants resolutely manage to keep such killing frenzy tigers at bay. No animal on earth is as cruel as that of man, who resorts to butcher elephants for ivory and poisons them when crops are raided. Elephants being highly social and emotional, occasionally they may attack humans as a revenge of killing their relatives. For self-protection and for the safety of their young, the elephants make all possible attempts to keep away natural enemies, like tigers. In the collective memory of humans, their mothers, as great bed-time story tellers and teachers, as part of curricula at schools, might use a standard line, 'if any one attempts to tease or harm the elephant, it would punish him'. The popular folklore story told among them, is the 'Tailor and an Elephant', the moral of the story being, 'as you sow, so shall you reap'."

"It is believed that old males have their body guards called *chela*, as a standby assistance. I had once, sitting on a *machan*, seen such an association of a tusker accompanied by a juvenile male at a salt-lick at Nagarahole. I too had formed similar opinion on witnessing, the way that juvenile provided care and affection to the bull. The bull was in his prime condition, looked hale and healthy. After a while, both of them visited the near-by water hole for a drink. While the bull siphoned water and squirted into its mouth, water was found jetting out through a hole at the base of the trunk. He had, perhaps, become a target to bullets of farmers/poachers. Such an association of a so called *chela* with a tusker was, I supposed, to assist in times of distress, such as this injured bull. The concept of *chela* was never encountered by me, thereafter, during many years of my association with the pachyderms in the wild. In their response to dangers of the wilderness, every bull usually, looks after himself. This makes all the more reasonable that young males do sometimes provide helping hand by associating themselves with their elders who have been found sick or suffering from injuries, just as cows assisting a helpless member of the family. There is a widespread belief among hunters that when a bull becomes old and feeble, he is attended by a young bull called *chela*, who looks after him in his senility. The belief in protective young *chela*, probably, originated from the experiences by hunters, who tried to get closer to an old tusker with prized ivory, might have charged by a younger male or probably, a more alert bull in their temporary association".

"Elephants do mourn the tragic death of a fellow animal of their species, irrespective of their relationship, unlike other animals, which take no notice of the injured/dead. I have seen elephants standing in silence for a long time, when they came across partially disintegrated carcass of a cow that had died due to old age, on the bank of river Kabini. Legendary of a secret burial ground of elephants does not have any scientific explanation. Elephants do possess many of the human qualities, like caring the injured, mourning the dead, living in family groups with strong bonds, exhibiting high level of intelligence and highly emotional expression, disciplining the youngsters while bringing them up and so on. As required under 'law of the jungle', elephants do not believe in sparing the cane and spoiling the young".

"As to your question whether Indian elephant would join the fate of dinosaurs, my reply is in the negative. As long as, we the enlightened folk are able to provide them compassion and safe habitat; and not, until natural disasters struck or regional upheavals on the face of the earth occur, the Asian elephant has little chance of meeting the fate of dinosaurs or even reaching the threshold of extinction. Ivory in Asian elephants is found on males only, unlike African elephants, where both male and female possess. Even in the worst situation, females and their young males come to the rescue of saving the species, even if all the existing bulls are shot out by habitual poachers. Dinosaurs, which reigned the earth surface 60 million years ago disappeared, perhaps, due to tectonic movements of the continents or upheavals on the earth surface, such as, earthquake followed by tsunami or volcano eruption. But Palaeontologists do not yet confirm whether *Homo sapiens* or his ancestors were, in any way, responsible in their sudden disappearance both from the face of the earth planet and ocean planet".

And as to your prudent question, why tigers are smaller than elephants, my considered answer is, "A supreme predator on earth, due to its manoeuvrability coupled with extraordinary perceptions, the tiger rules the Asian jungles. However, an answer could be that the evolution has never fashioned a tiger to the size of an elephant. Nor, is it likely to, because such a "supreme carnivore" would be unable to catch its prey fast enough to fuel the energy demand of its enormous body. As a carnivore, one can only be so big. Larger predator like the tiger tends to catch prey roughly of its own size or even larger one. Hunting and killing of large prey demands power driven energy; more than twice as much, after accounting for the predator's body size. Moreover, larger carnivores seemed to be having difficulty getting enough to eat within each of the banquet and feeding strategies. They spend much of their time in conserving energy by resting or moving slowly and their total rates of energy intake and expenditure tend to be lower than expected, given their body size. Carnivores may be unable to make a living at body size greater than their present size, say maximum of 500 kg. This is how tigers are cut to perfection".

If you believe that most of your questions are suitably replied in brief and if you have no more question to ask, let me now take you over to "the land of the elephant" – the Bandipur Reserve, about which we are going to continue our discussion on "Human rights versus Elephant rights Controversy", I repeated. The projector switched on, while the lights were put off. The transparencies on the habitat and wild animals of Bandipur Reserve continued sliding one by one, followed by my brief and crisp narration on each of them:

"An argument could be made out that the elephants are not poaching into forbidden areas, but are helping themselves to the bounty of the land that had been traditionally their feeding ground, since the dawn of human history. Elephants were here, when Rama's army passed this way on its march against Ravana in Lanka (presently Sri Lanka); they were here when the Chalukyas ruled in Badami; they were here when Iron Duke defeated Tippu Sultan; they were here when the British Raj folded up and Independence dawned over India".

Soon, I over heard a feeble voice some where from the audience and I asked, "pardon me?"

The voice repeated; repeated rhythmically; and repeated loudly. It did not take much time for me to realize that it was a snoring, like a guttural mating call of the 'Green barbet'.

Seeing my predicament, one of the staff member stood up from the last row and asked, "Excuse me sir, does elephant possess a 'pearl' in his head?"

Next one came from another corner, "May I have the privilege of knowing about *Gajaprana*?"

Thrilled by the level of questioning by the audience, it came as a blessing in disguise for me to again deviate from the current topic of my talk. The topic had, by then, turned to "Epics and Mythology".

"Switch on the lights, please", I signalled to the person in charge of the switchboard. "Let me talk to you about, 'epics, mythology, art and folklore, in which India is richer than any other country in the world, so as to accentuate elephant's long association with man, its obedience, power and steadfastness in the war field, apart from so called 'elephant pearl' and *Gajaprana*", I declared.

Continuing my discourse, I went on to comment on "elephant pearl", followed by various facets of epics and mythology that are dearer to me:

"As long as Indian mythology, epics and folklore remain alive in the minds of our children and great grand children, through great story tellers of yesteryears, the survival of elephants in the country is ensured. The elephant will remain the pivotal subject of enriching our art, culture and poetry", I contended.

3.1 Elephant Pearl

Sanskrit Pundits of letters in the bygone era believed that occasionally, an elephant might be found having a pearl inside its head. As the story goes, this rare gem was called *Gajamukta*, the elephant-pearl. According to Devi purana, the ancient legend (7th to 9th centuries A.D), there was a belief that a lion tore apart the head of an elephant and took away the elephant-pearl. The kings, who joined forces with Lord Krishna, had launched an attack on the Raivataka, who had set up camps in lions' dens that were filled with elephant-pearls. The lions had eaten the flesh of elephants and left the pearls, as described in Sishupala Vadha. Magha describing elephants in the army of Lord Krishna, narrates that these animals plunged into a river to refresh themselves and when they splashed water with their trunks over their backs the sprays of water looked like showers of pearls.

The *Ardhanarishwara*, a form of Shiva (person with half female), according to the poet's imagination (*Vidyapati Ke Sau Gita*), wears on one side a garland of elephant-pearls and on the other a garland of skulls.

It has been observed, however, that the *musth* fluid of some elephants is so thick that flowing down the elephant's face it becomes encrusted. It is then scraped off and ground into granules to serve as pearls. But the present-day Zoological science, however, dismisses the belief of the 'elephant-pearl' as a mere fantasy.

3.2 Gajaprana

In ancient India, elephant was believed to enjoy long life. Men, who were healthy and long-lived, were compared with elephants and called *Gajaprana*. The elephant was the symbol of strength. The might of a warrior was measured by the number of elephants each could subdue. Bhimasena the second Pandava in Mahabharata was considered to have the strength of ten thousand elephants. Those familiar with jungle lore believed the elephant as 'lord of the jungle' and that lions and tigers, generally, gave him a wide berth.

3.3 Epics and Mythology

During the time of *Ramayana*, the kings were fond of keeping elephants. They had sanctuaries and parks called 'Nagavana' for the protection and upkeep of elephants and for improving the breeds/stock.

Viswamitra had offered Vashishtha, in exchange of Kamadhenu, the cow of plenty, fourteen thousand elephants decked with gold chains and garlands. In the city of Ayodhya there were elephants of Airavata, Mahapadma, and Vamana breeds. These were the finest breeds and handsomest of all; these breeds were called 'Priyadarshini'.

On special occasions and festivities elephants were used for processions. They were adorned with elaborate care. Elephants while passing through public paths and highways, had their tusks decked with gold plates, their necks decorated with garlands, their foreheads painted with variegated patterns; the bells fastened to the huge chains of gold that girdled them tinkled as the animals moved in 'regal majesty'. They were provided with *howdah* of gold with parasol and flags fluttering over them.

When Bharata went to visit Rama at his Chitrakuta *Vanashram*, the elephants which his entourage used for crossing the river Ganga were reported decked with banners and as they swarm across they looked like winged mountains. Rama specifically, inquired Bharata, if his Nagavana was looked after well. In the stables of Ravana in Lanka too there were elephants of some of the finest breeds that were well trained in warfare.

The foot hills of mighty Himalayas and the Vindhyas were famous for excellent breeds of elephants during the time of Mahabharata. In historical times, elephants occupied the same place in warfare as tanks do today. In the battle fought between Rama and Ravana, the latter's army possessed thousands of elephants. According to an account in the battle of Mahabharata, no less than 27,000 elephants had been engaged in the combat.

3.4 Elephant in Folklore and Legend

The elephant has figured prominently in Indian art and literature. It has appeared in Jataka stories, in the fables of the Panchatantra and in folklore. According to *Gaja* Jataka, Bodhisattva was an elephant in one of his incarnations. He was then the leader of 8,000 elephants. He had two consorts — one of them for some reasons was roused to wrath against her lord. Determined to teach him a lesson she gave herself up to penance and austerities with the aim of making herself the queen of Kashi. She succeeded in acquiring that position. Then she could have her revenge too. She ordered a *shikari* to fetch her tusks of the elephant, Bodhisattva. The *shikari* was unable to pullout the tusks, with all his might. But Bodhisattva was not enraged. He had only compassion for the *shikari*. He himself pulled out his tusks and handed them to *shikari* to be taken to the queen. The sight of the tusks moved the queen to repentance. She felt miserable. Bodhisattva then went to console her. In the cave paintings of Ajantha, this story is graphically depicted. Of all the animals brought out in the Ajantha frescoes, the elephant figures the most.

According to another story, Bodhisattva was a prince called, Vishwantara in one of his incarnations. He rode an elephant, which was white as Himalayan snow and magnificent in stature. His temporal glands were wet with rut fluid with docile strides. He was called, '*Gandha hasti*'. The prince used to go all over the town and visit his charity homes, riding this elephant. Once a neighbouring king thought of teaching the prince Vishwantara a lesson, for he had become jealous of the rapidly spreading fame of the prince, as the most charitable. He dispatched some wise Brahmins to get the elephant from Vishwantara. The Brahmins showering benedictions profusely upon the prince told him that they had come on hearing of the virtues of his magnificent elephant and of his own generosity. They begged of him to gift away the elephant to them. Although the prince knew that the Brahmins had been egged on to ask for the elephant by neighbouring king, who was envious of him, he at once got off his mount and taking up in one hand a golden vessel filled with water and holding the elephant by the trunk with the other hand stood humbly before the Brahmins. "Please accept the gift", he said to them and gave away the elephant. But his subjects resented this action. In their eyes the elephant represented the glory of the kingdom. "One could give away cows, gold, food and clothes to Brahmins but not the white elephant", they contended. The resentment of his people became so loud and unbearable that the prince had to go into exile. The scene is graphically depicted in a stone carving at Bharhut.

Elephant carvings on rocks at Mahabalipuram of Tailnadu.

3.5   Elephant in Art and Culture

In a Kumargupta coin, the king is seen riding an elephant. He is prodding elephant with the goad to make him tread faster. The animal's trunk, legs, tail and tensed up body show that he is running with all his might. Hyder Ali's copper coins also show elephant with his trunk raised.

According to Abul Fazl, in the Mogul times, one of the playing-cards was named after elephant. It bore a picture of the king of Orissa riding elephant. Another playing-card introduced by Akbar carried a picture showing the king on elephant.

Elephant motif has also inspired painters of this country. Elephant has also been variously represented on postage stamps in India and other countries. The seal of the Delhi University bears the impression of elephant.

In ancient India, one of the four wings of the army used to consist of elephants. *Gaja* (elephant), *Turaga* (horse), *Ratha* (chariot), and *Padati* (foot-soldier) were the four wings. According to a narration, "It was a spectacular sight, when innumerable elephants decked with chains of gold and banners flying over their heads moved in battle formation. It was like a cluster of rain bearing dark clouds moving in the sky. These elephants were, carefully, trained in the art of warfare. They could smash huge doors of forts with head thrusts. The museums of Sultan of Turkey contain specimens of the shields and nails that were used to protect elephants in battle. Warriors on elephants were armed with bows and arrows, long spears and shields for protection. Shields were also fastened to elephant heads and body. Elephants were also used in transporting war material".

The temple of Konarak (1238-1260 A.D) also known as temple of sun god, abounds in carvings depicting battle scenes in which elephants figure. The Temple of Khajuraho, also known as, Temple of *Kama Sutra* of medieval India, depicts the carvings of elephants

The mode of punishment as prevalent in ancient India was to have the culprits trampled to death by elephants. History books are full of records of executing such death sentences in this manner. Similar evidences are also found in stone carvings. There is a huge stone sculpture showing tusker trampling men to death at one of the gates of the Konarak temple. Narasingh Deo (1238-64 A.D), the valiant king of Orissa, had the sculpture exhibited, as a warning to his subjects. He had decreed that should any of his subjects entering the precincts of the sun-god with an impure heart would meet the same fate, is so graphically depicted in the sculpture. Yet another sculpture in the same temple shows an elephant in battle. The pachyderm has lifted enemy soldier with its trunk and is about to thrash him on the ground.

Devadatta, a cousin of Goutam Buddha, was jealous of him and was perpetually devising ways to kill him. Once he had a mad elephant let loose at him. But when the elephant found himself near Goutam Buddha, he became calm and bowed his head humbly. The incident is graphically depicted in one of the Ajantha frescoes.

Sikhandar Lodi, the Afghan ruler of Delhi, had ordered Kabir to be thrown to an elephant to be trampled upon and killed. But the elephant in the presence of Kabir became docile like a lamb and sat down near him with bowed head. Kabir must have been an ardent lover of animals with compassion to appease such elephants.

I concluded my discussion with the remarks that so rich are our epics and mythology; so fabulous are the folklore, art and culture. The importance and role of elephants in man's life could be called 'man's mighty companion'. Because of rich heritage of our country, since ancient times, the elephant is able to hold on to its status in India against continued holocausts by anti-elephant communities. No other country in the world is so a rich in its epics, mythology, art and culture than India has!

3.6   Elephant in Ancient Times

In Ancient India, the elephant was held in high esteem and ranked only after the cow and the horse among animals, useful to man. The *Shastras* forbade killing of elephants. Even today we worship Lord Ganesha, who is represented with the head of elephant attached to human body. Elephant could, therefore be described as more holy, since directly connected to Ganesha than cow. The temple ruins at Bodh-Gaya, Bharhut, Amaravati and Udayagiri are strewn with carvings in which Lakshmi, the Goddess of riches figures along with the elephant relating to good fortune. Pushpaka vimana, the famous flying chariot of Rama, had the picture painted on it, showing Lakshmi seated on the lotus with elephants on either side, sprinkling water on her with lotus blooms held in their lifted trunks. In *Puranas* the four guardian Gods on the four directions are represented as elephants. Among the Sumerians, the common belief was that the elephant was the protector and regenerator of plant life. There was the celestial tree, the *Arbor vitae* that fulfilled wishes of worshipers. A seal belonging to the time of Nebuchadnezzar found in Mesopotamia bears the image of elephant with the torso of an ox. The animal is shown as standing by the tree of life protecting it from attacking hordes. Mesopotamia did not have any elephants and the Sumerians probably took the idea from the Sindh Valley Civilization.

In the tablets found at Harappa and Mohenjo-daro, the elephant is profusely depicted. There is a tablet showing on one face, the scene of a tiger hunt with some inscription and on the other face a unicorn, an elephant and a rhinoceros, one behind the other, doing obeisance to the 'tree of life'. On another tablet found at Mohenjodaro are depicted such animals as a rhino, an elephant, a tiger, a leopard, an ox with short horns, a wild ox, a goat, a dolphin, a tortoise and a fish – an odd assemblage of carnivorous and herbivorous animals – all going to do obeisance to the 'tree of life'. Yet another tablet, rectangular in shape, also found at Mohenjodaro shows a tree-faced deity seated in yogi's posture and flanked on the right by elephant and tiger and on the left by rhinoceros and buffalo. Below the seat are two deer, facing each other, but with their heads turned towards yogi. The representation is believed to be that of Pashupati. The interesting thing in this depiction is that, except for the elephant, all the three other animals are facing the God. Near the elephant stands a man – may be a warrior –

trying to restrain the elephant from running away from Pashupati. Another seal bears the scene of attempts being made to subdue an elephant with the help of black magic. They do not seem to be finding it easy. Ignoring the commands of the warrior, the elephant is raising himself on his hind legs and charging with his head. A Harappa seal has a scene showing how the elephant frightened a warrior who could vanquish tigers. An elephant is quietly moving away from the sight of a warrior who had killed two tigers.

The elephant sculpture appearing in the temple ruins at Amaravati is a curious creature; his hind part resembles that of a fish. In the Mahabharata such *Ichthyo proboscidea* are described as 'minavaji' or '*Gajavaktrajhasha*'. This idea of *Ichthyo proboscidea* finds support by Valmiki, when the poet compares a battle field full of elephants to a sea teaming with sharks and fishes.

Elephant images were incorporated in different idols: Ganesha – the elephant headed God of wisdom, good fortune and prudence is one of the most beloved Hindu deities. Elephants have not only been worshipped, but are believed to be worshipers themselves: the sun, the moon and the stars are just examples of what the elephants supposedly have worshipped.

Kalidasa, the priest of poets makes very interesting observations on wild, as well as, domesticated elephants in 'Raghuvamsham', 'Kumara Sambhavam' and his play, 'Abhijnana Shakuntalam', where he describes, "elephants as debarking trees and occasionally as depredators of secluded human settlements in forests, known as *Vanashrams*".

Bana's 'Harsha-Charita', (7th century A.D) describes the entrance to the royal camp of King Harshavardhana of Kanauj in northern India (A.D. 606-647) as, "dark with congregation of elephants, presumably, for use at the Royal court, some for tying up with silk ropes, some for carrying on trumpets, some freshly captured, some received as revenue, some received as gratis, some to satisfy the emperor's curiosity to have the first look, some sent by the Chief of the Nagabana forests, some borrowed for elephant fights and games and some as gifts to be sent through ambassadors". The passage of time offers a remarkable overview of various uses; the elephants were put to, in varied periods.

When we turn to the South, however, we come across the most impressive visual account of elephants in the rock-cut works of the Pallava dynasty (A.D. 600-740) and later in the temple sculpture and base relief of the Hoysala period (A.D. 1110-1138), as well as in the sculptures and relics of the temples of Orissa. Similar contributions are also seen in Belur, Halebidu and Somnathpura temples of Karnataka.

Ancient Tamil literature of the Sangam period (1st to 3rd century A.D), offers a wealth of information about elephants and shows elephants, as a part of culture and way of life of the ancient Tamilians. 'Nigandu', the old poetical lexicon, has 44 names for the elephant species and four separate names for elephant calves. Each part of an elephant's body is separately named. There are also indications that domestication of elephants was indigenous to India, and the Aryans picked it up in the process of assimilating the culture of the country they had overrun. There are many references too to the training of elephants. In 'the Tamilnadu Ahananoory', verse 13 describes, the Pandyan Hero Panni, catches elephants using pits and after training them to understand commands, gifts them to Mendicants who beg of them.

3.7 White Elephant – Signifies Holy, Prosperity and Peace

From time immemorial white elephants have been known in the east and are still believed to be so, as an incarnation of Lord Buddha. White elephants are, generally associated to bring fortune and power to the king. In spite of this, the kings of Burma, Thailand and Cambodia used to present white elephants to people who had incurred King's displeasure, as a mark of punishment. Their owners were obliged to maintain them without giving them any work to do and the drain on family resources and fortune, often led to starvation and death; the economic ruin came to be known proverbially as, "maintaining a white elephant". Innumerable stories are told about white animals and birds: for example, on the day of judgement, "all crows become white". In Assam it is believed, anyone who kills a white tiger will die soon.

There are white elephants (not albinos) in some parts of Asia. White elephant is a misnomer, in that, it need not be completely white; it may be of slate colour, brown or grey, having some specific attributes. The attributes are:

i. **Long tail with long tuft of hair.**

ii. **Eighteen toes from all the four legs put together-five in each of the forelegs and four in each of the hind legs.**

iii. **White penis.**

iv. **Colour of nails white/pink.**

v. **White retina surrounded by bluish shade.**

vi. **The roof of the mouth and tongue pinkish without blotchy.**

vii. **Straight neck with prominent forehead.**

viii. **Colour of the animal could be gold, grey, slate-grey or white.**

ix. **From a single follicle two or more hair are found to grow.**

x. **A long pink line running down the anus.**

Out of the above ten characteristics, at least 3 characteristics should meet the requirement to recognise the animal as 'white elephant'.

The sacredness surrounding the white elephant, possibly, has its origin in the dream of Queen Mahamaya (185-72 B.C), the wisest and the most beautiful woman in the world, where she reported to have conceived, Lord Buddha in the form of a white elephant. Queen Mahamaya, the mother of Goutam Buddha, in her dream saw a white elephant enter her body. The royal astrologers, interpreting it, said that the offspring that the queen was to bring forth would be either great ruler or great seer. The story is depicted on a *Stupa* at Bharhut (second century B.C).

In Asia white elephant is treated with special reverence. Hindus reckon it as representing Airavata, the mount of Indra. Valmiki imagined white elephant as magnificent as mount Kailasa having four tusks, bedecked with all kinds of ornaments and sweet-sounding bells. He also describes how the white elephants resembled white clouds in the stables of Ravana.

In 1961 a white elephant was reported captured in central lowlands near Beegethu Ot, in South Vietnam. The Vietnamese believe that a white elephant is the incarnation of some celestial king.

A white elephant captured in North Siam reported to have an interesting journey some years ago, when he was taken to the Royal stables. The story runs like this:

"A wide path was first cleared in the jungle along which the elephant was taken to a nearby river, where a floating house waited to receive him. The house had a straw roof and was draped all round with red hangings. The journey was long and fatiguing. When the elephant wanted to rest, troupes of singers and dancers entertained him. When he landed, he stepped on to a carpet interlaced with gold. He was bathed in water scented with jasmine. Then he was given a huge quantity of rice flour cakes and sugar cane to eat. The King, the courtiers and the priests had gone all the way to receive him. Arriving at Bangkok, the elephant was taken into a well decorated harbour, ceremoniously rubbed with oils and adorned with chains of gold. For nine days continuously, people made offerings to him and worshipped him before he was taken in befitting procession to the Royal stables".

White elephants are reported to have been found in the jungles of Burma too. The last white elephant born in Myanmar was in 1961. Here also white elephants once used to receive the same ceremonious welcome that was accorded in Thailand. Princes and courtiers were in attendance on them. They were fastened to their posts with ropes made of red silk. They were given food in gold and silver troughs.

Even today there are about half a dozen white elephants maintained in the stables of the King of Thailand. Traditionally, they are held in high esteem by the Royal family. White elephants are considered religiously symbolic by the Kings, as incarnations of their ancestors.

In August 1966, a white elephant was reported to have been the victim of mishap. He was being taken to USA as a gift to then President, Johnson from the Government of Thailand. He broke away disorderly, while in the boat. The boat sank. Since then no more white elephants found in Cambodia.

One such white elephant was acquired by London Zoo in 1926. He had been captured in the jungles of Burma. In Mogul times also there is a mention of the white elephant. Rajah Mansingh had promised Akbar that he would subdue the ruler of Arakan and get his white elephant for the King.

The white elephant also figures in a number of Jataka stories. Stories featuring white elephants have been depicted in stone carvings at Bharhut and Sanchi. One of the Ajantha frescoes shows an elephant-cow of normal colour with two calves which are white. Another cave shows a six-tusked elephant with a young one which is white.

Since the white elephant is treated as a sacred animal, it is not used for riding or as work animal. It is believed that a country possessing white elephants would have plentiful rain, abundance of riches and prosperity. Kings in the earlier days loved to acquire white elephants. Many wars were fought over white elephants. White elephant was never put to work, except maintaining it as a symbolic showcase, sparingly used for royal processions and religious functions of the Royal family. As already narrated, keeping of such an animal meant a considerable financial burden on the owner. Consequently, the white elephant myth has remained the most persistent and factual of the curious fables.

Many light coloured specimens have been called 'white', although they are not true albinos; but the real white elephant, like any other albino, has a pinkish skin and light coloured hair and eyes. Such an albino tusker, called Ganesha was maintained at the Mysore zoological park, until his death at the age of 70. He was reported caught in the year 1948 at Dubare forest of Kodagu District. He had serviced a female Padmavati twice in the zoo. Gajalakshmi (F;18-5-79) and Rajendra (M;3-5-92) are his offspring.

Albinos, in real sense, are "freaks" of nature occurring due to albinism. Albinism occurs in one out of more than 20,000 births in any species of animal, bird, man or plant. Albinism is no disease but a congenital degeneration or deficiency of pigmentation in various tissues on the surface of the body. This tendency is inherited as a Mendalian trait, caused by the recessive gene. Albinism occurs more frequently among domesticated animals than among wild animals. Owing to absence of the mask of pigmentation in the iris, albinos are extremely sensitive to the sun light. Bereft of the natural colours of camouflage, they are easily spotted by predators in the jungle and killed sooner or later. Perhaps, these are some of the reasons for their rare occurrence in the wild.

As a general rule, more albinos are found in arid regions than in humid regions, where darker melanistic specimens are common. In some cases, aging also brings about de-pigmentation. In many adult elephants, especially, in old bulls, there may be much light pink speckling on the face, trunk and ears; the tip of the trunk is usually entirely pink in such animals. One such elephant Biligiriranga was maintained in Royal stables of Maharajah of Mysore as a ceremonial elephant. Sometimes a lacing of light pink may form a conspicuous border to the lower edge of the ears, head and trunk. Partial or full albinism is also sometimes acquired due to skin diseases.

Zoologists and genetic scientists will pay any price for acquiring a rare "albino" in the hope that they may propagate a "new freak strain", which could be the only one of its kind in the world. Albino animals are, however, more expensive.

In general, elephants are expensive to feed, maintain and to train. White elephants, in particular, are the most expensive and are maintained by kings and emperors as decorative/ornate and status symbol.

A white elephant from the wild would bring to its captor in Thailand fabulous wealth, besides royal honours. For, Thais consider white elephants as incarnations of the Bodhisattva and venerate them.

3.8 Auspicious and Inauspicious Signs in Elephants

The Asiatic elephant has five toes each on fore feet and four each on hind feet, totalling eighteen. If an elephant has more or less than the above number, it is considered inauspicious. An elephant that has only sixteen toes is considered, particularly, inauspicious so much so, often it is impossible to sell him. While buying or disposing of an elephant, this characteristic never ignored, nor in the case of elephants meant for export.

Usually, when a newly captured elephant is brought into the camp, the first thing the people throng round it and try to ascertain the number of its toes. If an animal is found defective in this respect, the catchers do their best not to let it be disclosed to the buyer. The buyer for his part normally insists on the animal being brought into the open, so that, his feet could be examined. Some clever but unscrupulous owners stick mollusk shells on to the animal's feet to deceive the prospective buyers.

In Akbar's time, an elephant having pale white eyes with a slightly reddish tinge was considered auspicious in his conduct. Present day trainers consider such an elephant as dangerous and undependable. In times of crisis such animals become panicky. There are cases on record where elephants having this characteristic had made such a nuisance that they had to be shot at.

Paste Image Mysore.tif :A cantankerous sub-adult male which had strayed into Mysore city from neighbouring forest along with another belligerent sub-adult male, went aggressive, killed cattle and attacked humans. Note the tip of his tail touching the heal of hind legs.

We have seen some camp elephants, particularly males behave in an erratic manner. There are many instances of males going amuck, killing their *mahuths/kawadies*. There is a general belief that the animals that are ill-treated, not cared for and not fed properly, attack them. Such a behaviour is frequently noticed, when they are in *musth*.

There are yet other categories of males which by birth are belligerent; such animals are described as abnormal. They will have some kind of physiological abnormalities/disorders. While this author was camping at Bhimeshwari Fishing and Nature Camp, run by M/s Jungle Lodges and Resorts, the manager, Mr.Sunder Raj narrated an instance. It runs as follows:

"A young male of about four years is behaving cantankerously from his early days. He had twice attacked *kavadi*, who takes care, gives bath and food. Recently, while fetching it back from the forest, where it was let off for feeding, its *mahuth* was gored at his thigh, using his spiky tusks, causing severe injury. This was the third such attack on *mahuth*. His attacks were deliberate and with revengeful attitude".

I got interested in examining the aggressor and soon visited its camp with some fruits and hand outs. On scrutiny of juvenile male, it was noticed that he had four nails on his front feet and a blotch at the roof of its mouth. Tuft of hair at the tip of its tail was touching the heels of hind legs. "These are few of inauspicious or undesirable signs in elephants. Such animals, though appear sober, are described as undependable and unpredictable in their behaviour. Such animals pose danger to human life. *Mahuths* and *kavadies* handling such animals should always be cautious. Their sudden attacks may come with lightening speed, when least expected. Such animals turn out to be dangerous killers and never be used for safari riding" I elaborated to Sunder Raj.

Soon the assailant male was asked to be shifted to BRT Hills sanctuary. After a while, there were reports that he created a scene there too, attacking forest staff and tourists.

It is also considered inauspicious if the tongue of an elephant is black or it has black blotches. Such a mark on the palate is equally bad.

Some elephants have two teat-like protuberances under the throat as in goats. This too is an inauspicious sign. An elephant with a straight neck is considered superior to an elephant with a drooping neck. The latter would not be able to see very far. The same holds good for the tusks. An elephant whose tusks curve downward is not considered good. It is obvious that in a fight an elephant whose tusks curve upward would be in a more advantageous position for an attack. It is also true that the taller wins in a combat, just as the faster wins.

An elephant which has the eyes like that of deer, a prominent forehead, large ears with tusks projecting parallel to the ground like that of a cradle is considered good and auspices. A well developed forehead and hair on the head are good signs. The ears should not be too small. The epidermis is to be thick, wrinkled and hanging loose, so that it can be gripped by hand. A pie bald elephant is also much fancied. Such an elephant has black and white spots all over the body. The tail needs to be long and supple and should have twenty seven joints. It should be thick at the base, thin at the tip and curved with tuft of long hair. It should be long enough to reach the knee joint of the hind legs, but never touch the heels. The elephant should constantly move his tail except, of course, when he is asleep.

Elephant with stubby tail does not fetch good price and the elephant with a tail so long that it seems to sweep the ground as the animal walks (almost touching the heels) is considered the most inauspicious. Such elephants sometimes are found to turn dangerous killers.

3.9 Elephant-The Religious Symbol

Even if the elephant was made redundant as a war machine, its image, however lived on in the minds of the humans of south-east Asia. It was several thousand years ago that its great power and placid nature were first harnessed by man. Out of this relationship grew assured great prestige and status symbol for the owners of elephants, especially, the white elephants. The beasts were decorated and paraded for all spectators to see and admire. The graceful sweeps of the solid body lent themselves to artists who carved them out of wood and stone and by degrees they were incorporated into religious beliefs and ceremonies. The elephant, as an art form or as a symbol of religion is as strong in the East today as it ever was in ancient times. It stands proudly with raised trunk in many temple gate ways, religious and non-religious buildings; decorates countless palaces, buildings and star hotels through carvings, motifs, tiled floors, walls and ceilings of living rooms.

3.10 God of Good Things

The beneficent 'Ganapati', or 'Ganesha', is the beloved god of millions of worshipers. Ganesha *Chaturthi,* which is celebrated in Bhadrapada Masa, the sixth month of the Hindu lunar calendar, is associated with the birth of Ganapati, the elephant-headed God. Pot-bellied Ganesha a rat as his *vahana,* the vehicle, is known by several other names, like Vinayaka, Gananayaka, Vakratunda, Ekadanta, Gajanana, Gajamukha, Siddhidata, Lambodara, and so on. The Ganapati is worshipped as the *vighnaharta* (remover of obstacles), who keeps evil forces away and showers prosperity. Ganapati happens to be the most widely worshipped deity throughout India and many of the Asian countries. Devout Hindus from most parts of the country believe that no undertaking will bear fruits, if the *Vighnaharta* is not invoked and propitiated first and the foremost. And Hindu custom dictates that the first *aksharabhyasa,* the initiation ceremony to learning of a child begins with *Shri Ganeshaya namaha,* an invocation to him. He is also, probably, the only god in the Hindu pantheon, who has devout followers from other religions and several other countries as well.

When did Ganapati come into his own prominence as deity and was he co-opted into the Hindu pantheon? Scholars and historians, basing their conclusions on available art and literature point out; there are references to him much before he became an independently worshiped deity.

Vedic literature refers to an elephant-headed God, but he appears to be nowhere mentioned among the Vedic Gods. One hypothesis is that he was unacceptable to the Aryans and was probably worshiped by a tribe with an elephant totem. As far as structures go, there is a torso with an elephant head carved on the railings of the Amaravati *Stupa* (2nd century A.D) in Maharashtra. Other temples in states of Andhra Pradesh, Madhya Pradesh, Chhattisgarh and Karnataka dating back to the fifth to ninth centuries have Ganesha on their panels, albeit in subordinate positions to the main deities. It was only in the 10th century, however, Ganesha was elevated to an independent rank, as it were, from which date his popularity began to increase.

Once Ganapati began to be worshiped as an independent deity, efforts to integrate him into the pantheon of Hindu Gods began. His ungainly, once bare body began to acquire jewels and silks, the mythology began to be woven around his unnatural appearance. The adaptation, which is said to have begun with a description of him, as the son of Ambika in the Yajnavalkya Smriti, reached its apogee in the *Puranas*, the ancient literature, which described him as the son of Shiva and Parvati.

3.11 Ganesha-The Elephant-Headed God

Different *Puranas* have different explanations for Ganesha's elephant head. One of the most popular among them is the one, as told by my mother, when I was young boy on *Ekadantha*, during her bed-time story session that is still green in my memory. The story goes as:

"Ganesha, the son of Goddess Parvati, the spouse of Lord Shiva, was asked to sit at the door step to keep a watch, while she had a bath. Parvati had prepared Ganesha out of her body sweat, duly filled with life. Parvati had also asked Ganesha not to allow any one inside, until she finished her bath. As an obedient and disciplined son, Ganesha did not let Lord Shiva in, when he arrived. In spite of his persistence, Ganesha was adamant in not allowing him to step in. In his thwarted fury, Shiva struck his *Thri-shula*, the triple-pointed – device and chopped off Ganesha's head. The head fell after travelling beyond the seven seas. Surprised and annoyed Parvati got furious, when Shiva entered her privacy unceremoniously. Having come to know that her beloved son's head was chopped off, Parvati, vehement as she was, asserted that her beloved son's head be restored. Lord Shiva placated her with the ominous oath that it would be restored. He asked his men to go and get the head of a first creature that they might find sleeping with its head in the direction of north. They could find none but an elephant sleeping with its head in the direction of north, chopped it off and brought it to Lord Shiva (it is because of this belief, we find our grand parents, even today, asking youngsters not to sleep placing head in the direction of North; leave alone sleeping, even burial of human body is not done positioning head in the direction of north). The elephant's head was screwed to the body of Ganesha and life was recharged. Parvati was pleased".

"On the night of festive Ganesh Chaturthi", further the story goes, "Ganesha indulged in feasting at *bhaktas*', the devotee's houses. He went, after the banquet for an evening ride on a rat's back, his vehicle. When confronted with a snake, which loomed out in the moonlit night, the rat bolted off for safety. Ganesha was tumbled down with such a force that his inflated belly burst opened, spilling the contents around. The snake, by then, had become Ganesha's prisoner, was required to make good the damage it had caused. Ganesha collected all that was spilled around, stuffed back into his belly and tied it tightly by the snake. When this happened, the night sky blackened and filled with the echoing of the moon, said to have rocked with laughter at the scene of the rapacious conduct of Ganesha. Hearing the echoing, so great was the Ganesha's fury and so much hurt was his pride, that he tore out one of his tusks and hurled it at the moon, simultaneously, admonishing a *shapa*, the curse that whoever, looks at you on this festive day, bad things would befallen to them'. It is this curse, *bhaktas*, the devotees desist looking at the sky, leave alone not at the moon on this festive day of Ganesha *Chaturthi*. Having lost one of his tusks, came to be known as *Ekadantha*, the single tusked Ganesha".

We, as Foresters, when we encounter a male elephant with single tusk in the wild, christen him, as Ganesha. Elephants are thus related to as holy and are used in religious ceremonies in India and other South-east Asian countries.

3.12   Ganesha – The Spirit King of Elephants

Ganesha is usually shown in a pot-bellied, joyous attitude; folk stories relate him to have had a zest for good living and cunning wit. Come Ganesha Chaturthi, whole India gets jubilant with celebrations as one of the most popular festivals. It goes without saying that Ganesha is the most popular God of the Hindu pantheon.

Along with Buddhism, it is said; Ganesha travelled to other south-east Asian countries, like Nepal, China, Burma, Japan, Java, Afghanistan and Thailand and became a part of their traditions and myths. In the Mahayana school of Buddhism, Ganesha is believed to have been disclosed to Ananda by the Buddha himself, according to Nepalese's belief. In Buddhism, neither Shiva nor Parvati is credited with the parenthood of Ganesha. The earliest known appearance of Ganesha in the Buddhist art is from a frieze of the Gupta period, where he appears as a Gana or Yaksha.

In Tibet, Ganesha is a rare god. He appears as Vinayaka, the destroyer of malevolent demon. In the Buddhist monasteries of Tabo, he is positioned above the entrance. At Lakang, he is seen painted on the doors of the monasteries.

In the region of Chinese Turkistan, he is seen as four armed figure, attire in tiger skin. In figures seen in this region, Ganesha wears a coronet and holds a radish in his hand. In the rock-cut temples of Bezalik, there are several frescoes of Ganesha with six arms, holding the sun, the moon, a banner and a *modaka*, said to be his favourite dish.

Ganesha can also be seen in Mongolia, as *Nrithya Ganapati*, the dancing form. In China, on a stone image of 531 A.D, one can see Ganesha sitting in Indian style of squatting cross-legged, with four arms, holding the lotus in the right hand and the *Chintamani*, the jewel in the left. An inscription describes Ganesha as the "Spirit God of Elephants".

Amongst innumerable distinct forms of Ganesha, a sculpture found in a temple at Barasur of Bastar district of Chhattisgarh is, perhaps, the first of its kind, depicting conjugal relation with Sri Shakti. Chaturbhuja Ganesha in *musth* state is seated in Lalitasana, his genital exposed, while Sri Shakti seated naked with her legs wide open on his lap. Both appear to have been involved in pre-conjugal pleasure. Exited Sri Shakti is engaged in masturbation holding Ganesha's genital, while Ganesha is stimulating her sexually inserting his finger. This rare artifice said to be of early mediaeval times, is reported smuggled out of the country. This strange artifice is said to have great artistic significance.

Another sixth century depiction is a fresco from the Tun-huang rock-cut caves. Here Ganesha holds *navagrahas*, the nine planets along with the sun. Vinayaka, as he was known in Chinese and Japanese traditions, has two hands. He holds a radish in one hand and an axe in the other.

Ganesha sculpture found near Kabul in Afghanistan bears a strong Gandhara, the flat coronet on his head. He is worshiped here by the local Hindus. He is believed to have been worshiped in Japan in the ninth century. The Japanese Ganesha figures are happy, smiling and sitting on a mountain. Here Vinayaka is known as the "King of Elephants".

Ganesha travelled to Sri Lanka and Burma. I have seen a charming figure of Ganesha carved on a pillar of Shiva temple at Pullanaruva, in Sri Lanka. The Ganesha legend travelled to Thailand with Burmese Hinduism. Between the period of sixth and eighth centuries, Thailand was ruled by the Hindu Mon dynasty, who built many temples of Ganesha. At a Hindu temple of Bangkok, Ganesha is seen holding a manuscript in one hand and a broken tusk in the other. The legend about Ganesha being the scribe of Mahabharata has travelled so far.

Cambodia is the country, where one can find many Hindu temples. An inscription dated 611 A.D. records the grant of slaves to a temple dedicated to several deities, one of whom is Ganesha. He can be seen in many temples associated with Shiva, the "God of Mountains".

3.13   Ganesha – The Unique Representation

India's contacts with Indonesia dates back to Ramayana, which mentions, *Yava Dweepa*, the Java Islands. Though *Shaivism* is the predominantreligion here, Ganesha statues can be seen in almost all Shiva temples. The early sculptures of Ganesha in Java are extremely primitive and proper dating has not been possible. These statues represent the elephant-headed God – Ganesha with two arms and no attributes, such as head-dress nor the elephant like ears.

A stone statue from Dieng depicts the deity with four hands holding the axe, rosary, broken tusk and a bowl of sweets. In Java Islands, Ganesha statues may be found at river crossings and other places of danger/disaster, probably, in his role as *Vignaharta*, the remover of obstacles. Bali is the place, where all major Hindu deities are worshipped. One can find Ganesha statues in standing posture, with a third eye and a serpent-shaped thread around his waist. A statue from southern Bali shows, Ganesha seated on a throne surrounded by flames.

Ganesha has travelled, as far as, Borneo in the East. In a cave at Kombeng containing both Brahminical and Buddhist images in stone, Ganesha stands in all his glory with his axe and rosary. Ganesha idols in Borneo have straight trunks and Jata Mukuta, the hairstyle in the form of a crown. The Buddhist influence is seen in the *urna* or the protuberance of the eye brows, a mark of greatness. The ears are fan-shaped and the face is elongated.

It is possible that from Cambodia Ganesha travelled to Mexico and Central America as the elephant-headed God is seen in the Veerakosa in rare sculptures of that region. Ganesha figures are also found in Munich, where he is seen with ten-arms holding his attributes with those of Shiva. He is known as Heramba there. Panchamukhi Ganesha, with five heads is sheltered by five-hooded *Naga*, the serpent. Beneath the right leg is a lion and a rat lies beneath the left leg.

During the period of Guptas, Hinduism and Buddhism spread through Asia and Ganesha travelled far and wide, appearing in different *avatars*, the forms of incarnations. The calm and majestic Ganesha has enchanted us since the 5th century A.D. Considering the popularity and the spread almost globally; no wonder Ganesha occupies a special place in peoples' heart.

Back home, in all his glory.....

3.14   Gaja Gambhirya – The Stately Gait of Elephant

The elephant is deeply rooted in the traditions of eastern life and nowhere more deeply than in the lives of royalty. Preparations of the royal elephants for stately occasions are a lavish affair even today. They would be bathed in pure water and then liberally doused with eastern perfumes. Once their body is dry and smelling sweet, artists would set to work, carefully painting their heads and ears with brilliant colours in shapes following the contours of their muscles and bones beneath. The tusks are scrubbed clean and adorned with gold bracelets and hornet/coronet. When the paint was dry, a splendid cloak of royal scarlet, gold, purple and yellow is spread across the back. When the final trimmings of necklaces and pendants are all put in place, the full splendour of the animal and its proud *mahout* were paraded in public. Such elaborate decorations are performed for elephants, taking part in the procession of world famous *Dashara* in Mysore

In the bygone era, it was considered an honour to ride caparisoned elephant. Everyone could not aspire for such an honour. However, it was the prerogative of kings and nobles, to sit on *howdah* and go in procession. Common people could enjoy an elephant ride only on their weddings or on some other special occasions. According to Patanjali, scholars who had fully mastered the discipline of grammar of the language had the honour of sitting on the mount of elephants on special occasions (perhaps, honoured by their kings). The King of Magadha had thus honoured Panini.

Mysore, as it was called after *Mahishur*, traces its history back in times of the mythical past, when *Mahisasura mardini*, the Goddess Chamundeshwari killed wicked Mahishasura, the buffalo-headed demon. Mysore Dashara or Dashahara is the celebration to mark the victory of good over evil. The culmination of *Navaratri Habba* is the legendary Mysore Dashara procession with *Gaja gambhirya*, the stately gait of caparisoned male elephant is the centre of attraction. Mysore Royalty reported to have had association with the Mahabharata and King Ashoka of the 3rd century B.C. During the Wodiyars dynastic rule (established in 1270), the Mysore Royalty had reached the zenith of its glory, as the fabled centre of oriental splendour. When republic India was put in place, the dynastic rule faded gradually, while festive rituals are continued as *Nada Habba*, the world famous celebrations with Goddess Bhuvaneshwari, astride 880 kg *Ambari*, the Golden hauwdah carried by specifically nominated male elephant during the procession over 5 km long distance.

Caprisoned elephant marching majestically carrying Golden Howdah weighing 800 kg during Dussera festivity in Mysore.

3.15 Tiger Hunting From Elephant Back

The elephant makes an ideal and safe vehicle for riding in the jungle, wildlife safari, particularly, to see tigers and other carnivores. The sport of tiger hunting was the delight of Indian princes and Maharajahs for centuries and later became one of the grand events in the gilded era of the British Raj. The elephant was an ideal mount, but risky for tiger-shooting parties. In a comfortable *howdah* strapped to the elephant's back, the hunter had excellent mobility through tangled jungle or tall grass savannah and bamboo thickets; *shikaris* also had perfect view points to take fairly good aim at their quarries. The size of the elephant gave the hunter the illusion, at least of a safety from the savage tiger, when it was pitted. The elephants were, particularly, trained for such an obedience and steadfastness in the face of danger, although in a large hunting party the sheer number of elephants pitted against one or two tigers made the combat pitifully unequal.

With the arrival of more sophisticated and telescopic fire arms in the beginning of the previous century, Indian tigers were massacred in stupendous numbers. Can you imagine of a ridiculous act of one Maharajah killing well over a thousand and one hundred tigers during his life time? The Victorian empire-builders enthusiastically joined in this native big game hunting and elephant-mounted tiger hunts were the lavish entertainments offered to visiting royal guests, such as the Prince of Wales and others. More recently, rugged overland vehicles, fitted with spot lights for night hunting, replaced elephants in the tiger shoots. Thanks to the transformation from tiger hunting to tiger watching on elephant back, that brought about hopes of survival of tigers in the country. But this trend was short lived. It almost opened floodgate for traders in trophies and poachers, when they came to know of tiger in the country put on the path of recovery during the first decade of Project Tiger. Tiger population dwindled to mere 1411 by the year 1994 from that of 4500 during 1984. When elephant and tiger come face to face in the presence of *mahout*, the third party, both these mighty adversaries exhibit tolerance, by which tourists can have an advantage of seeing magnificent tigers at close range. Paste Image No.BIGTIGER.TIF: Caption : Tiger safari on elephant ride; gone aer the days, when elephants used for big-game hunting like tigers, leopards during pre-independence period. Modern generations prefer to go on elephant safari to spot and enjoy tigers in the wild.

In the display of kingly affluence and splendour, the elephants have played a prominent role. Kings, feudatory chiefs and *zamindars* in the country used to keep elephants in hundreds, just more than hundred and fifty years ago. Maharajah Jung Bahadhur, the builder of modern Nepal and founder of the Rana dynasty, reported to have had one thousand elephants in his stables. All the princes of Nepal kept elephants whose number varied according to the status of each of them. The use of elephants for hunting was a long-established tradition in Nepal. In 1961 one of the greatest assemblies took place at Chitwan when 376 elephants were brought in from throughout the Tarai region. A media report of the day described, "Nose to tail they would have stretched for over two miles! The reason for this incredible gathering was a 'grand tiger shoot' organised by the King of Nepal for Her Majesty, the Queen Elizabeth II and His Royal Highness, the Duke of Edinburgh. Never was there another such spectacle".

Although the merger of the states with the Indian Union and abolition of *zamindari* had adversely affected the demand for elephants, the Sonepur *mela* which is the largest elephants fair in India at the confluence of GandakRiver with the Ganges, used to attract more than thousand elephants until early sixties. Now hardly 150 to 200 or even less elephants are brought there for trading. Most of them return without being traded. Price of an elephant varies between `1.5 to 2.0 lakhs (US $ 2400 to 5000) each, depending upon age, size, sex and quality. Good female elephant of a proper size and age has become a rarity in recent years.

3.16 Elephant in Service of Man

A properly tamed elephant is one of the most useful service providers to mankind. In religious functions, national festivals and other important State/Royal parades, the elephant is used in leading the procession. In British Raj, elephants were largely used in jungle cleaning and as a means of timber transport, loading, rolling or dragging. Generally, state forest departments where timber was available in large quantities did maintain a taskforce of working elephants. Some of the famous temples and religious heads would like to maintain certain number of elephants as a social cause and/or status symbol. In Kerala state of South India, Guruvayur temple maintains as many as thirty males(mainly tuskers) for being exhibited during its famous *Onam* festivity, which is celebrated annually. But the temple, however, has to depend on the natural sources of the country to replace them, when needed, thereby exerting pressure on country's elephant population.

3.17 Elephant V/s Man

Occasionally, one hears about wild elephants knocking down and tearing off men into pieces. A stone carving at Hampi temple of bygone era of Vijayanagar Kingdom shows an elephant thus dealing with human beings during 15th century A.D. From the distension of its eyelids and the dark streak of *musth* fluid flowing down its face, the animal seems to be in a state of excitement of the five men trying to bring him under control, one has been grabbed by the tusker. He has crushed a man's legs under the left fore foot and wrapping his trunk round the other leg is pulling at it. The ungula of the right foreleg of the animal rests on the man's groins. With one of his hind-legs the elephant has secured another man who is being pulled by the hair by one of his companions.

It can be seen that age-old relationship between the elephant and human is intertwined since the dawn of human history. Elephants can at times, pose danger to human life and even kill him mercilessly. They attack in many ways. Man when he is careless and arrogant in the domain of elephants, with or without weapons, he is attacked and invariably trampled to instantaneous death. Elephants may kick the victim down or they may lift him up with the trunk and thrash him on the forest floor. They may trample him, reducing the skull and ribs into pulp. They may also pierce their sharp tusks into human body to take revenge. They may rip him open holding limbs by the trunk. Such is the aggression elicited, against the terrible experience the elephant might have suffered in the hands of man for it to hate or fear so much. Paste image No.Exhibit_73.tif Agressive matriarch :Caption:

It is an established fact that an elephant never forgives its *mahout* who resorts to torturous treatment and robs its ration. There are innumerable such instances in the living memory, when unscrupulous *mahouts* meet with tragic deaths by their frontal attacks.

3.18   Elephant Graveyard

There is a common belief, still current among tribes and even among educated people that the elephants go to some unknown places to breathe their last. Since skeletons of dead elephants are rarely to be seen, the question as to where or how elephants die has been the subject of speculations.

In his book, 'Wild Elephant', Sir Emerson Tennant narrates of a belief that prevails among some aborigines in Ceylon (Sri Lanka). These people think, according to him, that there is a secret graveyard of elephants in a valley that lies to the East of Adam's Peak and the elephants, when their death is imminent, make for that area, passing on their way along a narrow pass between the rocks. Similarly, tribal communities around Bandipur forests also believe that elephants end their lives in a collective graveyard. However, I have not come across such a place during the discharge of my duties there. I have, of course, found some remains of skeletons and skulls at different places of the National Park, infrequently, near water holes and reservoirs.

Another interesting belief is that elephants often like to die at a place where there is water nearby or even in water. In the wild, nature has its own way of disposing off the carcasses. This happens within a shortest period possible. Carnivores like tiger, leopard, hyena, and scrap hunters like jackal, wild boar take part in disposal of carcasses. The vulture, the last member of the food chain have, of course, larger role to play in cleaning up the system and maintaining the ecological balance. While they exercise their rights in "scrap business", the remains may get scattered leaving only skull and big bones. Subsequently, these bones may also be tampered by human being.

In case the carcass of elephant is noticed by the park staff in the forest, the remains are either buried or burnt after a post-mortem examination by a veterinary surgeon. Of course, removal of tusks, if any, is the top most priority. Such things are immediately reported to immediate superiors, along with copy of first information report (FIR) filed before the local police. Simultaneously, detailed records are maintained as to its sex, age, cause of death, after conducting investigation. If tusks found, their weight and length are recorded and immediately dispatched to the central treasury at the District Forest Head Quarters.

3.19 Elephant in Poetry

Kalidasa describes elephants, "when rains come, elephants gain in vigour and vitality and their minds too become filled with desire....".

In describing the rainy season, Kalidasa writes, "look sweet heart, the season of rains, dear to love-loran hearts, has come arrayed in kindly splendour, riding on *musth* elephants of water-bearing clouds, flashing banners of lightening and sounding kettle drums of thunder".

"Clouds bring rains, rivers flow, *musth* elephants trumpet, wood lands put on lustre, love-sick hearts blossom, peacocks dance and monkeys crouch into shelters", Kalidasa narrates nature and natural history in the monsoon season.

"The cheeks smeared with *musth* fluid and with clusters of beetles clinging to wild elephants intoxicated by the rumblings of the first rain-clouds and trumpeting again and again, shine like fresh lotus blooms", Kalidasa continues his description of nature!

"From the fighting of elephants, the lake there has been rendered desolate: lotuses are uprooted, fish are afflicted and the frightened cranes have taken to flight", as having watchful eye describes Kalidasa.

"The tusker Nalagiri, having run amok, has wrenched out in rage the post to which he was tied and now roams about in the stable", describes Meghadoota in Poorva Megha.

Magha describes elephants in the army of Sri Krishna in Shishupala Vadha, thus:

"One great tusker beholding his own limbs reflected in the surging waters of the lake and mistaking the image for another tusker coming to attack him, began to run helter-skelter in rage. The mistake seemed unnatural".

"Remove thyself with speed from the path. That great tusker, seeing the abundant breasts and mistaking them for the projections on the forehead of a rival tusker, is making for a side thrust. Thus in jest did some people address a maiden going to fetch water".

"The spray of water, bright as a *Kasa* bloom thrown by the elephants over their temples to assuage the burning bright by the intensity of *musth* and reaching the ears, shine like white whisks".

"The crocus painted on the elephant's body had dissolved in water, while the purple of the pollen of lotuses had coloured the body of the elephant. It was as if the river and the tusker, at the end of their love play had exchanged robes".

"The eyes formed by the oil-like *musth* fluid spreading into moons on water, with which the elephants were decorating the river, they were promptly getting back from the river in the shape of *Nenuphar* petals that clung to them as they emerged from water".

"To control a tusker intending to attack another tusker, the *mahout* gave him so deep a thrust with his goad near the ear that the animal began to bleed, yet he could not hold him: the mighty animal will not be subdued by force".

"The lines of beetles clinging to the forest tree against which some tusker had scratched him and which had some *musth* fluid sticking to it looked like a garland of Sapphires".

"A great tusker wrenched out the post to which he was tied, exuded a great deal of *musth* fluid which made the trunk wet and broke the chains that had been put round his hind legs thus making himself wholly free".

"A captured tusker neither picked up pieces of sugar cane repeatedly offered to him, nor did give so much a look to the elephant-cow near him. Closing both his eyes, he brooded on the joys of his former freedom in the jungle".

The love-loran exiled Yaksha by Kalidasa too saw the first monsoon cloud as a massive elephant. Addressing the cloud in Meghaduta in Poorva Megha, he says:

"You are welcomed there to cover the Devagiri Mountains by a soft breeze laden with the fragrance of the earth made joyous by your juices, while trumpeting elephants will inhale it with their trunks".

The Yaksha tells the clouds that after it has passed the river Rewa, "Elephants sniffing the scent rising from the woods will guide you along your path".

Describing his home-surroundings in Alakapuri, the Yaksha says:

"O, cloud while you are black as finely ground mascara, the mountain Kailasa is white as a freshly-cut tusk".

"You will see elephants of Alakapuri, as massive as mountains; exude *musth* fluid as profusely as you exude sweat" (Meghaduta; Uttara Megha).

Valmiki, describing the coming of winter in Ramayana says, "Languid of movement have become tuskers, who were beloved of their ladies, who loved water-lilies and forests, whom flowers filled with joy and who were intoxicated by *musth*". (Kishkindha Kanda)

"The elephant-cow in heat languid of movement and accompanied by her calf follows the *musth* bull through the wood".

When Sita was kept captive in Lanka, Ravana had instructed *Rakshashas,* the demon women guarding her that they should employ with her all the cunning tactics, used to domesticate a wild elephant that is captured. Sita in captivity has been compared to an elephant-cow having strayed from the herd, has been captured and tied to a post where she is heaving long and distressed sighs. Elsewhere too, Valmiki has compared the lot of a distressed woman with an elephant-cow separated from the herd.

In the Ramayana, a well shaped thighs of a woman have been compared to an elephant's trunk.

Basaveshwara or Basavanna – a great visionary and social reformer of the twelfth century A.D. in his revolutionary preaching, through *Vachanas*, the speech of expressions, describes elephant:

"Immense is the elephant, but does that make an *ankush*, the goad, small; nay we say." And "The mirror images the elephant even so, I contain Thee!"

Basavanna practiced what he preached and attained the status of the Man-Universal.

Basavanna further urges, "Compassion must be shown to all living beings; compassion is the root of all religious faith".

Compassion towards elephant, signifying global recognition is more relevant today than ever before and hence, the constant beacon for its conservation by this author.

Chapter IV

Elephant That Was in Soup Rescued!

The Asian elephant, unlike the African, is usually the one carrying man or doing his bidding. These are found in four distinct sub-species: the Indian is the commonest and the beast found in Malaysia is the hairiest. Indonesia has the highly endangered Sumatran variety, whilst the herds in Sri Lanka have the fewest number of males with tusks and dominated by *makhnas*.

Asian elephants inhabit many ecosystems, including tropical wet evergreen forests, grasslands of Western Ghats, open grasslands (savannah) and mixed (moist and dry) deciduous forests and scrub and thorny forests of India. They have even penetrated Himalayan ranges up to the snow level, apart from Tarai-Babbar region of Himalayan foot-hills.

The elephant tracks at Sumatra have been reported to be found nearly up to 3000 ft msl. It may be realised how valuable elephants are in maintaining the plant community of the rain forests and other vegetation types. Thanks to their size, their power and their 'all purpose' trunk, they gain access to practically every plant food from the floor up to the tree canopy. Incidentally, what they possess in strength lack in agility, being incredibly large in size. These gentle giants of the Asian land mass knock down the trees with ease. They rip the bark off the trees; pull down the branches to feed on them. Elephants help create openings in the forest canopy where regeneration is stimulated and undergrowth is pushed up to provide fresh food sources for other animals. These feeding-machines like, if confined to an area will transform forests into grass lands. They need, therefore large expanse of forests with enough browse spp. and grass and drinking water. Elephants are the first creatures to suffer if the forests are depleted or shrunk under anthropic pressure. It is, therefore, necessary to protect and manage large expanse an area and interconnect 'Potential Island' like elephant forests by insulated corridors, so that they get an opportunity to exchange their genes with distant herds.

4.1 Distribution of Elephants in Asia

The present-day distribution of the Asian elephant covers only remnants of its former extensive ranges of distribution. Six thousand years ago, its ranges extended from the Tigris-Euphrates Basin in Western Asia, eastward up to the Yangtze-Kiang and perhaps, even beyond this, in northern China. This distribution covered present-day Iraq and nearby countries, southern Iran, Pakistan, the entire Indian sub-continent, south of Himalayas, continental south-east Asia, a substantial part of China and Island countries, such as Sri Lanka, Sumatra, Borneo and possibly Java.

We find the elephant has disappeared from Western Asia, a major part of the Indian sub-continent, substantial areas of South-East Asia and almost entirely from China. The domestication of the elephant is believed to have been first achieved by the people of the Indus Valley Civilization, about 4,000 years ago and its regular capture in large numbers in the Asian continent might have played a major role in the decline of wild elephants. The loss of habitat due to deforestation, expansion of human settlements, extensive agriculture and infrastructure development had been the most important factor causing a decline in elephant populations. As settlements spread along river valleys and plains, the elephants were forced into remote forested hills which were relatively inaccessible to people. During the twentieth century, even these last strongholds of elephants have since been opened up for settlements by exploding human populations and uncontrolled logging in many regions.

The rough estimates of wild Asian population ranged between 36,000 and 53,000 individuals and their habitats covered an area of about half a million sq km some decades ago. The elephants are now found, however in as many as hundreds or more distinct populations, with little or no possibility of natural genetic exchanges. For many Asian elephant populations, viability is thus, severely constrained by smaller populations. This has further strained by insufficient and island like habitats situations. Only about 10 populations or so seem to consist of over 1,000 elephants each. These include: Nilgiri Hills complex, Eastern Ghats complex and possibly Silent Valley, Anamalai-Parambikulam, Periyar plateau, including Kalakkadu-Mundanthurai Tiger Reserve in the southern most India. Uttarakhand, Uttar Pradesh, Jharkhand, Orissa and South of West Bengal in the northwest and central India regions, and north West Bengal, Assam-Garo-Khasi hills and Arunachal Pradesh in North-Eastern India.

Asian elephant herds are also found distributed in Sri Lanka, Myitkynia-Bhamo and Irrawady-Chindwin in Myanmar, Tenasserium Mountains along the Myanmar-Thailand borders and Laos-Cambodia-Vietnam borders and Sabah in Borneo and China. In addition, some of the smaller populations, including Taman Negara in Peninsular Malaysia and those in Sumatra, are important as they may represent genetically distinct populations sub-species that have evolved in the rich rain forests. Initiatives for long term conservation should pay special attention to these populations.

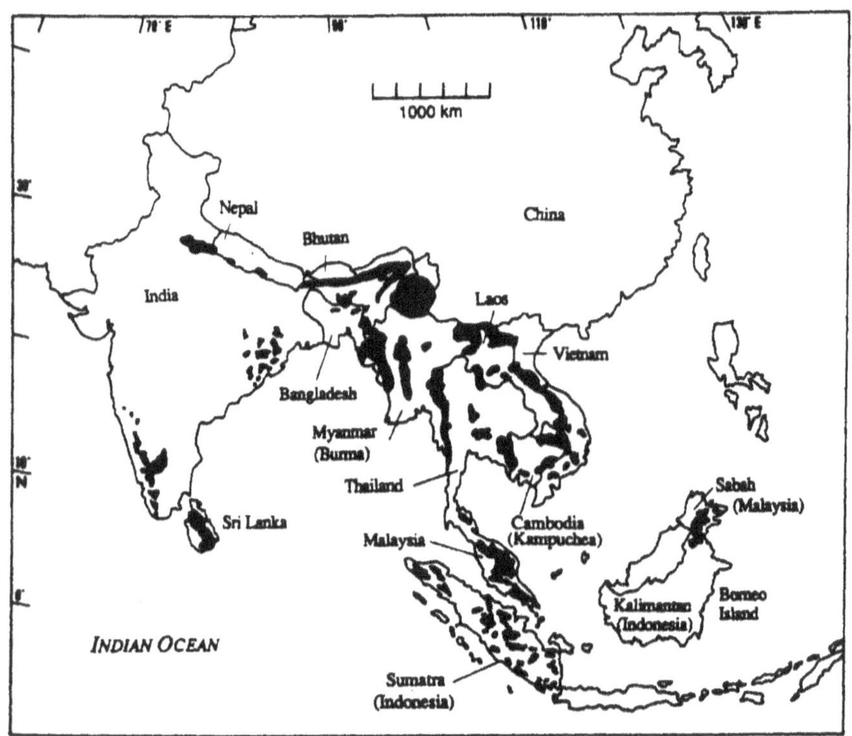

The Asian elephant is, however, more commonly referred to as the Indian elephant. It is popularly thought that India is the stronghold for the Asian elephants of southeast Asia. But it is their former distribution here and the strength of their association with man that has perpetuated such an attribute. Today, the Indian sub-continent includes India, Andaman Islands, Nepal, Bhutan and Bangladesh. The national parks and sanctuaries in these regions were surveyed during 1979 by Southern Indian Task Force of the International Union for the Conservation of Nature (IUCN) – Asian Elephant Group. It is only with effect from 2002 and 2007 and subsequent periods regular census of elephants are carried out in India. The overall trend shows that there is gradual increase in their populations by about 1000 elephants, from 26,000 in 2002 to 27000 in 2007 and 30,000 in the subsequent period. This increase might be due to the protection afforded to their habitats.

4.2   Distribution and Status in India

The elephant inhabited all but the most arid areas in the Indian sub-continent. Elephant had been recorded even from the dry tracts of Punjab and Sourashtra in the fourth century B.C. Kautilya's Arthashastra mentions eight Vanas in the country as abodes of elephants that existed. Since that time, the loss of habitat and capture of elephants by Emperors and Kings for warfare in their armies reported to have led to the depletion of elephant populations

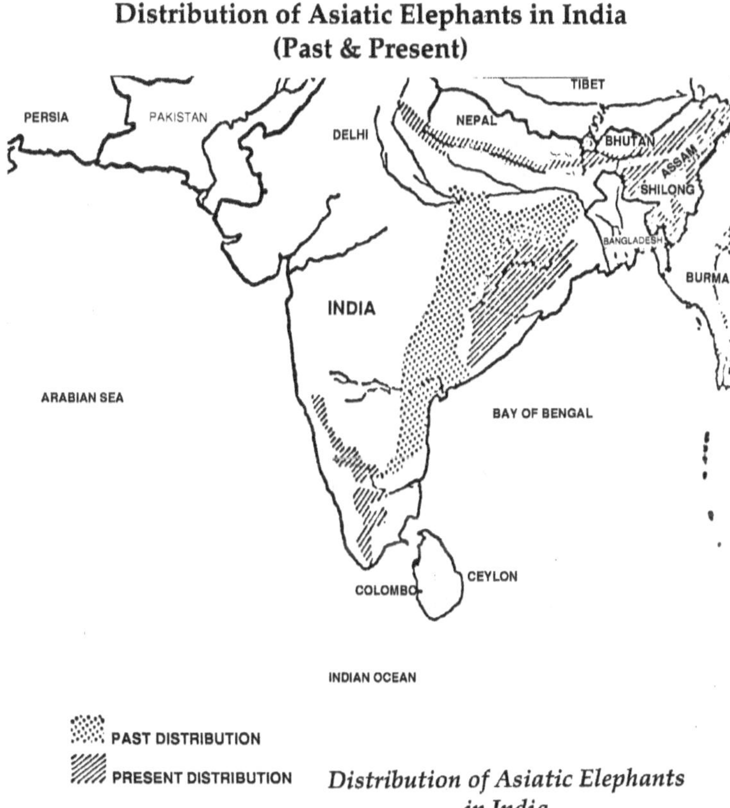

*Distribution of Asiatic Elephants
in India*

Precise information on the distribution of the elephants in medieval India is available from the memoirs and the writing of the Moghul Emperors of the 16th Century A.D. Emperor Babar (1526-1530) writes in his memoirs, "elephants inhabited the district Kalpi (UP) and as one advanced towards East, they increased in number." Abul Fazal's Ain-i-Akbari, a chronicle of the times of Akbar (1556-1605), recorded the presence of elephants in many parts of central India including Narwar, Chanderi, Satwar, Bijagarh, Raisen and Panna (all in present Madhya Pradesh). Jahangir (1605-1627) describes elephant hunting in Dohad in the Panchmahal hills in Gujarat. Jerdon (1874) gives details of elephant's distribution at the Himalayan foot hills from Bhutan westwards to Dehradun, in the east and the Central India, from Midnapore (West Bengal) to Mandla (Madhya Pradesh) and towards the south of Godavari. In recent times, it is reported that the elephants had disappeared from Rajmahal hills only in the 19th century. By the end of the 19th century, four distinct elephant regions had emerged; Southern India, Central India, a narrow-belt along the Himalayan foot hills from Dehradun in North-West and North-East India. Each region had further fragmented populations. In the south certain hills of Eastern Ghats, such as, the Sheveroys and Kollimalai still hold some elephant herds and elephants were also seen in the Kalrayans during the mid-nineteenth century although they had disappeared by that time. Imperial Gazetteer of India (1907) refers to many isolated herds of elephants in northern and central India, like Nahan and Ambala (Punjab), Udaipur (Rajasthan), Bilaspur district (Chhattisgarh) and Parkal (Warangal district of Andhra Pradesh), all of which, alas, have since disappeared!

The past and the present distribution of the elephant in India is an indicator of the drastic depletion and the fast changes in the habitat conditions. These factors have led to a progressive decline in the elephant populations of the country. Nothing illustrates better, the need to maintain viable elephant populations with their habitats intact and prevent their ongoing fragmentation than the above telling facts.

An estimate of the elephant population in the 19th century can be made from the number of elephants captured during the last 200 years. My guess-estimation is that between 30,000 to 50,000 elephants might have been captured throughout the Indian sub-continent during this period. Jardin (1836) puts the number of elephants in captivity at that time at 40,000. These numbers give a rough indication of elephant population in the past.

Right up to the times of Lord Curzon and Rudyard Kipling, if not quite within living memory, in India a man's wealth was judged by the number of elephants he owned.

Presently, India holds the largest number of Asian elephants in the wild. There are between 27,000 and 30,000 elephants distributed over four widely separated regions – North-western, North-eastern, Central and Southern India. In addition, there are reported to be 3,500 elephants in captivity.

4.2.1   North-Western India

The moist forests along the foothills of Himalayas – Terai-Babber region in the states of Uttarakhand and Uttar Pradesh hold an estimated population of 1500-1600 elephants. Among the important elephant areas are Corbett and Rajaji national parks and Lansdowne Forest Division. The habitat has been fragmented by an irrigation canal and recent human settlements including an army cantonment. Frequent accidental killings of elephants by railways are common around Rajaji national park.

4.2.2   North-Eastern India

With 9,000-12,000 elephants, this region is believed to hold the largest number in the country. Large population of 3,800-5,800 elephants roam along the Himalayan foothills from northern West Bengal, eastward through Assam and Arunachal Pradesh. The vegetation includes tropical moist deciduous and evergreen to cloud forests. Key conservation areas include, Manas Tiger Reserve, Buxa Tiger Reserve of Assam and Namdapha Tiger Reserve, Eagle Nest Sanctuary and Kameng Valley sanctuary of Arunachal Pradesh. To the south of Bramhaputra River, another large population of nearly 2,000 elephants inhabit the alluvial floodplains of Kaziranga National Park, Karbi Anglong and Naga Hills. A third population of 2,500-3,500 elephants occupy the Garo hills and Khasi hills of Meghalaya. All these populations are under severe threat from habitat loss due to extensive *Jhoom* (shifting) cultivation and encroachments apart from massive illegal cutting of trees in the guise of Bodos movement. Small scattered populations have been observed in the Jainti hills, Tripura, Manipur and Mizoram. Here elephants are also threatened against hunting for big meat by local tribes and extremists.

4.2.3 Central India

The elephants are largely confined to the states of Jharkhand and Orissa, although in recent years, they are reported to have been moving into Sarguja, Jeshpurnagar and Raigarh districts of Chhattisgarh and southern West Bengal. About 65 elephants in the Palmau Tiger Reserve, 200 in the Singhbum tract and 70 in the Dalbhum tract of Jharkhand are found roaming. Orissa has an estimated 1300 elephants in a number of isolated populations, of which only 375 are found in Simlipal Tiger Reserve and 300 in Satkosia Gorge Sanctuary (longest gorge over 20 km). Since 1987, large numbers of elephants from Dalma Hills, in East Singbhum district of Jharkhand, have been entering the densely populated districts of Midnapore and Bankura in West Bengal. Predictably, this has resulted in human-elephant conflict of enormous proportion. The loss of traditional transit corridors through Paschmi Singbhum in Jharkhand and into Keonjhar district of Orissa – is one of the reasons why the elephants had selected such unlikely places as post-monsoon habitats. The elephants have to cross two canals near Dalma Wildlife Sanctuary in Jharkhand, railway crossings, human habitation and finally a web of iron ore mines. Small groups of elephants have started venturing south of Dalma into the Seraikella Forest Division, and then further down towards the jungles of Saranda in Jharkhand, bordering the Orissa highlands. This has forced the wild elephants to move into areas where they had not been recorded in the recent past and resulted in a phenomenal rise in human-elephant conflicts. The enormity of the threat to the survival of wild elephants in eastern India can be clearly seen by comparing records of elephant mortality, before and after the increase in mining activities in the region.

4.2.4   Southern India (Plate:---)

The elephants are distributed in the hilly forests of the Western Ghats and adjoining regions of the Eastern Ghats in the states of Karnataka, Kerala and Tamilnadu. The largest population, conservatively estimated at 6000 to 8000 elephants inhabit the Nilgiri Biosphere Reserve and surrounding forests including parts of Eastern Ghats. Nagarahole, Bandipur and Biligirirangan Hills tiger reserves of Karnataka and Madumalai, Mukurti tiger reserves of Tamilnadu. Silent Valley national park, New Amarambolam sanctuary connecting Mukurti and Madumalai national park, boast considerable elephant populations. Beyond the Palghat gap down south lie the Anamalai tiger reserve of Tamilnadu and the Parmbikulam reserve of Kerala, where elephants drift from place to place. The Periyar tiger reserve of Kerala connecting Megha Malai sanctuary of Tamilnadu also inhabit elephants. Few herds of elephants range in Kalakkadu – Mundanturai tiger reserve of southernmost regions of India. Elephant densities in some of the reserves are among the highest in Asia and comparable to those for the African bush elephants, having densities in the range of 1-2 elephants per sq km. The diverse vegetation types – evergreen forests, mixed deciduous forests with grasslands and bamboos, available to elephants within a relatively small area, are no doubt, an important factor in supporting these higher elephant densities. The main threats to these habitats come from encroachments, poaching for ivory, development works such as hydro-electric projects, industries and mining, tea and coffee plantations including extensive agricultural practices.

4.2.5   Andaman Islands

Andaman Islands are the forest clad chain of hills in the Bay of Bengal. When colonization started in the islands during early 1850s, a Bengali timber contractor, P.C. Ray, was leased a part of the forest area of 200 sq km of Interview Island off the West coast of North Andamans, which is separated from the main island by few km of shallow reefs and channels. He started an ambitious timber extraction programme equipped with trolleys and his own ships, supported by about 50 working elephants. In the early 60s, Ray went bankrupt and died soon after. The labourers received no wages and walked off; *mahouts* also joined them after letting the elephants free in the lofty jungles. There are now estimated to be 70 feral elephants on this 131 sq km. island. Some 8 elephants are also found in Diglipur of Andaman Islands.

While the elephant conservation efforts in India have been able to mitigate direct and more obvious threats from poaching and unplanned capture (both illegal and legal) for domestication, the most potent threat to the long-term survival of the elephant comes from the diversion of elephant habitats for non-forestry purposes and degradation due to excessive exploitation. Even strengthening of national parks and sanctuaries with the buffer and core concept, has proved to be inadequate to provide safe havens to this long-lived, largest of living terrestrial mammal. It is here that the 'Project Elephant' has come up with an objective of protection of elephant ranges of distribution of identified populations in Karnataka.

For hundreds of years dialogue between elephant and man was limited to arms warfare. Exploding human civilization, extensive agricultural practices, expansion of cities and towns, coupled with infrastructure development have been the causes of shrinkage of elephant habitats. Crop protection guns and high velocity rifles available with farmers and poachers, respectively, are responsible in massacring elephants. Sky-racketing prices of ivory in the domestic and international markets have taken heavy toll of tuskers. It is seen, a woman buying an ivory article from a curio's shop, an elephant falls victim to the poachers bullets.

Elephants are the master pieces of nature's creation. A living elephant is indeed a treasure trove of Indian jungles than a piece of ivory carving in a show case. By catching glimpses of these living animals in nature, we have experienced man gets thrilled and feel better.

Of late poachers' guns have fallen silent due to total ban on ivory trade in the country. It is no doubt a temporary respite, but as long as ivory commands value in the domestic as well as in the international trade our tuskers are going to be the target of trigger-happy and anti-elephant community. A tusker in the wild becomes a victim to poacher's bullets, at every carved ivory item bought by a tourist. We may have to fight a loosing battle, if we fail to provide safe space for elephants. Think over it.

4.3   Distribution and Status in Karnataka

Back in times, the elephants Uttara Kannada were reported to have shown a declining trend by the turn of the century, though not critically towards threshold of extinction. After the country got its independence, the picture became somewhat blurred. It was a devastating experience, when we looked back the desperate past that lasted until the time of states reorganization. The new game laws took time to bite in Uttara Kannada district of the state, where more weightage was given to commercial logging, rather than conservation forestry. The wildlife protection in this region had taken a back seat. The present north Karnataka region that came into erstwhile Mysore state from the erstwhile Bombay Presidency, the Wildlife Protection Laws could not be enforced until recently, when a separate wildlife divisions were created there. Licit and illicit hunting was rampant. Here wildlife protection and timber harvesting always clashed. Wildlife conservation and forest management never go hand-in-hand, according to a long standing experience of this author.

On the contrary, wildlife protection laws were more effectively implemented in parts of erstwhile Mysore State. Elephant ranges in Kodagu District and Malai Mahadeshwara hills of Kollegal Taluk that were merged from erstwhile Madras Presidency, were reported to be managed fairly well due to which elephants were found safe in these regions. Together with measures of protection, some natural factors also played a significant role in re-establishing favourable conditions for elephants, but they too acted unevenly. The first of these was the cattle plague, the Rinderpest disease (RPD), which swept down Bandipur and neighbouring reserves during 1967 and 1969 killing hundreds of gaur, including sambar. The corpses of immense number of gaur and sambar littered the ground; even hyenas, vultures and other scavengers could not cope in disposing off carrion with their "scrap business". Elephants, however, were not susceptible to this deadly disease.

Fortunately, Mysore and Kodagu districts, unlike Uttara Kannada and Shimoga districts had no problem of pastoral tribes (*Gowlis*). Infiltrations of pastoral tribes from Maharashtra into Uttara Kannada and Shimoga have had intense ecological disaster in certain forests.

The most important region of Karnataka from elephant conservation point of view lies in the Mysore plateau along the south and south-west borders of the state and adjoining to the northern borders of Kerala and Tamilnadu states. The present distribution of elephant population in the forests of Karnataka state is estimated to be ranging between 6000 and 6200, as against 3500 to 3800 around the time of independence. Some of their habitats have turned out to be mostly island like and severely threatened, due to submergence of vast stretches of forests. Elephants here, in particular, are fighting for their survival with their back to the wall.

4.3.1 Mysore Plateau – The Paradise of Elephants

The region includes Bandipur, Nagarahole; Biligirirangan hills tiger reserves, Kaveri elephant sanctuary carved out in Malai Mahadeshwara Hills. These are interconnected with the foothills of Nilgiris in the south by Madumali and Mukurti; Bannerghatta National Park of Bangalore District in the north and Sathyamangalam, Anchetti, Denkinkota and Palmner forest ranges in the east. These form parts of western spur of the Eastern

Ghats. This expanse is connected by fragmented chain of hills, comprise mostly, sholas, dry deciduous and scrub forests, except a small patch of semi-evergreen forest around *Doddasampige* tree near Burude Forest Lodge of Biligirirangan Hills. Here too major wildlife species occur fairly in good number and hence the elephant becomes the prominent species. These hill ranges can sustain a large population of elephants, because of the flow of perennial River Kaveri and its tributaries. This entire stretch of forest, spread over an area of about 2500 sq km has, perhaps, the highest density of elephant population in the whole of South India, harbouring about 6000 elephants, with density @0.5-0.8/km^2. These areas are also rich in other wildlife, such as gaur, sambar and chital, wild pig, Grey langur monkey that coexist with elephants and are hunted by tiger, leopard and wild dogs. The above reserves are scientifically managed for more than a quarter of a century. Despite the fact that they are managed systematically, they are still facing increased anthropological pressure. So far as, Biligirirangan hills and Kaveri sanctuaries are concerned, the problem of rehabilitation of tribal communities outside the PAs remains a challenging task. If this is done successfully, sooner or later, the future of elephants, including other wild animals becomes a win-win situation. However, perseverance and driving force of park authorities need reassurance with dedication, apart from participation of local communities.

The above extensive expanses of forests are contiguous to forest areas of Vellore district of Tamilnadu that form corridors connecting Koundaniya sanctuary of Chittore of Andhra Pradesh. Elephant herds are frequently sighted, but an estimation of their number is rather difficult, because of their seasonal migration and their home range being quite extensive. Some of these elephant herds visit Bannerghatta National Park and even stray over to outskirts of Bangalore city during their annual migration, because these suburbs, once belonged to them as part of their migration range. There are about 200 elephants that range this region according to a rough estimation. Habitat loss and fragmentation coupled with poaching for ivory, have threatened their survival in these ranges.

4.3.2 Elephants in Soup in Malenadu Region

The Malenadu region lies to the East of Kardibetta, Agumbe, Bababudengiri and Kuduremukh hills of Western Ghats. There are two important rivers, the Tunga and the Bhadra that drain the Malenadu region. As many as three wildlife protected areas (PAs), namely Settihalli, Bhadra and Kuduremukh are located here. These were the forests almost regularly haunted by elephants before the country was liberated from British Raj. These PAs also had better concentration of gaur, sambar, chital and wild pigs, apart from carnivores like tiger, leopard and wild dogs. The Bhadra Wildlife Sanctuary faced a disheartening plight when large herds of gaur were wiped out due to Rinderpest disease during 1989-90. It took nearly 10 years to rebuild the lost gaur population. Presently, Bhadra is the only haven for elephants in the region. The presence of Bhadra reservoir as a perennial source of water, supported by plenty of Bamboos, Ochlandra cane, grass and other browse species to feed on, makes this region an ideal habitat for elephants. There are good numbers of herds of elephants with a population of about 200. If the security in the sanctuary remains good, these stable family groups are likely to prosper.

4.3.3 Extinction Looming Large for Fragmented Herds

In parts of Kuduremukh wildlife sanctuary, there appears to be a small herd of elephants of about 10, moving around in the forests of Balehonnur, Mudigere and Kalasa Ranges. One animal of the herd was found electrocuted accidentally while it raided crops, some years ago.

There were 10 male elephants wandering in the deciduous forests of Doddabetta of Hassan district. Having been separated from the main herd after the inundation of forests by Hemavati reservoir, the bachelor group had turned out to be notorious in the region, damaging crops and property, even killing humans. One of the tuskers had turned out to be a rogue. It deserved mercy death. Despite the efforts made by the local forest officials for its extermination, the marauder could not be traced.

Its body was found floating in Bhadra reservoir, with tusks in tact, after three months. The remaining bachelor herd of 9 (nine) was captured by "operation tranquillising". They were trans-located to Nagarahole National Park over a distance of about 100 kms during Nov/Dec 1987.

Similarly, another bachelor group of 8 (eight) male elephants from Kattepura forests (on the southern bank of Hemavati reservoir) of Kodagu District were found isolated due to submersion of reserve forests of Maldare and Dubare of Somwarpet Taluk. This notorious bachelor group aimlessly wandered causing damage to crops, property and human life. These were also trans-located to Nagarahole forests over a distance of about 120 km. by tranquillising during March/April 1987. In the above process some two tuskers died, while transporting and due to suffocation. Surprisingly, all of them were found back-tracked their way and arrived in their original places-Maldare and Dubare forests, within few days.

All of them were recaptured and this time most of them were disposed off by public auction sale. Among the captives, a huge *makhna* was retained with the Forest Department for being harnessed in forestry works. Unfortunately, after few months this unfortunate one died of mental depression and agony. The only survivor among them is the tusker, named Balarama that was nominated to succeed Drona, in carrying golden *howdah* during *Dashara* procession.

The above "operation translocation" was the outcome of the meeting of the Southern Indian Task Force of the IUCN – Asian Elephant Group, which met at Bandipur during my tenure as Field Director. I was also involved in decision making process in the month of November 1985.

In recent years, increased Human-Elephant conflict in the above regions is found to have recurred, due to shrinkage of their home-ranges. Hydro-electric projects, release of forest lands for agriculture and rehabilitation of people, infrastructure development and encroachments are responsible in creating island-like elephant populations. As the anthropogenic pressure, such as, destruction of forest by local communities for small timber and fuel wood, uncontrolled livestock grazing, setting fire to forest, poaching, grass cutting, etc., is on the increase. There are no enough forests for these elephants to feed on. They venture to stray out in search of food and water, where they come upon farm lands causing damage to crops and property and frequent human deaths. Consequently, farmers and coffee estate owners resort to take revenge by shooting, poisoning, electrocution and trapping. Thus, never ending war over there was going on causing deaths on both the sides of elephants and humanbeings. Some 7 human deaths and 15 elephant killings reported to have occurred in these regions alone between 2007 and 2010.

It was suggested, among others, to acquire coffee estates, so as to enlarge the area sufficient enough to facilitate in *situ* conservation of elephants, rather than attempting to *ex-situ* protection. The existing area of about 62 sq km, where 25 elephants are drifting from place to place is insufficient to provide shelter, food and water. This is the main reason for the elephants to create havoc around Alur forest of Hassan district. The existing elephant population needed at least 100 sq km chunk of safe forest and free from anthropic interference. Another group of 10 elephants affected by 'Harangi Irrigation Project' were reported creating similar problems in Kodagu district.

In view of socio-economic, political and emotional issues involved, it was impossible to put an end to this age old human-elephant confrontation. However, in respect of elephants around Alur of Hassan district and those in Kodagu district, the following immediate remedial measures were considered appropriate:

i. **The key to successful elephant conservation in the region was by reducing deforestation and forest degradation. This could help maintain, enhance and replenish in** *situ* **forest cover and ensure a positive relationship with local communities. It was, therefore paramount to consider "in** *situ* **conservation of elephants, rather than attempting** *ex situ* **protection elsewhere, by capture and translocation".**

ii. Habitat development, such as grasslands creation, rainwater harvesting, water conservation, removing of weeds, apart from total protection needed be undertaken, so as to provide elephants enough food, drinking water and shelter, through the year.

iii. Effective protection of the habitat by continuous stone-walling with dry rubble stones wrapped by expanded steel mesh/rough stones with cement – would help prevent elephants straying out (eg. continuous stone walling around Ranthambore tiger reserve in Rajasthan and elsewhere has considerably solved the problem of wild animals straying out).

iv. Coffee Lands/Paddy Fields around the area needed to be acquired and declared as add on reserve forests (RFs). This would help provide resident elephants with additional feeding grounds. The wisdom lied on authorities to interconnect this area with nearest reserve forest by insular corridors.

v. Indian government was then in a position to foot bill of conservation of elephants. Required budgetary requirement for the items iii & iv needed be requisitioned from the Ministry of Environment, Forests and Climate Change, New Delhi, which had expressed willingness under the directions of Hon'ble High Court of Karnataka.

vi. School children and teachers, including local communities around the area needed to be educated in environmental conservation awareness.

vii. Initiating massive eco-development programme to gradually wean away local communities from entering forests for their daily needs was proposed.

viii. It is the systematic management practices with scientific and technological inputs followed by effective protection of habitat, with committed personnel on the job would help bring about desired results.

Continuing the discussion of fragmented populations, a small herd of 5-6 elephants was reported in the Ghat forests of Mudigere, Belthangadi and Uppinangadi ranges of Chikkmaglur and Dakshina Kannada districts of Karnataka. These elephants had caused severe damage to crops in villages adjoining to reserve forests. Partially decomposed body of a tusker was found floating in the flood waters of Netravati River near Uppinangadi in the year 1991, with one tusk missing. Their future, thus seemed bleak.

Further down south, there reported to be another herd of 10-16 elephants ranging in the Ghat forests of Bisle, Pushpagiri forests of Hassan district and Subramanya and Sampaje forests of Dakshina Kannada district. They often raid paddy crops and areca gardens and got shot at.

Yet another herd of 20-25, was reported to be roaming about extensively in the grassy slopes with sholas and evergreen forests of Bramhagiri, Makut and Bhagamandala forests of Kodagu district. They were a fragmented lot into splinter groups and they too raided plantation crops, paddy crops, including pineapple, jack fruit and tapioca.

Fate of these isolated and fragmented herds was gradually narrowing.

Extinction was looming large for those pachyderms. Their days were numbered.

It became rather police-eying on those splinter groups.

4.3.4   Dramatic Come Back in Uttara Kannada Elephants

The news of tragic end of a two-and-a-half-month-old male calf in the herd of elephants, when a speeding vehicle knocked it down on the high way near Kolikere village, about 10 km from Yellapur in the early hours of the night of 14th December 1997, shocked the entire community of foresters and animal lovers. Soon after the ghastly accident, its mother was reported to have dragged the carcass of her baby to the road side and blocked the traffic for more than 14 hours. The visibly upset cow was so adamant and tried to attack truck drivers who ventured to move their vehicles. The hostile mother even attacked and damaged wind shield of a public transport vehicle, the driver of which ventured to force drive the vehicle. A two-wheeler was also trampled by the sobbing pachyderm when pillion rider made futile bid to cross the accident site. The other furious elephants uprooted some of road-side trees, only to way-lay and stood guard. In the early hours of next morning six of the seven elephants left the site, leaving behind the female that stood guard over the carcass of her dear one.

The fragmented herds of Uttar Kannada District are reported to be wandering beyond the back waters of Supa reservoir, visiting paddy fields during harvest season. Considering the anti-elephant attitude of the local people and *Gowli's* menace, the survival of elephants had reached a slender fissure in that highly disturbed ecosystem. Patience and perseverance, followed by driving force of the Forest and Wildlife officials in providing safe habitat, were given reassurance for gradual revival of elephant population here. The present elephant population reported to be 45-70, has shown a dramatic come back in the region.

Dandeli-Anshi Tiger Reserve in Uttara Kannada District that boasts the richest evergreen to dry deciduous forests are aimed at conservation of elephants including tigers and other wildlife. Honey combing pattern of settlements and encroachments in the above tiger reserve, followed by heavy clearance of rich forest for release to encourage agriculture in addition to ecological disturbance by the gigantic 'Kalinadi' hydro-electric project, followed by clearance of rich forest to draw high tension electric lines and mining had negative impact on the elephant population. Another challenge the elephants in the region facing are that lack of grass lands and browse species as ground cover under large expanse of teak plantations. Unless grasslands are created and enough browse species are made available as fodder, crop raiding, leading to increased confrontation against man will continue. Though there is considerable recovery in elephant population, in the absence of enough fodder, the elephant herds are gradually migrating to the forests of Sawantwadi in Satara district of Maharashtra state.

According to Conservator of Forests, Wildlife, Kolhapur, during the visit of this author, in the month of June 2010, some three to seven elephants that crossed over the frontier line between Karnataka and Mahrashtra, about two years ago were reported to have been stay-put in Sawantwadi forests of Satara district. Initially, though protests by local politicians, followed by attempts to drive them back were made, local people in the region are understood to have accepted their arrival and learnt to live with elephants. They reckon elephant as revered animal, associated with Lord Ganesha.

In search of breaking new grounds, some more elephants from Dandeli forests of Uttar Kannada district of Karnataka in the process of spill over reported to have join them in the subsequent year. Local people with political patronage received them as welcome guests. Elephants are believed to bring fortune and good rains. Driven by instinct, these elephants have ventured to disperse into their historical migratory corridors. Elephants are known to drift back and forth during their seasonal movements in search of fodder, water and shelter. Authorities concerned need to ensure farmers' crops are given effective protection, if necessary, by erecting stone walls around newly created elephant sanctuary to prevent possible human-elephant conflicts. Wisdom of forest officials calls for educating people in the region that it is the responsibility of every citizen to protect and preserve our living national heritage.

4.3.5 Menace in the Elephant Country

Gowlis (pastorals/graziers) around Bhadra and Settihalli wildlife sanctuaries of Chikamaglur and Shimoga Districts respectively and Dandeli Wildlife Sanctuary of Uttara Kannada District know the behaviour of elephants too well. This nomadic tribe have had their homes around these forests for more than 75 years. It is their practice, everyday, to wander about in deep forests, herding their hundreds of buffaloes. These nomads belonged originally, to Maharashtra state. After the Western Ghat forests of that state were found bald, these pastorals gained entry into the state of Karnataka through the forests of Uttar Kannada District. The communities were given political patronage when they were found to be potential vote banks.

Those buffaloes are ferocious and capable of fending for themselves from the attacks of powerful carnivores like tiger and leopards. The impact of heavy grazing is too severe in those wildlife habitats. Wild animals, particularly pachyderms are the first to suffer for want of fodder and eventually, they are forced to indulge in extensive crop raiding. Large numbers of elephants get shot at in the process. There were even rewards for killing habitual crop raiders until the middle of the twentieth century. Officials of British Raj, as a privileged class of trigger happy people, hunted such elephants on the pretext of killing "rogues". Depredation on elephant population in these regions was faster than in other parts of the state, especially after independence.

4.4   Ivory is Theirs; Elephants Alone Shall Wear Ivory

Ivory is found best in its natural place – 'on live elephants'. Tusks are indispensable, multipurpose instruments to elephants. Tusks in male serve not only as 'status symbol', but also as deadly weapons against enemies. They help in establishing superiority over adversaries of its own tribe. They use their tusks to dig for a source of water, salt-lick and even to force free-flow of *musth* fluid discharge from their temporal glands. They are also used to debark that is used to subsist, particularly during pinch period of summer. In the wild, we know, the strongest will service the female in season in the process of natural selection. When an animal looses its protective weapon, it becomes depressed psychologically and could be challenged even by a youngster. Tusks in elephants are also for display as weapons in self-protection. They also serve for marking the trees in their home range, as trunk-rest and as protection for the trunk (comparable to a bumper in a car). Just as humans are left or right handed, elephants too are left or right tusked; the tusk that is used more than the other is called the 'master tusk'. Master tusks can easily be distinguished since they are shorter, worn out and more rounded at the tip. In addition, master tusks usually have a groove near their tip where the constant action of grass wears a transverse furrow on the ivory.

A strange, but sad act was reported to have been performed on a wild bull at Bandipur reserve during 1987. In their enthusiasm of saving tuskers in the wild from poachers, both the tusks of a bull were amputated by tranquillising at Bandipur reserve. Dr. Khadri, the Vet. of the park, explained that tusks are marked at a point, measuring the distance down from the lip-line, equivalent to the length between the edge of upper lip and an eye. They were sawn off. This was to avoid damage to pulp tissues inside the socket of the tusk and to prevent of possible infection.

This is nothing but an act of biological terrorism and short sighted vandalism against nature's own way of functioning. The unfortunate bull whose tusks were sawn off was found suffering from infection in the socket after few months. It was reported, the bull succumbed to *Haemrrhagic septicaemia* (a bacterial disease) caused by *Pasteurella multoceda*, after two years of sufferings. Its body was found along the periphery of the forest of Maddur range.

I have seen a camp tusker in Myanmar, whose tissues of the socket of an amputated tusk were totally eaten up due to infection and it looked hollow. It was cleaned daily by inserting a pipe and medically treated.

4.5   Who Needs Ivory, Any Way?

Government of India have imposed total ban on the trade of ivory and ivory articles, by an amendment, under the Wildlife (Protection) Act, 1972. Under this act, every dealer or trader in ivory and wildlife trophies etc. is required to declare to the nearest Chief Wildlife Warden, as to the stock position of ivory and ivory articles. This, however, had very little impact on illegal trade in ivory. Still ivory poaching and illegal trade carried on unabated.

In India raw ivory has never been stored as an investment or as a hedge against inflation, while it has been the practice in Hong Kong and Japan. Of late, in Gulf countries and in New York, traders have started hedging ivory against inflation. As a result, prices soared. Because of sky-racketing prices of ivory and ivory products, even Indian ivory (in the form of antique tusks), had entered the market. This author's memory is still green, some of the raw ivory kept as decorative pieces in Forest Offices and Forest Museums had been stolen and sold as antiques in the market.

After a piece had been carved, painted or used in inlay work it is extremely difficult to ascertain whether or not the ivory is of Indian origin or African. So, unscrupulous Indian traders could easily trick the authorities and tourists. While the ivory articles were shipped out of India, they should be accompanied by an export permit, granted by the officials in New Delhi, when they are satisfied that the raw ivory was legally imported from a known source. However, *bona fide* tourists are also required to obtain export permits for the ivory pieces they bought and took out of the country.

4.6 Say, No to Ivory!

Only in Gujarat and Rajasthan do girls still wear ivory bracelets and bangles and other ornaments during marriage ceremonies. Social changes are, however, showing in gradually; the younger generation are shunning ivory articles. But then why do we need ivory? Certainly Indian women do not need ivory any more. In view of dwindling tuskers in the wild, our women folk may perhaps, be the inspiration to the world community in total rejection of ivory and ivory articles, thus help participate to stop massacre of elephants.

Don't buy ivory and its articles! Say, no to ivory!!

Chapter V

Shadows in the Forest

Indian forests, inhabited by elephants and carnivores are safe for those, who follow "law of the jungle"; even safer than concrete/glass jungles of so called civilized society. When our forests are invaded by anti-national communities like, ultras, militants, naxallites, bodos and forest brigands, they turn out to be "jungle of the law"! – the most dangerous places, not only for entire gamut of life forms, but also to environmental decay and ecological degradation. It is time citizens of the country learn to live with the nature and participate in the conservation process. The mother earth needs your involvement to mitigate natural disasters.

The maxim, "*Mens sana incorpore sano*" (meaning, sound mind in a sound body), inscribed below the tiger face of the logo of my blazer during my training at the Indira Gandhi National Forest Academy, Dehradun, had an incredible influence on my developing mind. Later, while I was working as, Field Director, Project Tiger, Bandipur National Park, I was surrounded by the natural space. I was strong and healthy with a challenging aim and plenty of stimuli to create a balanced existence. I never craved for the humdrum life of suburbia and I loved my isolation in the midst of forest. Soon, I had explored every corner of the reserve and survived there without the worldly trappings of society. I was part of a continuum with the elephants and my behaviour often showed the same motivations as theirs, in similar situations. Though my principal duties were to manage the welfare of tigers including their potential prey species found in the habitat, I fell in love with elephants. It was easy for me to spot the elephants than the tigers, during my sojourn in the reserve. I could, however spend long hours in the company of elephants, which were not aggressive, if not friendly, by my presence. Eventually, whatever protective and conservation measures were adopted to develop the habitat, under the 'Operation Tiger', the elephants in the reserve automatically, became the beneficiaries, as the tigers could not be managed in isolation.

5.1 Wild Discovery

As the time rolled by, I grew closer to elephant herds that visited Bandipur reserve. But, I could not keep track of a particular herd continuously, as they used to be within the park limits for a few days, before crossing over frontiers between Karnataka and Tamilnadu forests or Karnataka and Kerala forests. The difficulty was that different herds visited the park at different timings. Unfortunately, my duties did not permit me to follow one or few particular herds throughout their stay at the reserve. Similar was the situation with tuskers. Every time different male or males visited and remained in the reserve for few days, then entered deeper into the forest or crossed over to adjoining reserves of Madumalai or Wayanad. Gradually, I learnt to stay put to a charging elephant and called him or her bluff by pushing forward my palm, while being confined to the vehicle or standing at a safe place. But, I never took a chance of facing the charging animal on foot during the initial stages of my acquaintance with different herds/ lone tusker. As I started recognizing the herds, recalling their previous acquaintances, I ventured to follow them on foot talking to them at close quarters. It was not the bravado; I knew what I was experimenting with. It was up to me to recognise danger and to get out of the way, or else, I would fall to a really hostile elephants' trunks in the same way that they would fall to a hunter's bullets. I could not help feeling a great admiration for them; I was, rather, drawn to them by shear love and passion. Was it their size, their power or their gentle behaviour or their body language that attracted me? I could not, however, pronounce markedly. I just knew that I loved being surrounded by elephants. This experience gave me a great joy. As far as possible, I always maintained a critical safe distance from them, constantly looking out with a watchful eye on cantankerous juveniles and making sure that there were more than one escape routes in case of exigencies.

5.2   You Can't Expect Wild Animals to Parade on Public Ramp?

After visiting nearby areas to Bandipur as Field Director, I visited Begur Range forests at the western most sector of the reserve. By then the implementation of programmes under the 'Project Tiger' in Bandipur was eight years old. I wanted to study, in particular the general health of the habitat and its recovery, including wildlife populations – both carnivores and herbivores, ever since the project came into being in the year 1973. Accompanied by Prabhakar (Sr), Range Forest Officer, I drove into the reserve. After driving a km or so, there came series of shattering trumpets, followed by growls and rumblings from a herd of elephants on either side of the jungle track. Our vehicle came to a jerking halt on my signal to the driver. A female, supposedly next in hierarchy to the matriarch stood in front of the vehicle, her head held high with coiled trunk, ears cocked, fixing her piercing look on us and advancing one step forward and two steps back.

"Isn't that a little dangerous"? I asked Prabhakar.

I had never been so close to an elephant before. I was very much surprised to learn about the dominance of the elephant lady, next in command to the Matriarch. Here, she conducted herself as 'in charge' lady boss, representing the Matriarch of the family. She actually stood on guard, while some members of her family crossed the road, amidst commotion and joined the remaining members on the opposite side, where the matriarch stood pacifying the agitated members of the family.

"I had believed, until then a big fierce bull, the Patriarch, was the boss of the herd", I raised my apprehension. "My belief proved wrong", I apologetically corrected myself.

The lady keeping an eye on our vehicle, her flank arched with raised tail and keeping her tip of the trunk in her mouth moved away to join the members of the herd. All the members joined the matriarch to greet her one by one, the sight of which was heart rending. Calm in the forest returned. We moved on.

A while after, we passed a herd of gaur crossing the road and then looked out for a tiger; crossed a dry *nalla* bed and drove through a herd of chital and finally turned towards Banur, a dilapidated hamlet right inside the reserve, along a narrow track. On reaching the village site, the Ranger explained the challenges he faced in relocating villagers of Banurgadde and Gundregadde, out side the reserve, under the relocation programme for a successful management of the Project Tiger.

On reaching the 'Forest Hut' at Banur, I deviated from the subject and inquired Prabhakar, "Why we had missed the tiger, during our drive through the reserve? As in the past, tiger had evaded me this time as well".

Meanwhile, our 'bush-breakfast' was served by the care-taker, belonging to local Jenu kuruba tribe. We sat on the parapet of the veranda with our tray, munching the bread toasted on burning wood. I began pouring out 'safari tea', which had a peculiar taste of smoke and powdered milk.

Prabhakar remarked, "Sir, every visitor to the park, like you, expects a tiger or a leopard to come and parade one after another, as if the wilderness is public ramp of a fashion show". "In nature", Mr. Prabhakar continued, "unlike zoo animals, one has to look out for wild animals and birds with eyes and ears open, but moth zipped, if he/she wants to have the thrill and enjoyment of the wilderness". He went on to say, "generally, visitors to the park come with high expectations to see all the animals in one go"!

I simply nodded my head, in affirmative.

"When tourists see a herd of elephants, next they expect gaurs, then a tiger and so on", asserted as an experienced Ranger.

Ironically, at the end of the trip, visitors remark, "Oh, hopeless; this park is disappointing, we could see only a herd of elephants, a leopard and few peacocks, that is all. Isn't it, you wanted to say"? I expressed based on day's experience.

"There are forest officers", he added, "who might not have seen a tiger in their life time".

"Why do you say so?" I asked, inquisitively.

"Tigers in the wild are shy and basically fear of humans. They reckon human as a "Master Predator". They are elusive and come out only after dusk and retire before dawn. Those who spot a tiger are considered as the luckiest, particularly, in the protected reserves of south India. The real excitement lies in looking out for one and spotting it", Prabhakar declared.

"Yes, you're right. Your assessment is in conformity with the law of nature. I appreciate your views. Accordingly, visitors to the park need to be educated as to the realities before they embark on wildlife safari", I concluded.

We continued our drive towards Kalkere Forest Lodge, through the jungle track, inspecting some development works en-route, such as rain water harvesting and road works.

5.3   Camp-Life in the Jungle

On reaching Kalkere, the remotest place in the reserve, I decided to stay for the night in the forest rest house (FRH), while Prabhakar was asked to return to his HQ at Begur.

I loved camp life, in particular, forest lodge at Kalkere, away from human habitations. It had certain toughness, though: the bare rooms no decorations, except a kerosene lamp and some old gaur and sambar horns hung on the walls, no curtains and every piece of furniture was used. Yet one ate from plates, drank out of glasses and had hot tea and coffee served in proper cup-saucers. There were good books to read, interesting things to look around in the surrounding prime forest. At the end of the day, there was hot water for a bath and clothes were washed every day. The water at Kalkere was a good fortune, as if 'liquid gold'. There existed only one water hole that was used by camp elephants and *mahuths* belonging to local Kuruba families stationed there. Even wild animals used the same source for drinking and wallowing. The water was wild and complex. The same water was used for drinking after boiling and filtering. It represented the minimum and may be maximum comfort needed for an officer on duty to stay in the depth of woodland.

I have heard visitors complaining of boredom, no radio, no TV, no network coverage for their mobile communication and no other entertainment in such a remote and godforsaken place. They chant as if they can't survive without them. People, who live in concrete jungles, I may ask them, "can't they afford to forgo such luxuries and earthly comforts for a day or two"?

5.4   Call of the Wild?

I was proceeding from Kalkere to Bandipur the following day accompanied by Srinivasa Murthy, the territorial Ranger. By the time we finished inspecting some habitat improvement works, the sun was descending fast in the westerly horizon. Dark clouds started hovering overhead. The Ranger cautioned about possible downpour, the stray shower of the season. I was also exhausted by the hectic work. Asking the Ranger to return to his HQ, the Waggoner rolled down the pot-holed, asphaltic-corrugated inter-state Sultanbattery-Gundlupet road. I felt the Waggoner was trotting. But soon the vehicle turned right and entered the jungle track that led to Bandipur camp. It did not take much time for the Rain-God to flood the forest floor. The vehicle, however, could negotiate that muddy forest road.

The green valley was, by then, lit by a strange light of a full moon covered by drifting rain clouds. When we reached a steep slope steering across Chamnahalla FRH, a flecked in black and white, the gaur bull propelled itself down the road. In that dimmed head lights of our vehicle, it looked like a wine barrel with a bull's white legs and a tail pinned over it.

We were still 14 km away from Bandipur camp, where suddenly the vehicle slumped to one side and came to a skidding halt. "I am afraid we have got a deflated tyre", Makbul, the driver warned me.

There were indications that elephants were feeding on the hill slope, hardly 15 metres away. "What about the elephants?" I asked the driver who was preparing to get down replacing the deflated tyre.

"They are all right, sir", but a man eating tiger or a man eating leopard is worse. Let's me try and get this tyre off", Makbul exhorted with confidence.

The driver looked for the jack every where, but could not find one. He was a new driver to this particular American Jeep, on a relief duty. The regular driver was on leave as his wife was to deliver their 9th baby.

We tried to drive on to the table-top road so that we could remove the flat tyre by lifting that metallic monster, but nothing seemed to work on that slippery muddy track. To our bad luck, we were not able to reach any of the wireless stations, as our positioning was such that the valley surrounded by chin of rolling hills. Finally, I offered the choice of spending the rest of the night in the jeep, in spite of being devoured by mosquitoes.

"Walk back to Chamnahalla Forest Lodge, which we had passed a few minutes ago and spend the night over there", came as a wise suggestion from driver.

Though, our presence had forced the elephant herd to move away from the road, so as to allow a wide berth, they seemed to be close by. No doubt, it was a suggestion worth taking risk, but how to avoid those dark shadows of the forest, the elephants? I asked him repugnantly.

"Don't worry about them, Sir, they will never hurt us", driver reassured me. He went on to kindle courage in me, saying, "Let us walk past them.

The best thing to do is to talk all the way or sing loudly to muster courage. Your leather-soled boots may also help add sound. Let us also have a walking stick and go on tapping the ground. The vibration of the forest floor will also scare away snakes, if any".

The moon showed up from time to time drowning by the passing clouds. Leaving the vehicle behind we walked down the slushy track, amidst intermittent chorus of Cicadas, followed by snorts, barks of denizens of the forest around and the trumpeting of distant elephant herds.

The sky turned dark, followed by drizzling on reaching a *nalla*. Soon, clothes got drenched and water had seeped through my boots. Further walking made me disgusted and sickly in that gusty wind. Nevertheless, I kept walking as there was no alternative. We reached a hump with dense forest, where tall trees swayed with whistling sound, triggered by westerly cold wind. All these had created in me nostalgia, in addition to fear phobia.

Dwarfed by the diminished light, we were confronted face to face with elephants just standing on the road, beating the mosquito menace. It was at this situation, I realised how vulnerable a man would be without a gun in front of an "army of wild beasts". All we had to rely on our senses and tactful avoidance of the situation. I imagined momentarily that the 'shadows in the forest' must be gazing at us standing in a single file and blowing out their nostrils. I felt, we were putlogs, potential target of their attack, if they decided to do so. Unarmed and unprotected, as we were, dwarf and weak in that immensely dark wilderness, we were forced to reverse backward few steps away and wait for the beasts to make way for us. Except for the sound of dripping rain over broad leaves of Teak and the rhythmic shrilling chorus of Cicadas, the forest was silent. We waited....?

"Dhank-dhank", a belling of a sambar echoed from behind. I got frightened! It was like a bolt from the blue, shattering the calm of the dreaded night!! The sound echoed through the forest canopy!!! I turned back to find the cause for that warning. Was there a carnivore on its prowl? No. It was we, who had surprised the sambar stag crossing the jungle track.

"On seeing our presence on the road, the sambar had sent a warning bell to rest of the denizens of the jungle", whispered Makbul.

I mustered my courage and started talking to my self loudly. Noiselessly, the 'shadows in the jungle' slid into the thick bush. But we had to wait for some time until we got confirmed that they had moved away into the depth of the jungle. At last, distant sound of breaking bamboo indicated that the herd had moved away. The path was made clear and we continued our tread fast.

"So much can go right in the wild, but so much can go terribly wrong too", I exhorted with sheer desperation.

Our long walk came to an end as we approached the staff quarters at Chamnahalla camp. We called out for some one present inside the forest quarters. No reply came. We desperately climbed up to reach FRH, atop the hillock. To our anguish and annoyance, we found the door was locked.

My frozen body through the bone marrow needed warmth and rest. I took out clothes and hung them to the door after squeezing. Squatting on the door steps, I kept talking to driver, so that we could keep awake for rest of the night.

We were woken up by Jayendrappa, Range Forest Officer, Bandipur, who had come with a 'search party' to escort us, since we had failed to reach our destination, even past mid-night. A night to reckon with – strained by horror and anguish. I couldn't realise, how soon my tired body was overtaken by slumber. Driver also had surrendered to deep sleep.

5.5 Forest Fantasy

The true mother of all life forms is forest – the gift of nature. With different ecosystems, the Bandipur National Park has not only gone through centuries of evolution but also turbulences of the history. Ecological terrorism has spelled disasters, time and again, leading to modifications/threshold of extinctions of certain species of flora and fauna. The floristic composition of the reserve is as diverse, as that of faunal composition. The Bandipur forests are classified as the "Southern Tropical Mixed Deciduous forests with bamboos and grasslands". Teak grows naturally and forms a predominant species of the whole ecosystem. Large extents of Teak plantations add to the economic value of the standing growth. The well known associate trees are: the Gum-kino (Honne), *Pterocarpus marsupium*, species of *Terminalia chebula* and *T. bellerica*, both yielding myrabolams; *Terminalia tomentosa* (Mathi), which has a much-fissured bark resembling crocodile skin, the Dindaga, *Anogeissus latifolia*, which some times forms gregarious stand, the Nelli *Emblica officinalis*, the Pathri *Stereospermum tetragonum* and the Bende *Kydia calycina*, notable for occurring gregariously in almost pure patches,while still in the sapling stage, where as, the mature trees are found spaced well apart and mixed with other trees in the forest.

There are also commonly found trees, characteristic of the more moist mixed deciduous forests of Western Ghats, such as, the darkly beautiful Rosewood (Beete) *Dalbergia latifolia*, one of the handsomest and costliest timbers in the world today. Nearer to forest pools and water courses, the Ben teak *Adina cordifolia* (Naked maiden) and *Mitragyna parvifolia*, both stately trees of the coffee family valued for their light coloured, evenly-grained timber.

Like the magnificent stature Rosewood, another tree of modest size, typical of the drier tracts and highly prized, the Sandalwood *Santalum album*, every part of the tree is so valuable, including the roots and the branches. It is a semi-parasitic plant and found declining everywhere owing to spike disease, said to have been caused by *Mycoplasma* like organism. On account of its high price and increasing demand for fragrant oil, carving and in burning as incense sticks, illicit cutting and smuggling have threatened its survival. Sandalwood tree is, therefore, declared as the 'endangered' species and finds its entry in the Red Data Book. Though the flora of Bandipur has been strictly conserved for more than four decades, since the Project Tiger came in, no mature Sandalwood trees are seen and not even saplings, due to smuggling and fires.

Shorea talura (Jalari) the southern cousin of the Sal *Shorea robusta*, yielding fragrant resin grows gregariously in places, as on Chamnahalla hill; the tree from which coat-button seeds are produced. *Strychnos nuxvomica* (Nanjana *mara*) from which Strychnine obtained is also found here, but sparsely distributed. *Randia dumetorum* (Kare) is a small, interesting tree; its arrestingly white flowers fade to most attractive pure yellow ochre and its round fruits contain a toxic principle and are used to poison fish in shallow pools. However, deer and sambar are fond of the fruits and eat them with avid zest and impunity.

The flower buds of *Bauhinia racemosa* are eaten by Bonnet macaque, Langur monkeys and Malbar giant squirrel. The nectar of the bloom of the Red Silk-cotton (Burga) *Bombax ceiba*, draws Mynah, Bulbul and even Parakeets and other birds; Giant squirrel and Langur monkeys also eat the young fruits. *Erythrina mysorensis* also attracts birds when in flower.

Deer and other herbivores, the sambar in particular, greatly fancy the fruits of *Gmelina arborea* (Shivani) and of *Terminalia bellerica* (Tare); the long, black, cylindrical pods of the Indian laburnum (Kakke) *Cassia fistula*, are eagerly crunched up by deer, gaur, monkeys and the sloth bear. The drupes of *Garuga pinnata* (Godda) are favoured by many wild animals, including squirrels and the mouse deer. The sour fruits of the Hog plum (Amte) *Spondias mangifera*, excellent in making pickles, are much liked by many herbivores like Barking deer (Muntjac), Sambar and Chital.

Many kinds of tall grass (all those appropriately and loosely termed as 'elephant grasses'), as also some short grasses are found along with herbaceous plants. Among the grasses, commonly found grown may be mentioned: *Saccharum spontaneum, Ischaemum pilosum*, species of *Panicum, Sorghum* and *Themeda cymbaria, Apluda mutica, Arundinella holcoides, Eragrostis gangetica, Hackelochloa granularis* and *Paspalum scrobiculatum*.

There occur two species of Bamboo namely, small bamboo *Dendrocalamus strictus* and big bamboo *Bambusa arundinacea*, both ofwhich form principal food source for elephants, gaur and sambar. *Ochlandra travancorica* (cane) is totally absent in this region.

5.6 Night Life in The Forest

The stars looked faintly in that moonlit night during summer, while I waited on the *machan*, a platform built over a tree branch. In an elephant inhabited forest, a safe place to sit and watch the activities of denizens and listening to the sounds of the jungle. My attention was drawn by an intermittent call of Night-jar. But the choruses of Cicadas around me drowned the complete silence in that open jungle. I was to keep my vigil the whole night, for which I had gone prepared physically and mentally. I sat without a blink of an eye, listening to the 'night language' – the sounds of rustle of a small animal in the under growth below, the snorting of gaur and distant roars of a territorial tiger and an occasional call of a peacock and an owl.

Night after night, I sat with watchful eye but could not escape the incessant braying chorus of the 'my-raid Cicadas' that seemed to permeate every nook and corner of the forest, especially during monsoon.

Yes. I was learning the secrets of night life in the jungle. Life in the jungle kept me in the state of high alert and excitement. Pragmatically speaking, at times, the night life in the jungle is at its zenith: A leopard on the prowl, killing his prey, feeding voraciously at his hard earned kill, intermittently resting and visiting water hole for a drink; a passing by tusker approaching the *machan* to investigate human presence, when I held my breath and maintained pin-drop silence; I would often hear the trickle of water from the nearby water hole, as it slipped while the tusker squirted into his mouth or the lapping sound of a carnivore; huge dark shadow of a bull gaur, emerged from the thicket, stood motionless, looked around and then wandered off past, testing the air around. Occasional distant calls of peacock, croaking of frogs and so on kept me captivating. There was no sadness or boredom, when nothing happened. On the other hand, I was nourished by total silence and felt nothingness on this earthly world. On occasions, my mind travelled back and forth between bush life and civilised life in those zigzag puzzles of moonlit nights. Once the moon was gone, I could absorb the long hours of nothingness amidst occasional hooting of an owl. I felt, I was blind folded in that pitch dark and total silence of the forest.

5.7 Human-like Qualities in Elephant

While watching elephants sitting all alone in the jungle, I soon discovered that they showed many of inherent virtues like loyalty, protective nature and respect to elders, love and affection towards an individual within the family group or the clans. As I stayed far away from my own species, the *Homo sapiens* and became deeply involved with the welfare of elephants, consciously or unconsciously, I drew parallels between their social behaviour and ours. At the end of the day, I could discover many similarities between theirs and ours. They are summarised as :

* **The positioning of breasts between front legs of elephants is just as humans, who possess them between arms.**

* **Anatomically, elephant's hind legs and front legs operate like legs and arms with wrists, respectively, like those of human.**

* **Brain of young and its progressive development in elephant is just as in human baby, unlike other quadrupeds, whose brain is almost as in adults.**

* **Maturity age in female elephant being 13-15 and in case of male 18-25, comparable with the maturity as in humans.**

* **Elephants are the intelligent animals next in order of humans and they live in social harmony. Elephants could be trained to remember nearly 200 commands and to perform, just as in case of humans.**

* **For *Homo sapiens* and *proboscidean,* death of a member remains as significant and emotional ritual for the survivors. In**

life, individuals of both the species are tied by strong emotional family bond.

* Frantic efforts are made to rescue the life of family member in danger and so also save a sick or a dying relative; departed soul is mourned by both humans and elephants.

* Incest is as much a taboo among elephants, apparently, as it is among humans. Throughout their bachelor wanderings the bulls harbour deep respect and affection for their female members that is equalled only as in human society.

* Considering these human like qualities in elephants, the lord Ganesha, perhaps, came into existence in ancient times (during fifth century A.D) to bring about cohesive understanding between the two most powerful living species on the earth planet. It is, perhaps, an alliance in principle and an affiliation in pragmatism.

5.8   Forest in The Height of Summer

During the months of February-March, the tropical mixed deciduous forests present parched look with trees becoming almost naked, as a result of wrinkling up of leaves and bushes leafless to beat the summer heat. Grasses dry up and crackle and the forest floor turning hot and dusty. The air blows dry and hot, the wind smelling dusty and the earth surface remains cracked. A thin layer of black waters sparkle and gradually fall into shallow pools from which trickles made their way along a sticky bed and stopped abruptly. Then one day one could see the bed of silt cracked presenting a mosaic art form. Contrary to the desiccated look, the 'Flame of the forest' *Butea monosperma* stood out bracing with bright amber glow.

Amidst the tree canopy, Teak, Terminalias and Naked maiden (Ben teak) covered in tender little green leaves and every day there after, I could count more trees, whose tops were becoming dark green and others filling out with more leaves, while the undergrowth remained still parched. This was the perilous sign, indicating that rains would soon be here, in a month or may be two.

When the park confronts mid-summer drought, in the heat of the day, I felt as if all eyes in the jungle were watching and waiting for the woodland to be covered in green spray. The elephants drifted from one patch of the shade to another like shadows in that drama of light and shadows of the forest floor. Their eyes and nostrils half closed, the elephants and other ungulates waited for cool hours to bargain for.

5.9 Arrival of Pre-Monsoon Showers

The month of May is the time of commencement of summer rains in the region. Rain bearing clouds start piling up the limpid sky, whirling around the horizon. Each day more clouds piled up the sky, rolling, tumbling and flying past the valley. But then the rain-god failed to dampen the valley. If there are no rains, no animals are seen around or no perching birds to watch. The entire forest including animals and birds become restless. I would just look up and watch the sky until the rainbow appeared on one fine day on the opposite direction of fast descending sun.

On one sultry day, a strong wind blew from the Nilgiri Mountains towards Bandipur forests, when tall trees stirred. The wind carrying summer dust whirled around madly, tree branches rustled, scattered animals came out and herded in the open glades, elephants trumpeted and langurs screamed, echoing between earth and heaven. It didn't take much time for me to realise it was the wind to gather rain bearing clouds. In a few moments, I could see dark clouds gather over head. The air turned heavy and the atmosphere tensed up with dusty winds. Lightening crashed around me followed by deafening thunder bolts. The air dampened. I felt heaven lay close to the earth and I stood between them, prepared to get soaked to the bone marrow.

Slanting streaks of grey and white swept away the valley with a rushing gush of rain drops that grew louder. Over my head, dried leaves from tree top rustled at the first drops and blown away. Thunder storm soon descended from heaven. Green leaves that remained attached to branches got cleaned of dust. This was the opportune time, the entire community of jungle denizens, including non-vertebrates beneath the forest floor waiting for. The air that blew hot few moments ago grew cooler and the smell of moist earth filled the atmosphere. My nostrils filled with that peculiar and pleasant earthy aroma, almost felt the beginning of new life emerging from mother earth. Filled with joy, I felt like singing, dancing and love making.

The hail storm pounded the earth. It poured and poured as if a cloud burst. Soon the whole forest floor was flooded. No animals nor birds called nor were visible. The entire forest was then found to be energized. After an hour or so of pounding the forest canopy the clouds passed over beyond the horizon. In the stillness of the valley, the soaked trees shook off drops that fell with loud splatters on the ground covered with dried, but moistened leaves. Mosaic of crystal blue sky then appeared through the cloud-scattered sky. Soon the sunlight flashed and the dripping bushes sparkled. The desiccated earth sucked in the water and steam rose up from the latent heat. Nothing could now stop the whole forest smiling with new life.

Insects came out from their pupal stage and frogs emerged out of their state of hibernation from the muddy ponds. The insects that emerged from eggs served as food for starved frogs. The snakes came out of their hideouts in search of their potential prey, the frogs and the rats. Prey-birds like serpent eagle and crested hawk eagle feasted on snakes and rodents. Peafowl, Jungle fowl, Blue jay and other prey birds called out with joy expecting a big feast in the days ahead. The park lost its fantasy of pale colours and turned to the realistic forest green. Life in the forest changed with the rains and so did the animals. The rains brought food for animals, birds and insects. And rains also brought new births. Before the rains only the mothers were fat with pregnancy and the males thin. In a month's time, they expected to be other way round.

Lush green forest giving fresh life to all life forms including parallel universe of underneath our feet

5.10   Life in the Green Valley

Citizens, who live in glass and concrete jungles, might find it strange about my lonely life, set amidst the valley of denizens. But, I was intently active and alert. There was life every where: peeping through the tall grass, hiding under bush-tunnels and vegetative cover or on tree tops or in burrows and in waters. Birds such as, Crows and Indian roller (Blue jay) fought in the sky against prey birds like Hawks and Kites that pounced on mice and insects. Snakes, eagles, mongoose, leopards, tigers, chital and elephants all visited water hole, while I waited in a hide or a *machan* on tree top, by day or by night. I had to be constantly vigilant against elephants for my safety. It was my one of the priorities of safety needs, while working in the elephant country.

On occasions, I was in the midst of violence, but it was one of necessities for me to push through my assignment. As the months passed by, I got used to witness killings of prey animals by carnivores and their intra-fights for survival. The beauty and the cruelty were part of the nature. Each animal and bird in the wild had its survival strategy. I was not living in the jungle with fear or under inhibition; on the contrary, it was a great joy to be part of the nature. Only I was to be alert all through from potential poachers and smugglers. Strangely enough, though I had to protect myself from accidental attacks from elephants, I knew, wild animals protected me, against human intruders, such as poachers and smugglers. I could not have found better security guards or night-watchmen than tigers, leopards and langur monkeys including peacocks. I kept myself well insulated from human intruders or accidental attacks from prowlers by their warning calls and signals.

5.11 Survival Camp

It was the *Dashara* festivity, during which time I decided to get into the depth of the jungle and survive with minimum ration. Accompanied by Keechanna, a Betta Kuruba tribal Guard, I got lost in the woods. Provisions that we carried consisted of a packet of tea powder, a ball of jaggery and two kilos of rice between two of us to last for 3 days in the jungle to survive. For the rest of our requirements of survival, we expected to source from the jungle itself.

We lived amidst the smell of the woods, the way our ancestors did thousands of years ago. There were no machines, no pollution, no women, no news papers, whose daily headlines whip up primal frenzies and terrors; riots, rapes, murders, political intrigues; just two men living under the green canopy amidst sounds of wild beasts and calls of colourful birds, that made it seem to be the perfect place to be.

While we wandered about in that green stretch of wilderness, first and the foremost thing, we could discover was the well beaten track and hide-outs that were regularly used for smuggling of sandalwood by *Chhatamars,* belonging to a christen community in Kerala. They were found smuggling of Sandalwood in large groups to Kerala from bordering states of Tamilnadu and Karnataka. Then we came across caves and dens frequented by tigers and sloth bears. We uncovered rock paintings of ancient times, perennial springs, ancient giant Teak and Rosewood trees from the depths of the jungle. Sitting at the mouth of a shallow cave, we cooked our lunch – rice mixed with wild fruits in freshly cut bamboo container. The nearby brook invited us to taste its fresh water. Left over lunch that was stored in green leaves of Muthuga, *Butea monosperma*, we enjoyed it in our moonlight dinner, watching down the valley. Soon, it was time to give rest to our tiered limbs.

The second day started with brewed tea mixed with jaggery in a *Gotta* (bowl made out of green leaves). When hungry, we followed troupes of langur monkeys and ate wild flowers, fruits and whatever they dropped from the tree tops. Berries, honey; mushrooms, tubers and tender bamboo shoots were mixed with rice and cooked on bon-fire. We relished the stubble on our faces, the greying and ripening of shirt and underwear. We took care, we were not crossing any frontier line between adjoining states of Tamilnadu and Kerala. I felt, I was the emperor in the wilderness without any clothes on self.

We wisely avoided devils fig, wild tobacco, poison peach, wild passion fruit that could be responsible in killing humans. I could prepare a list of hundred or more 'folklore cures' including heart leaf with the help of Keechanna. These folklore cures were handed down from tribal father to tribal son. Rest of the time of our survival in the jungle was, fruitfully, spent in tracking down mating leopards, flirting cow elephant with sub-adult male, which often dislodged by the matriarch of the herd in an abortive act to prevent inbreeding. Territorial tiger, colourful birds and rare flying lizard were also encountered at close quarters. More importantly, by sleeping on a bare rock, experienced the 'night life' of the jungle language under the open sky strewn with stars, which otherwise were denied to me always sleeping in Forest Rest Houses during forest inspection camps.

5.12 Telling Bull Stories!

In the third day of our *Vanavasa*, the jungle life, we witnessed an elephant cow deserting the herd and flirting with a tusker. When she stroked his pendulous penis, smelling and sniffing, the bull used to squeak, that aroused the curious young cow to shudder. Other cows in the family also became excited, when they saw the bull stimulating clitoris of the cow in oestrus. Whenever the bull attempted to mount the female, she used to move forward. Watching no cooperation by the female, other members of the herd trumpeted and growled and surrounded the pair. "Despite the fact that he had the largest penis of all terrestrial mammals, weighing nearly ten kg with skin on, the bull was found to be no great a lover in the animal kingdom", I told Keechanna, who was equally excited. As we kept watching, only the fraction of that long and pendulous penis could thrust into the vagina and it all over.

"The nature is full of sexy living beings, as I could see it; among animals, birds or reptiles, especially, the males are so attractive creating an environment of sex-appeal. The nature's dictum is that only matured males should sire the female in season. In nature, looking at those massive and beautiful male animals and birds, men in human society also occupy similar place of strength and beauty on par with animals and birds, so as to satisfy sexual hunger in fair women in the human society", I communicated to Keechanna in his dialect. "Of course, men are in no way inferior to so called fair sex-women", I asserted!

"Though there was more than one bull at the scene of breeding, the strongest automatically, took over the full control of the female in heat. There were brief skirmishes among the rivals, but the strongest bull could establish, 'who was the boss of the situation'. Once the hierarchy was established, he became the undisputed monarch. He could service the female to pass on his genes to the next generation. Thus the male's mission in elephant's society was over", I went on to preach him.

"There is no doubt that the bond between the cow and the bull was short lived phenomenon. At Bandipur reserve or at neighbouring reserves, there are no *salaga*, 'sire bulls', permanently attached to any particular family unit or kinship group, nor is there any tendency among the large bulls to establish such a long lasting relationship. The bulls mated until the females were conceived. Males' job was over. They went off on their own in search of other females in oestrus and bore no responsibility in raising the young or in the protection of the herd. Bulls in elephants keep changing from one herd to another with no rigid hierarchy", Keechanna narrated relying on his field experience.

"Even when a bull, casually, happens to meet a herd on his way, he stays with the herd for a while, sampling females, if any, in oestrus. After servicing such of the females in oestrus he moves on. He has his fixed abode, known as "Home range", ranging between 450 and 500 sq km. Some times, his area of operation may become flexible, depending on availability of food, water and mates. Though he fulfils the social obligation of passing on his genes to the next generation, his soul exists for the welfare of elephant species. He is free to move wherever his inspiration takes him. His movements are not restricted to any one forest boundary, nor confined to frontiers of man-created administrative states. The welfare of elephant community, at large, is his prime concern", I added.

To sum up, 'telling bull stories' in the middle of Kipling's own jungle, away from worldly pleasure and hustle-bustle of civilised world, was truly a great escapade. Three days of my jungle life in the company of Keechanna gave me incite that how our ancestors lived under the purity of nature. As a matter of fact, my indulgence in 'secret life of the jungle' had transformed me into an energetic and better informed person.

5.13 Elephant Quest

It was late afternoon. I stood in knee deep water watching through the binoculars, a pair of spot bills that were found fishing at Tavarekatte tank, about half a km away from Bandipur camp. Swimming and plunging their beaks into a shallow depth of water, as rhythmically as a trained technical team, they caught fish and gulped. I could feel fishes bumping their nose against my ankles. On the other side of the water edge, I could notice a sounder of some twenty wild pigs dozing in muddy ditches, obviously cooling their body in that hot sun. Keeping cool is high in the priority list of pigs. Suddenly, I heard the noise of water splashing behind me. I turned about to find elephants; a large herd lead by the matriarch. Unnoticed by me the thirsty elephants had strolled down as silently as the clouds moving in the sky. But, they had not spotted me yet; even if they had, their compelling thirst might have made them overlook my presence. To my good fortune, the wind blew in my direction. But then, it didn't take much time for me to realize that I was trapped like an idiot and would never be able to get out of their way.

Elephant cows with their babies were the most dangerous of them all. I knew that, but all I could think at the spur of the moment, was to vanish fast; and vanish I did. I slipped into knee deep muddy water. Taking a long breath, I swam under water, as fast as possibly I could. And when finally, lifted my head to take another breath, I turned around to see what was happening.

The elephants, no doubt were watching me intently, lifting their trunks to catch a whiff of my scent. I was in that filthy water, stinking awfully with full of elephant dung. All I could do was to swim across only to land at a place where naked children of Betta Kuruba tribe flashed in muddy water and women dried their clothes. I managed to walk out of that mess with dignity.

I was unable to find why the elephants had failed to mount a charge at me?

"The elephants are far too big and my memory is still green with full of stories, as told by elephant-hunting friends of the bygone era and 'old-guards' of foresters' family about their narrow escapes and people who had been squashed into pulp by enraged elephants. But, this particular herd had behaved in the manner of gentle giants, whose priority at that moment was to quench their thirst and cool their body", I guessed.

Note the matriarch seems to be in stress during summer as the dark fluid is oozing out from her temporal gland.

5.14 Approaching Elephants by Foot

To find a herd of elephants in the jungle one has to stop for awhile on his way and listen to the sounds. Elephants, in general, are never silent, whether resting or feeding or drinking, except when they freeze suspecting a danger from enemies or on sighting suspicious movement of a strange thing. A rumble from a member, who is separated from the herd, a squealed protest from a calf that is shoved forcibly away when he wanted to taste whatever his mother was eating or some youngsters trumpeting in mock fury are few of the signals, one can listen, while in the jungle. The winds are often tricky in the forest, particularly, at midday heat, when the air is sucked up in thermals and the cold air rushes under the lifting bubble causing eddies in all directions along the ground. Stalking elephants through the ground cover or under the tree canopy depends on vagrant air currents, which may well give them one's scent and one is lucky to remain undetected for long.

Approaching elephants by foot at close quarters is an art. When the wind is favourable, one can approach the animals by creeping through the bushes, until we are only few meters away from them. But often the wind is tricky in the forest floor, suddenly changing directions. A knotted handkerchief with ash or fine dust in it, is the best wind direction indicator. During warm weather even dried leaves/grass or forest soil may serve the purpose of testing the direction of the wind. One may find, in such situations, it is advantageous to smear the body with elephant dung or forest soil, as a means of disguise.

I had visited Bandipur reserve earlier in the year 1978 with my daughter, Keerti and Johnsingh, then a research fellow, working on wild dogs, joined us on a photographic expedition. We all went on foot leaving behind the jeep at the site of "rolling rock" falls, near Moyar gorge. Here, water from Kekkanahalla, a tributary of Moyar River, rolls down the steep slope, presenting its grandeur during rainy season. The water joins the Moyar River that cascades down the Nilgiri Mountains and flows turbulently as white water, through the most picturesque 'Moyar Gorge', the deepest in South India, next only to "Satkosia Gorge" of Orissa.

We were treading through scanty under growth strewn with rocky outcrops to reach a vantage point at the upwind direction for a photograph of the herd of gaur which we had seen crossing our way few moments earlier. We anticipated the herd to climb a saddle and relax in that tender sunny morning. As we advanced about hundred meters, we could hear a faint muffled sound. Assuming that it was the largest tree in the area, rustling to the breeze we continued ambling on tip-toes. My sixth sense warned of a precautionary gesture, I signalled Kirti and Johnsingh to bend down to get that hissing sound reconfirmed. We peered through the bush-tunnel. To our surprise, we spotted a huge tusker standing under the tree. The bull was busy in twitching off with green twig holding with his trunk to drive away flies. To our good luck the wind was blowing in our direction. Before the tusker could detect our presence, we ran for safety. A nearby herd of gaur was disturbed from our panic escapade. The gaur herd dashed off down the Moyar valley.

5.15 Monkey Business

It was late morning, while I was trekking alone. The day was already heating up. I was by then conversant with some of the prominent roads, beaten tracks, water holes and meadows. I knew that at that hour most of the animals would be quietly resting or enjoying their siesta until it became cooler by late evening or when their thirst pestered them to visit nearby water hole. Of course, I had my apprehension at the back of my mind that I might invite trouble myself, if by chance, disturbed them from their siesta.

While trying to encircle downwind from a herd of elephants that I had sighted and had been tracking them for some time, I came face to face with a wild pig bull, taking his nap underneath a thick bamboo grove. Each of us seemed as surprised as the other and after a pause that seemed like an eternity, we both ran; we ran, fortunately, in the opposite directions. The wild pig, which is unpredictable in its temperament, however, ran straight into the herd of elephants, which were panicked. Instead of chasing away the pig, the herd came charging straight in my direction. I managed to announce my presence with a loud shriek. They stopped. But I heard a loud crashing sound behind me. I turned in the direction of thudding sound, only to find, a troupe of handsome Grey langur (Hanuman) Monkeys. I saw them jumping down the lofty Teak tree to find a shelter on another tree. With their tails held high in the shape of '?' they watched me intently. Contrary to this phenomenon, the langurs in the northern half of our subcontinent hold their raised tails in the shape of 'C'. Why? No scientific explanation; one can only say, "It is a natural phenomenon".

When I reached the Teak tree from which monkeys had run away, a mat of tender leaves were strewn around on the forest floor. The leaf-stalks were nibbled at. It was the handy-work of langurs – the "monkey business, but not monkey politics", I concluded.

This amazing Hanuman langur, the 'naturalist-cum-forest watchman', possesses unlike as in human, three-chambered stomach that helps to consume difficult-to-digest leaves. Leaves constitute the bulk of langur's victuals. Evolution has also granted it forward pointing eyes to judge distances, so that a leap from one branch to another becomes less life threatening. On the contrary, the hare in the same jungle is gifted with the sight, it can see 360 degrees without turning its head.

I plucked a Teak leaf and chewed the petiole just as the monkeys did. It did taste like plain watery starch. I soon realised that the tender stalk of Teak leaf is another source of food, for humans when they get stranded in the depth of a jungle. "Follow a troupe of langur monkeys, if any one of you is found lost in the jungle". You eat whatever langurs eat and stay close to them; he/she can remain alert against carnivores. Langurs announce the presence of predators like tiger and leopard by their alarm calls; these warning calls echo through the forest canopy and may be heard from a km or more in cool hours of morn or night. They also alert the jungle denizens against an intruding man, reckoned by jungle denizens as master predator. But they will not announce the approach of herbivores, like elephants.

As I tread fast the elephant path saw to it that my boots made no sound. Every few hundred metres, I would stop look round, yell and clap my hands. When nothing stirred around, I resumed my tight walk. Suddenly, a grey shadow in that thicket caught my sight. I quickly stepped aside and crouched behind a tree-stump. Slowly lifted my binoculars to investigate, what the shadow was? The grey shadow soon focused into a familiar wrinkled and pitted pattern, at magnification of hundredth time. I felt thrilled with awe that I was confronted with a gentle giant, a magnificent elephant. It did take much time for me to realise that the pachyderm was *makhna*.

The *makhna* was standing tall and head-on in my direction, not even ten paces from me. He had a broad head and a powerful trunk, the tip of which rested lightly on the forest floor. The only movements were the frequent slapping of his ears and blowing of forest floor. He was resting on three feet. Fortunately, he had not noticed me. The wind was blowing towards the animal. This, I could make sure by picking up dried heap of leaves from the ground and slowly dropping it.

I was in a fix and my heart started pounding like a drum beat. I cursed myself for walking so nearer to the animal. I knew perfectly well that elephants relied little on their sight, but mainly on sense of smell and hearing. I apprehended that what little breeze there was, would carry my body scent before I could smell the animal. I would have blundered, if I had bumped head on with the giant. My sixth sense must have worked at that critical moment. As I wanted to observe the *makhna* under better lighting, I decided to retrace my steps towards an open glade and waited for him.

After reaching the meadow, I took up a safe position facing the jungle track, in anticipation of arrival of the *makhna*. From that vantage point, I could have a clear view of nearly a quarter km radius. I expected it to be a long wait for me. But, better luck prevailed; I was rewarded by his appearance at the edge of the tree-line in a short time. I realised then that the nature had gracefully compensated the *makhna* at the absence of tusks with large head and powerful trunk to fight against adversaries, particularly, while competing for a female in oestrus. He paused, lifted his trunk moved it like radar sniffing the air to test. Having satisfied himself that no danger lurked around, he stepped out in the open.

The *Makhna* began to feed, keeping himself close to the edge of the tree line. The grass was so short, that it had to scrape into a file by his toe-nails of the forefoot. Using his trunk he would grasp a parcel of grass and beat it against a raised forefoot to shake off the dirt before pushing into the mouth.

In the mean time, I was also rewarded by the emergence of a big herd from the opposite direction. This herd was joined by the *makhna*, who sampled potential female in oestrus one after another, after going through the ritual of greeting each other. I was able to recognise many individual elephants in the herd. No two animals shared the same combinations of sex and size; there were a multitude of identifying features. Among them were the tears and holes in the ears, de-pigmented patches on the trunk and ears, warts and scars over the body, the presence of tusks or tushes in various shapes and sizes and disfigurements of tails in sub-adult bulls, but not in females.

5.16 Control Over Waterhole

One afternoon, I was waiting inside a hide built of thatch-grass and surrounded by elephant proof trench at the edge of Erekatte water hole. Cow elephant, the matriarch arrived at the scene with a family of twelve heavy weights, followed by half a dozen of youngsters. They soon entered the water hole for a drink. Other smaller animals and peacocks which were resting under shade were quickly driven off one by one by youngsters in the herd. The herd virtually took over the control of the water body, rather at the cost of others. The matriarch stood guard, while other members of the family squirted water into their mouth rhythmically, drawing water lifting their trunks, letting part of water drop back into the pond.

The height of the matriarch was estimated to be about 8 1/2 ft. on legs like pillars with cushioned sole. Each forefoot adorned by five smooth nails and four on each hind foot. These thick nails gave the leading edge of her feet, hard and shiny appearance like well-polished shoe caps. Using the edge of the inner toe nails, she scratched delicately, the side of her other leg with great care. Then as if the sole of her foot was itchy she rubbed it over a tree-stump. I caught a glimpse of the hard pad with criss-a-cross fissures. These fissures differed from each animal, enabling skilled tribal trackers to follow one particular elephant through the footprints of a herd. While the matriarch continued to remain on guard, another female who had those hypnotic eyes, was mowing the grass at the edge of the water hole, with her trunk grasped one tussock at a time, and then gave a forward kick with her foot, the toe nails of which sheared through fibres as neatly and efficiently as cutting with a scythe. Then she popped the little bunch of grass into her mouth. The tips of grass blades were dropped on the ground.

Suddenly the wind changed and a whiff of my scent swept up matriarch's trunk. She wheeled and within seconds loomed up in front of me, trumpeting and kicking up dust, shaking her head and then looking down as if she were aiming through the tip of her trunk searching for the intruder. Her face was a mixture of grief and anger, tensed up as I was, I did not move. This enormous animal was powerful, confident and co-ordinated in her movements – there was certain completeness about her. Then quietly, looking like a grand old lady who had been offended, she moved away kicking cloud of dust behind her. The fifty-two thickly padded feet trailed her made hardly any sound.

5.17   Baddie in the Meadow

Never be over confident, while you are in an elephant country for, one of those juvenile elephants could turn out to be a 'baddie', a characteristic of which is very difficult to recognise in time. Then no hand clapping or waving of arms or showing palm would deter him from triggering out threat aimed at you. One should always have a sense of fear at the back of your mind. After all, being an intruder in elephants' territory, danger might be lurking in any corner of the thicket. While you are keeping an eye on the surroundings, several eyes might be spying on you in the forest. You are expected to be alert, treading cautiously keeping your ears, eyes and nose open, but lips zipped. In case the elephants are aware of your presence, it is advisable for you to stand visibly in the open and watch from a safe distance. The line of critical (LoC) danger to watch a herd or a tusker should be about fifty metres or more. While they are police-eying on you, they will study your psychology, before deciding their next move. It is not wise to try to hide behind a tree, bush or an ant-hill while they intently keep an eye on you. They are likely to develop suspicion, in case you try to hide yourself.

One of the teenagers may slowly move in your direction, while grazing and still keeping an investigative-eye on you. It is then safer for you to retrace your step, so that you maintain a sufficiently safe distance. While the elephants are crossing your path, give them due preference and wait until they clear the way for you. Some time they may test your patience. With due respect, you may tap a nearby tree trunk with a stick or a *matchu*, a machete, if you intend rush through your way. They relate the tree-tapping sound as that of a wood cutter. Alternatively, you can use bamboo clappers, if they are readily available. They would slowly move away, much against their annoyance. Once they give way, make sure they move sufficiently deep in the forest. Remember you are an intruder in their domain; they deserve priority treatment over the right of way. For heaven shake, never ever shout, beat drum or shoot in the air, burn crackers in an anxiety to drive them fast; they are likely to protest or get enraged and turn their attack against you. Let them take their own sweet time to move away. Another point to remember is, never carry a gun in an elephant country. You are likely to be negligent with over confidence and may commit blunders.

5.18 Wildlife Hunter Without a Gun

I am a hunter of wildlife, but without a gun during my photographic safari in the jungle; a camera with tele-lens was only my weapon. One will never know what is in store, while in the jungle. Always be prepared for an unexpected....? Remember, in the dynamics of world of nature, it's always "law of the jungle" prevails. Many a time, as a man at the threshold of better life in wildlife photo shoot, one is likely to get disappointed, when nothing interesting or worth-a-while happens. On many occasions, one may not find even a single opportunity to photograph any animal, even after waiting or hunting for a photo the entire day. And yet, illusion clings on for a better day ahead of you.

I had to figure out what the elephants were up to, seconds before they appeared near about my hide/*machan*. For every good action picture or to catch a sharp expression, I had to struggle a lot. In the end, I learnt to sit for hours in the van or in a hide with my camera, ready to shoot, watching out and making notes. I began to understand what the elephants and other wild animals were doing, what they do? And why they do? Occasionally, I was rewarded too. On many occasions, I used to take up my position in advance, anticipating their arrival at a particular place – a meadow, a water hole or a crossing of a jungle track, so that I established my rights, claiming due priority. This helped me in getting close shots, when they approached my vehicle with their inquisitive mind to investigate as to what was in the vehicle.

5.19 Watching Wildlife From a Hide

To sit alone and watch from a hide is a great experience. As long as one is motionless and keeps his lips zipped for a day or two, one can acquire bush eyes, bush nose and bush ears. The faintest sound can be detected and the smallest details sighted apart from smelling animals like elephants or tigers present in the vicinity. While waiting for the elephants to arrive, I had plenty of time to look around for other animals and birds. When none came around, I could make best use of the time in bird watching and recording sounds of birds and other denizens. While in wait, I also learnt lot many bush language, such as, when Grey langurs came to the water hole it was safe for the shy Chital herd to come out of their hideouts for a drink. The females were herded by one male, his head adorned with huge sized antlers. The stag kept busy in chasing away other potential males. They knew then that there were no prowling predators around. It took no more than ten minutes for the Grey langurs to settle down after their quick drink; then a twig or two under a bush would crack and through the leaves a pair of horn or a face appeared, followed by a sambar or two would appear majestically and wander past the Grey langurs, straight into shallow waters. Next, another batch of three or more would follow and play with langurs, before joining the group. Meanwhile, a pair of Red wattled lapwing, emerging from their nest would make frantic efforts to chase away a Peacock which also had appeared for a drink. At the end arrived a herd of gaur with their ears twitching ceaselessly at the water edge. Thus the prey animals have learnt through evolution that the water holes are highly vulnerable from potential predator-a tiger or a leopard, who keeps in wait for an ambush.

After a long wait, there came a herd of elephants, accompanied by one or more tuskers. Then suddenly the entire water hole was converted into a congregation of elephant clan. They went through fast ritual of a drink. Each adult elephant must have squirted at least 90 to 100 litres of water. It was entirely a family affair. No other animal or bird was tolerated or allowed to share the water hole, as long as they remained there. The interesting moment was that when babies were introduced to the water for the first time, they were reluctant to enter water. Such babies were kick-started to enter by pushing them lightly by their respective mothers or sisters. '*Gaja snana*', the elephant bathing is strictly a private affair, followed by rituals of wallowing, mud-slinging and mud-pasting. Then quietly ambled off to the edge of the tree line, where they splashed dust over their body, as if it were a talcum powder. Even the calves were learning this as though it was a technical job. Water, mud and dust are important components of cosmetics in the daily life of elephants. While water helps to keep the sensitive skin tender, mud and dust work as anti-insects apart from keeping the body cool. These rituals of elephants at the water body reminded me of my mother often warning me, "Don't you attempt, *Gaja snana*", whenever my efforts were likely to be ended in fiasco.

I found myself in the middle of the elephant world, after spending a year in the management of the park, as Field Director. Watching from a hide, I had the same excitement, as sitting in a theatre just before the curtain went up, watching people arriving, recognising each other and exchanging greetings, some of them listening to the musicians tuning their instruments and so on. I knew that all sorts of things were going to happen, when different herds of elephants congregated at a water hole or a grazing ground. Elephants from each herd, walking up and down, occasionally stopped to greet each other with their trunk to mouth gesture, with no caste system, while young babies walked up to a big bull and greeted him one by one. In return the bull touched their heads in the way elderly *Soliga* tribesman blessed children. None of them showed any sign of aggression or caste politics, nor did they exhibit any kind of egoistic attitude. Each member of the herd approached the other with affection and greeted with perfect harmony and fervour.

5.20 Retreat, Better Than Valour

In the following year, there were some unexpected turbulent moments in Bandipur tiger reserve, such as, a prolonged drought had caused concern; drying up of tanks and ponds, frequent wild fires, scarcity of food and water affected general health of ungulates, including elephants. These concerns had an adverse impact on the management of the park. During this time many aged, weak and diseased elephants died. Matriarchs exhibited stress and strain, affecting the welfare of their families/clans. Exuding of dark liquid from their temporal glands (but not *musth* flow) in females was an indicator of stress they underwent.

Along the Kerala borders killing of elephants became rampant using locally made explosives hidden in tapioca tubers, while they attempted to raid crops.

A tusker was found limping due to fracture in his left hind leg. By the time we organised treatment after tranquillizing, he had crossed over to Madumalai sanctuary.

A Juvenile male elephant was found trapped into a borrow pit, by the side of Bandipur – Tavarekatte road. He was extricated by roping out with the help of camp elephants.

While the field staff were kept engaged in organising supply of drinking water to animals through tankers, extinguishing wild fires day in and day out, in addition to controlling of poaching had added pressure as the responsibility of park personnel. Luckily for the park, some late pre-monsoon showers brought great relief. The entire forest was rejuvenated with new life within a month.

In the course of my evening tracking in the reserve, I came upon a bull elephant face to face at a sharp turning point. He was found feeding on tender shoots of bamboo just on the road side, near the "shooting box". This tiny shed was used for tiger shooting during Maharajahs' times, according to a headman of local Betta kuruba tribe.

As soon as the bull saw me he stopped eating, perked up his ears and waited without making a slightest sound. I stood like a pillar, a couple of metres away, glued the tongue to the roof of my mouth and fixing my eyes on him all the time. It was a moment of great tension for both of us. After a while, he lent out a loud snort, shook his head, flapped his ears in a cloud of dust, and twiddled his trunk in knots, in much the same way as I wring my hands when nervous. I stood firm my ground, exhibiting that his gestures of threat had no effect on me. He began a little dance with his trunk curling like a snake. When I took a step backward projecting my palm, his head went down. He snorted, chewed the bamboo shoot that he held in his mouth, rubbed his eye with the tip of the trunk and next used it to dig in his ear, sniffed the air and kicked up dust, but he never tried to advance in my direction. It looked as if he were playing to buy time, unable to make up his mind what to do and in the meanwhile, using his trunk to distract my attention. Plainly enough, he could not muster enough courage to chase or attack me, I guessed. We stood watching each other for quite some time. It was an exciting moment. I soon realised, "retreat is better than valour". I then, turned and walked back a distance of 50 ft – a historic achievement in my life, I presumed. That noble, powerful, graceful and magnificent male seemed to be egoistic. He asserted his absolute right of way in the forest. He was a fantastic male; and I loved him. I blew him a kiss, which he reciprocated promptly by raising his trunk. He soon resumed his search for another tender shoot, amidst a congested bamboo grove, when I had a second look at him.

5.21 Desist Carrying Firearms, While in Elephant Jungle

Shooting any animal in the jungle is like hanging a man, the worst thing one can think of. Mercy killing (Euthanasia) is a different issue, which could be thought of, if the animal is undergoing endless trauma and intractable suffering due to injuries or incurable disease. If I ever shot at in the reserve, something terrible ought to have happened because, I never shoot any animal, unless I myself would otherwise die. Firstly, I never carry a gun when I enter the protected areas (PAs). I avoid firing in the air as well; even occasional firings may threaten the peaceful environment of the reserve and the animals might loose heart and feel insecure. I am also aware, when I carry a weapon, I can't save myself or even the person accompanying me, when dangerous animals are encountered by surprise. If I carry one, I am likely to neglect myself against impending danger with my audacity or over confidence. Rather, I find pleasure to shoot with my camera. I also find pleasure in doing so and help conserve nature and natural history. While dealing with anti-elephant community it is a different matter.

5.22 Accidents in Elephants

It is perhaps, not surprising when attempts to revive an elephant might continue long after it's almost dead. It was the month of June. The rainy season had just started. On that day in the afternoon, while I was busy organising a workshop on "Capture of wild animals using Cap-tur™ drug" for Vets, working in the Forest and Wildlife units, I got a wireless message that a young wild elephant cow had met with an accident in the Reserve Forest of A. M. Gudi, near Kalkere Forest Lodge. The message also was that the animal was unable to get up and move. I decided to seize the opportunity and rushed immediately along with Vets. and medical aid.

Dr. Sivanna, a senior among the Vets., present there, on detailed examination declared, "The victim had severe external and internal injuries, in addition to critical damage caused to spinal chord. Perhaps, this might have been caused by a fall from a height".

After a brief discussion with the Vets, we arrived at a consensus to provide field treatment with a view to revive that victim. Dr.Sivanna along with Dr.Khadri, the park Vet. started treatment.

Female met with an accident is being treated in the jungle, but failed to respond to the treatment.

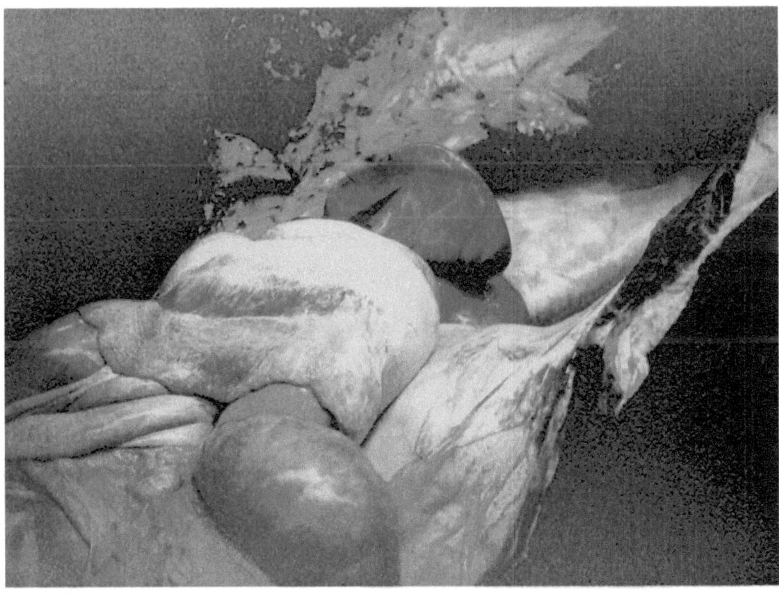

Post-mortem showing internal organs of the female elephant after the death. Investigations showed the broken spinal chord due to fall from a height.

Immediately, an anti-shock injection, followed by glucose water drip administered. She was looking pale around the jaws – either from loss of blood or shock – and at this stage, effective treatment was too valuable than to ponder for the possible reasons of accident. Vets. also gave her an injection against blood clotting to stop further loss of blood.

"Will she survive? I asked Shivanna.

"It is impossible to say anything at this stage, how seriously she was hurt? She was very badly injured and I don't want to speculate any thing at this stage. But I would like to know what it was that caused her injuries? An anaesthesia could cause her deeper shock; her breathing is already very depressed", remarked Sivanna.

"Chasing about animal's body for damages and injuries without an x-ray was no use. It is necessary to keep her under observation", Shivanna added.

"I am afraid, she is loosing battle for survival and there was nothing we could do now, but to wait and watch", opined Khadri.

While the treatment was in progress Sivanna wanted to drain off urine, since she was not passing any urine for the past few hours.

"Will you please insert catheter by opening the vulva, Khadri?" Sivanna inquired.

Khadri took his own time in attempting to pass catheter, as if the whole world was at his disposal.

"It appears, you enjoy keeping your hand inserted in that thing Khadri?", Sivanna remarked.

"I opened the thing and inserted the entire length of the catheter. I feel it got lost. I am, frantically, trying to locate it. Once, I catch hold of it, I can pull out myself you know", retorted Khadri.

Preliminary field diagnoses continued in that wilderness, until late night.

5.23 Death, Only Means of Escape For The Wounded in Wild

While the treatment was in progress, the victim's breathing, heart beat and body temperature were recorded. Recordings were found to be abnormal as against normal breathing of an elephant @12 per minute, the heart beat @40 per minute and the body temperature @36-37°C.

The treatment continued for three days relentlessly. But, to our shock, the whole exercise failed to yield encouraging results. At the end of the third day Khadri came to know that cow's cadaverous jaw had sagged; she went pale and then dirty green.

"The cow was showing all the signs of a terminal struggle and was having considerable difficulty in getting her breath. By about midnight she gave last shuddering gasp and it was all over", cried Khadri with tears.

It was like a nightmare for all of us. Of course, we had taken a calculated risk in the gamble. The failure in our efforts had taught us a lesson, "death is the only means of escape for the wounded in the wild".

"There was, however, a greater stumbling block to the future of veterinary glory. However, could you carry out post-mortem, so as to investigate causes, leading to her death?" I asked Sivanna.

"But what earthly good is it going to do? It won't bring poor pachyderm back", came the answer.

"It was an accident case and FIR is registered, followed by the medical treatment with desperate hope of her revival. We have collectively discharged our responsibilities, but her survival was not in our hand. By carrying out post-mortem, let us give a concluding touch to the records of treatment, so as to give her a clean chit and the case be closed respectably", passed on my verdict.

5.24 Postmortem of The Elephant

The Vets, Sivanna and Khadri started post-mortem investigations on the following morning. I also joined them to assist. The marathon process of opening that huge body was a Herculean task that took hours. The findings of the internal organs were beyond my inquisitive eyes. Soon we had heart, lungs, liver and assorted organs that were found healthy, laid out in neat piles. But there were neither old wounds nor a diseased organ, which could have explained the female's untimely death. Paste here post-mortem of Elephant

I could not help being impressed by the size of the elephant's huge intestine that tumbled out, taped about 30.0 cm in dia. The intestine of the elephant exceeded the length of those in any other mammal: the victim's small intestine taped 25.0 m; appendix 1.5 m; large intestine 6.5 m and the rectum 4.0 m. The coagulated blood had covered the ground all around the carcass like a thick red carpet. According to an estimate, the blood is about 9.5% to 10% of the body weight. The blood vessels were quite large – arteries leading to the head had a diameter of nearly 2.0 cm. and the heart weighed about 7 kg with length at 44.0 cm and breadth at 32.0 cm.

I had never seen the internal parts of an elephant before. We wanted to know if she were pregnant. Running along the back – ribs where it was cut open, her body cavity was a white tube that emerged from the pelvic girdle. Its front end thickened and split into two horns at the end of which were the ovaries, about the same size and consistency as of sheep's brain. We carefully dissected these organs by slitting open the tubes along their length, examining every inch minutely. At last, we were rewarded with the discovery of a tiny elephant, no bigger than my little finger nail. It was still in the first stage of development with gill pouches, but had four perfect elephant feet, and a tiny pointed nose which could have been the trunk. We put it in a bottle containing alcohol to preserve it. I asked the Ranger to bury the carcass, since it no more required for further investigation.

5.25   Mishaps in the Forests

On that warm evening of dreadful day, while I was camping at the Forest Lodge at Begur, Prabhakar (Jr), the local Ranger brought terrifying news that a cow elephant was found trapped in a mud-flat at Kabini reservoir-bed and that its baby was bawling desperately for help. I could, immediately, corroborate an instance of continuous bellowing calls heard from across the river course while trekking in the burning heat of the day.

On hearing frequent elephant groans from across the river course, while we were riding elephants during the day's inspection, I could recollect having told to Ranger, "when the animal is in distress or in pains it squeals". But at the spur of the moment, I considered those distress calls as natural phenomena of the jungle lore and did not venture to verify, since we were also in a distress condition, due to certain mishap that took place during the day. By the time, Ranger had brought the above news of trapped cow elephant, the scanty sun had already signalled the coming night fall. So, we decided to visit the spot the following morning, fully prepared, for the "Operation Rescue".

5.26   Rescue of a Pachyderm From a Death Trap

Next day, at the sun dawn, we set off with Jayaprakash and Bhanumati, the camp elephants stationed at Begur, to support the rescue party. We crossed the river Kabini at the tail-end of the reservoir beyond Nai halla stream, where water flow was knee-deep, before reaching the site of trapped elephant.

The golden rays of the sun had burnt the morning mist, by the time we arrived at the spot. The scene was a horrifying one; the cow was found trapped deep into the quagmire. The trunk, the head and top of back only were visible; a constant struggle of the victim in her attempt to wriggle out of mire had caused her sink deeper and deeper. The heavy weighted pachyderm was sinking inch by inch in that thick silt-pit, whenever it tried to move desperately, while battling for life.

Female elephant supposed to be a matriarch that was bogged in quagmire at the backwaters of Kabini reservoir was rescued from death trap.

She was extricated with the help of camp tusker and freed to join her family.

"My good God, the elephant is in soup", exclaimed my son, Sanjay, with horror! He too had joined the rescue party.

The cow was found to be piteously terrified and seemed exhausted and undergoing cramp and tribulations. I tried to reassure her safety with confidence in saving her life, trying to reach her trunk with a white kerchief. She moved the tip of her trunk, as if to acknowledge my message. The atmosphere was quiet, but tense; total silence had over shadowed the rhythm of jungle songs.

The rescue party swung into action: the first thing was to free the victim from the slurry, by scooping it out by hand. No human being could approach the cow, lest he too could get trapped along with the animal. Even the *kumki* could not be given a trial. As the removal of slurry progressed, the poor animal showed signs of response; a ray of hope of its extrication and eventual survival brightened, when it could turn its flank. But, our concern was that how to retrieve the heavy armour from the death-trap of thick slough without any one of our rescue party or work elephants getting trapped?

Among many options, suggested by our friends in the rescue party were: summon a slurry mixer, a crane and so on, from the nearest city, Mysore, about 90 km away. Those suggestions were impractical and time consuming. The only practical way, I thought, at that moment, was to improvise a technique for its immediate retrieval. Any delay might cost her life. Immediately, an SOS was sent to the nearby elephant camp at "Belle" to get a big tusker with thick ropes, since none of the elephants we had with us could be harnessed for such a stupendous task in that rugged and inhospitable landscape.

Every thing looked progressing well on silt-removal front. There was no logic for me to come to immediate conclusion as to the circumstances, under which the innocent cow could have entered or forced to step into the mud-flat, though elephants are known for their cautious treading by tapping the ground with their sensitive trunk at every step. Meanwhile, to satisfy my inquisitive mind, I decided to read through the "news reel", left behind on the forest floor by previous day's events. My investigations of the locale revealed valuable information. It trickled as under:

"A herd of elephants, had arrived at the river site for a drink and to cool off their bodies, some time in mid morning the previous day; this I could guess because, we had heard yelling calls in the afternoon and the information the Ranger got through a local tribe was that a baby elephant was, desperately, roaring for help standing on the bank and keeping a grim vigil over its mother that was struggling for life".

5.27 No Sympathy for the Unlucky in the Wild

The rest of the evidential information, I could record from the forest floor from the available spoor was as followed :

"That one of the boisterous youngsters in the herd, while getting down the slope of the reservoir bank had strayed out from the 'sanctuary of the herd' and ran straight into the mud-flat and got trapped. Its mother, whose first priority was to rescue her kid, rushed only to be caught into quagmire. While mother succeeded in pushing the calf out of the wet ground, she got stuck".

Disaster had struck instantaneously. Alas, her instinct had, in fact, become stupid in her efforts to save her calf. The warning had come to her too late. She had failed to sense the impending danger, in a fit of maternal love and care. As the cow attempted to negotiate the trap, she sank deeper.

Having seen the chain of events of that horrifying mishap, no other animal of the family perhaps, ventured to provide a helping trunk to the unfortunate victim. The family remained there for quite some time, helplessly watching a relative sinking with no hope of rescue, had reluctantly, abandoned the cow and moved away to continue their routine".

"There is no sympathy for the unlucky in nature; eventually, there is no guarantee of its survival", I deplored.

"The calf having refused to join the herd, had to stay-put with fond hopes of its mother coming out to suckle. Having learnt a lesson from its pit-fall, the calf was now at the mercy of the God. The cow had become the victim of emotional ties. While it was a long drawn battle for the mother to keep herself alive, the baby had prepared to weather the storm out of grim situation".

The kid, desperately, hung on to its mother for the rest of the day, groaning for help. But the family never returned thereafter, leaving the cow and the baby high and dry.

In such a disaster, as it happens in civilised world, there are always beneficiaries in nature too – the predators. The twist of fate had played its role in this case also. The calf's yelling was finally answered by the response of the territorial tiger – the master of ambush. The striped predator, after a drink in a nearby puddle, had arrived at twilight and picked up calf in distress. The predator had dragged the body after it was knocked down for nearly 300 meters, deep into the thick bamboo brakes, where it had devoured in peace. The remains of the victim were found covered with bamboo leaves, where the tiger planned to return for its next meal. The calf was about a year old male and mud-flakes were still seen on the carcass.

It was mangled by the torrential striped cat out of sheer brutal superiority, but not necessarily as part of the food chain, while, mother weathered storm with lady luck.

Before the day warmed up there arrived Bharat, a huge tusker carrying a strong rope and accompanied by Devsetty, Kakankote Range Forest Officer. By then a substantial quantity of slurry had been removed by the rescue party. The cow's face and part of the body was freed from the slough. One of the *mahouts* jumped over to the back of the cow and sitting on the animal he succeeded in inserting the noose over to its neck, passing through the trunk and the head. The other end of the rope was tied firmly to the saddle of Bharat. Due care was taken to see that noose did not cause constriction of the cow's throat. The tusker, Bharat was now ordered by his mahout to climb an unnerving steep bank steadily and cautiously, pulling the cow gently out of the "slurry pit". Immediately, I grasped her trunk and held it raised and tested it; she was breathing normally. I felt the warmth of her breath. I shook the trunk firmly suggesting, "You are the animal I wanted to know. And know well"! I also conveyed our appreciation of determined desire to live her life. She had survived to pass on the genes to next generation. For me, it was an unforgettable experience of 'trunk shaking' with a wild cow elephant that could reinforce the unspoken words, "don't, of course, go wild gesturing, just be yourself, the elephant lady"!

The cow was, then persuaded to stand up and climb the bank with the assistance of Bhanumathi, the camp lady. She was held in position with support of Bharat and Bhanumathi together and served a bucketful of water to quench her immediate thirst. Simultaneously, the noose from the neck was untied. The tension that reined the air was eased. The lady stretched her crumbled muscles and tired limbs, lifted her trunk towards us, as if to convey her gratitude. I could glean through her eyes an element of affection. We kept watching that great lady moving away woefully, much more nimble on her feet.

"May her tribe increase", all of us gathered there wished in a resolution.

A peacock called out from the distant meadow and the jungle reverberated by a rutting call of chital stag.

"Rescue of elephant – the lady boss", was timely; or else, the poor pachyderm could have joined the mastodons of prehistoric times, possibly to be retrieved as a whole skeleton, by our future generation", I declared. Not many animals in the wild get a second chance of survival in life. But this "Elephant – the Lady Boss", had perhaps, greatest desire to live through agony and ecstasy of her loving child – her unfinished business. Alas, the disaster had struck only to snatch her kid.

Looking at her size and guess-assessing the age, I arrived at a conclusion that she must have been the matriarch, the guardian of the clan. We were proud and happy to have availed of an opportunity of giving a lease of life to this 'Lady Boss' – the noble and the magnificent. The proverbial saying goes, "The boss is always right", but it had proved wrong in her case, contrary to the belief. It is also true, "Triggered by instinct, her long term investment on her offspring had proved worth risking her life". We had just extended a helping hand to this lady, the matriarch for another chance of enjoying her share of planet earth.

Chapter VI

Sanctuary of the Herd

Watching the social life system of the elephant family is indeed an enchanting way to experience the nature's phenomenon. The elephant herd led by the matriarch, adult and sub-adult cows, including juveniles enthusiastically look after calves, which are playful and some times boisterous. Elephants are skittish and very protective of their young. Elephants are innately peaceful and are easily spooked. It is our responsibility as civilised society, to respect their social system and provide protection to their living space, where they can lead a peaceful life.

During one of the training programmes on "Non-formal Environmental Education to rural school teachers" at Bandipur, the first question I was asked to answer was, "What constituted a stable elephant society in Bandipur Tiger Reserve?" Once, I could explain this convincingly, I would be able to interact with rural school children, who were to attend similar type of training, the following week. Further, "How these basic social bricks of elephant herd remained cemented even under adverse seasonal conditions and withstood the test of time against increasing human pressure on their habitats?"

A gist of discussion with rural school teachers during field visits is reproduced here, as under:

6.1 Social System and Behaviour

"Elephants visited in family units of closely related cows and their offspring led by the matriarch to Bandipur reserve. The kinship groups, I encountered usually had several cows with their young at heels, those tightly related or loosely strung out as extended family or overlapping from another kinship group. It was impossible for me to differentiate, where one kinship group ended and the next began. The large kinship groups were in the order of 14-22 elephants, sometimes with juvenile and sub adult males loosely strung on the outskirts."

"Similar family units in their social system that were related to kinship groups also visited the reserve. The average size of such a family unit was 12-15 elephants and most of these belonged to a larger kinship group, called 'clan'. Family units who are members of a clan/kinship group might split up for a few days and go in opposite ends of the reserve or adjoining Madumalai or Wayanad sanctuary, but they would always join sooner or later and continue to keep in contact, through ultrasonic communication system. Such temporary splits did take place, particularlyduring summer, when scarcity of food and water confronted."

6.2 Stable Family Unit

"Although there had been a hypothesis that the cow-calf groups might be stable family units, it had never been suggested that larger herds were anything but aggregations of family units joining and leaving at random. My observations, as in case of Iain Douglas – Hamilton's on African elephants, provided the proof of family unit a stability and showed that family ties were far wider and long lasting than hither to thought."

"Individual elephants varied greatly in body structure and character. Although the oldest cow elephant, the matriarch functioned as boss', the female next in hierarchy takes over protecting the herd with the fiercest threat displays. And within the same family unit, some may be gentle and curious and others suspicious. While juvenile males continue to remain in the herd, the sub-adult males are booted out by the matriarch to prevent inbreeding. Such ousted males form bachelor groups of 3-5 animals and wander about until they prove their winning streak.

"Elephants continue to grow throughout their life span of about 60 years; by the age of thirty, they are within ten cm of the height they would reach, if they lived for sixty years. Also some are comparatively taller for their age, while others are shorter. A cow elephant at 55 still actively participates in reproduction and accompanied by a small calf at heel. She is in an excellent physical condition, well-padded on the back and thighs with rounded contours but cheeks and head sunken as associated with ageing".

At the end of the training programme, I felt satisfied by a series of questions that were put across by teachers, backed by mature minds, simultaneously, clearing the doubts and mysteries surrounding elephant-the lady boss.

As observed by me in many different reserves, such as Periyar, Madumalai, Wayanad and Nagarahole, in addition to Bandipur, normally exclusiveness is a feature of elephant herd associations. Very old animals as well as very young calves and elephants of all intermediate ages, may be found in a herd. Where there are more than one adult bull in a single (not composite) herd, one may be in his prime age and 3-4 sub-adult males or when there are two lesser bull's acceptance of the dominance of the big bull may be evident. However, it is only rarely that two big bulls are found in a single herd; all records showing several bulls probably pertain to composite herds.

In the present day situation, a herd composition may be described on 3 counts:

1. **Grand mother – the matriarch by age and experience – the unquestionable authority to guide and protect the family group comprising of her daughters, their offspring, including her sisters and their offspring".**

2.   **Social hierarchy – The matriarch, associated mothers and their offspring – juveniles and babes.**

3.   **A stable family unit with extended family group – mothers and their young.**

For social animals like elephants, the survival is very much a family affair. One evening at Erekatte tank of Bandipur, I happened to count about 60 elephants, the largest congregation, I had ever seen. When herds met they never exhibited egoism, audacity or hatred attitude. All of them showed love and understanding through exchange of greetings. They had their drink at a common water pool, remained feeding together for a while, before parting away in their respective family units. The congregation, I could make out was of kinship group or a clan consisting of three families. However, I have never seen a bigger herd than 22 elephants in Bandipur and adjoining reserves like Madumalai, Wayanad and Nagarahole.

MATRIARCHAL FAMILY IN TIPICAL ELEPHANT HABITAT

Sanctuary of the herd-calves, sub-adults are well protected cuddled in between by all elders-by their mothers and aunts-moving gracefully in tandem led by the matriarch at the backdrop of typical habitat, the dry deciduous forest.

6.3 Sanctuary of the Herd

I was proceeding to inspect an accidentally burnt patch of a meadow. While I arrived at a spot accompanied by a tribal tracker, Kala, a group of 18 elephants was about to cross the road just in front of the van. On seeing our approaching vehicle, they changed their mind and started walking fast parallel to the track. Their heels scuffed the ground; there were bursts of incandescent dark dust. Some ten animals crossed the jungle track hurriedly and then the younger females scurried over, turning to look in our direction with heads held high and flanks arched.

I asked the driver to switch off the ignition, simultaneously, signalling Kala to get down and push the van forward. The driver took the vehicle just adjacent to the herd before coming to a sane halt. As the slanting evening light began to turn the bushes and trees into golden colour, the long-awaited moment took me by surprise. A silent armoured column of cows towering above the young of all sizes filed in single line, some ten meters in front of us, which, I supposed was their critical and a safe distance from any vehicle. Their flanks blue-grey in the shadow of that failing sun, indicated that they had just then come out of their mud-wallow from a nearby forest pool. They wheeled about in unison, as if, at the word of command, as soon as they were safely across and almost hidden by bushes. A gust of wind wafted our scent in their direction. Ears flared and a row of trunks performed snake dance, waving sinuously above the line of their massive heads, sampling our smell, afterwards expelling their breath with a whoosh. Although their faces were relatively static the infinite variety of trunk postures and movements lent the elephants, all the expressiveness of a primate's visage. I could no longer see the youngsters apart from glimpses between the legs of large cows, which had formed a solid fortress like. Our presence was obviously worrying them.

After a while they became nearly composed, the young ones peeped out inquisitively. I was able to examine the whole herd carefully, while I photographed them, though lighting seemed imperfect. The youngsters wanted to venture out in the front line. But their mothers prevented them from doing so by the barricade of their trunks. The Elephant herd looked as a perfect 'sanctuary' for the youngsters.

Thus, the youngsters were found to be disciplined from their childhood. The cows, I was impressed, did not believe in "sparing the cane and spoiling the young". They punish kids by extremely tender actions, when they tempt to do mistakes. Mothers have every right to punish their children as much as they have the right to love them. At the same time, mothers protect their young at the cost of their life. On sensing danger, mothers alert their young through "bush-telegraphic message" or "ultrasonic communication" or simply by slapping ears; young ones immediately push themselves underneath their respective moms' belly and remain glued until the environment thins out. Thus, every member of the family takes part in protecting the youngsters. The herd is truly the sanctuary in itself.

6.4 Deep Attachment

It is well known that in a herd, certain adult cows develop a deep attachment (which can be termed as 'friendship') to certain other cows. Young males too, keep together; it is a common sight to observe two or three juvenile males together. The attachment of one cow to another has been observed both in the wild and among captive elephants as well. This type of behaviour is also seen even between a cow and a male among camp elephants. Indeed, this is so well recognised by *mahouts* that they are not separated from each other even when put on job work (e.g. logging works). It was noticed at Begur camp of Bandipur reserve, that the male elephant, Jayaprakash, a fine upstanding male in his prime could not be used singly, as a safari riding or on protection duty, unless the elderly cow, Bhanumati was also taken along with him. Among wild elephants, the tendency of certain members grouping together when the herd splits into parties for foraging may be noticed.

6.5 Sleeping Without Lyingdown

Elephants are likely to take a brief nap in the middle of the day when it is too hot. The elephants need not lie down for the purpose of a brief nap.

The adults take a nap standing while young ones lie down under the shade and security of their mothers or aunts. Elephants normally go to sleep early mornings between 5 and 9 or they may rest any time of the day or night, depending on the circumstances, place of convenience and security. Once, I took my position, while I was waiting on the main *machan* at Nagarahole reserve, at 0500 hours. I saw a herd of elephants crossing the view line at 0530 hours and remained inside the forest without any sound. Evidently, I was getting strong smell, though from the direction of elephants confirming their stay, perhaps having their snooze. They came out of their siesta at about 1000 hours, heading straight to nearby water hole. They spent about half an hour at the water hole, drinking, bathing, followed by other rituals, such as mud packing and dust gathering. By about 1100 hours they passed by the *machan*, where I was waiting for them the whole morning.

Once, I saw a herd of elephants sleeping behind the tree line off the Mysore-Ooty highway passing through Bandipur reserve at 0600 hours. On hearing the sound of the approaching vehicle, cows got up only to demonstrate their resentment.

On another occasion, I came upon a tusker taking a nap, standing underneath a tree at about 0830 hours at Nagarahole reserve, while I was riding a cow elephant in search of a gaur herd. Mahout silently back-tracked the elephant from the site avoiding head on collusion. These *mahouts*, though they serve as masters of massive tamed elephants and are responsible in controlling and commanding them, are however, found to exhibit inherent timidity against wild tuskers or herds. They are terribly scared of them and retreat to safety at once. That is how, tribal communities are able to survive in elephant inhabited country for so long.

The Jungle covered with tall grass and thick undergrowth, inhabited by elephants is not safe to walk through, according to tribal communities. They warn one must be cautious while treading, looking around at every step, listening to jungle language and signals, if any. The lone tusker resting under the shade will be flapping its ears incessantly, producing twitching sound by swinging twigs held in its trunk, engaged in driving away flies/

mosquitoes. This is why, local tribes or graziers invariably, attempt in setting fire to tall-grass lands in order to avoid elephant menace during their illegal movements. Once the grass/ground cover is gone, they can fearlessly wander about in the jungle even during odd hours of nights.

6.6 Body Language of Elephants

While face-to-face confrontation with intruders or adversaries, such as, humans or tigers within her home range, the matriarch of the herd sends a clear message of her dominance through her body language. With determined staunch advancing towards an enemy, she demonstrates with aggressive body language. Indeed, matriarch's body language could be spoken through the way she moves is formidable.

How does a matriarch send a message of aggression against an enemy or an intruder?

It is indeed frightening!! Her body posture with raised head, cocked ears, a grim face, eyes turned red, raised trunk, swaying, swinging; kicking the dust frequently, throwing dirt overhead, twiddling the trunk, tossing the head, the body angled forward, eye contact held firm as long as necessary, she exhibits formidable size by spreading ears at right angles and with terrifying anger against an intruder or an enemy. In an extreme case, she sends repeated growls followed by series of trumpets that are really blood curdling.

The defensive posture of an elephant shows with flanks arched, raised tail, loosely folded or coiled trunk, head half turned away and avoidance of eye contact with ears tucked in to the nape, back tracking with squealing sounds.

6.7 'Palming' – Its Effect on Elephant in Aggression!

We know how animals, birds, amphibians, reptiles, could be hypnotised by applying different methods in captive mode? We also know how humans could be put under a state of hypnosis? All members of the cat family including captive big cats (tigers and leopards) could be hypnotised by rubbing/patting their scruff, while members of the canine family could be hypnotised by stroking their ventral side of the neck. Each animal/bird has its specific part or point on its body being used for the purpose. But in case, of wild elephants there is no possibility of accessing them physically. They need to be dealt with from a safe distance.

While facing a matriarch with aggression in a family an open-palmed gesture sends a forceful message to calm down against serious intention of an attack!

While facing a matriarch with aggression an open-palmed gesture sends a forceful message to calm down against seriousness serious intention of a charge. Any man pushes forward his open palm with fingers pointing upward, drives home the effect of hypnosis. This act of man sends a placating message to the elephant in aggression. The elephant will be influenced to sober down momentarily. It puts its head down at the show of the palm with raised fingers extended by man in its direction. Even an elephant in its instantaneous charge would come to a halt lowering its head converting its aggression into the defensive posture. However, I can not categorically say at this stage whether this leads to conclude to have an effect of hypnosis or just a soothing effect. While trying this technique over an elephant, one must be at a safe place, either in a vehicle or on a *machan*. Safety requirement is the foremost in an elephant jungle. Just a word of caution for dear readers: never try it out over denizens of concrete jungle.

Eventually, one morning I caught sight of a new family group of elephants standing placidly in a tall grass meadow, adjoining to Madumalai reserve. A strong wind might have drowned the noise of my vehicle, while the herd remained undisturbed. Just as the driver switched off the engine, they swung their fierce heads round, with ears cocked like hostile radar scanners about to launch missiles. One cow shook her head, may be a matriarch, I pushed my palm forward and she lowered her head and backed out. The family watched me intently for considerably long time and slowly uprooted from the spot.

"With such amazing experiences, I would like to keep up traditional tracking of wild animals as long as I can, because it is an integral part of human culture. If not, ancient jungle-culture would die out. The practice of tracking wild life stretches since the dawn of human history. I could develop curiosity in jungle tracking, as part of my wilderness study over the years. While, I ventured into the jungle during my inspections, I always found joy and delight in watching birds and wild animals; I witnessed deadly games of prey and predators. Some times, I found trails of good and bad events in the park: firstly, bad deeds – foot prints of smugglers and poachers, followed by counter action; secondly, good things-saving of animals in distress, followed by remedial measures and so on. Bandipur reserve is an elephant country, just as much famous as for tigers and one of the most enchanting landscapes in the country. Unlike the Lion that is reckoned as a stanch enemy of elephant (*Gaja Vyri*), as described in ancient history, tiger and elephant, being adversaries, use the same habitat. This is where, I spent much of my time in the company of elephants, rather than tigers; experienced romance and adventure, infrequently, wondrous and treacherous events too" I concluded.

Thrilled and impressed as she was, of my just few experiences and my responsibilities, as the Field Director, she gratefully offered me a whole lot of publications and teaching material on 'Environment Training' brought out by the Smithsonion Institute.

6.8   Ticks Politics

During the inspection of Ainur Marigudi reserve forest (RF), accompanied by Srinivasa, the territorial Range Forest Officer and his staff, we parked our vehicle on the bank of 'Soolekatte' (an *Aanicut* – the barrage of historical times) built across the river, Nugu, before getting on checking of formation of elephant proof trenches (EPT). The EPT is meant to prevent elephants from crossing over to adjoining farmers' fields. "Why this barrage is called, Soolekatte?" I asked Ranger while wading through waist-deep water.

"The loose-stone barrier is said to have been constructed for irrigation during the regime of Heggadadeva, the chieftain under the dynasty of Hoysalas. This historical barrage provides perennial source of drinking water for elephants and other wildlife, even during prolonged summer. The river Nugu, also known as the Brighu, is an important tributary of the river Kabini, which has its birth at the Nellambore hills of Wayanad in Kerala State. The river Nugu enters the borders of Mysore District at Moolehole of Gundlupet Taluk. It flows towards North cutting across the Bandipur reserve into two halves, before joining the Kabini near Hampapura. It is said, this barrage was built to please one of Heggadadeva's concubine", narrated Srinivasa briefly, based on whatever little knowledge he had gathered from local people.

We waded through waist deep water to reach the opposite bank. As we tread fast a narrow bush tunnels led us through thick under-growth beyond the bank. Winding path along the deep-cut eroded gullies, entered thickets of a scrub jungle infested with *Euphatorium* (an obnoxious weed) that had choked the forest floor. Looking ahead we could see not beyond three metres, but the width on either side was no more than arms stretch.

Some fresh elephant droppings lying on the beaten path warned us that we were not alone.

We trudged on up to a solitary boulder, where we sat and ate our packed lunch that consisted sandwich and sipped a cup of coffee. Nearby there existed a patch of damp and dark woodland with lichen draped trees, beyond which lay "green-ocean view" of vast stretch of forest of Ainur-Marigudi RF. On the opposite direction and beyond the edge of green canopy, scattered huts that were springing up had literally swallowed the rhythm of the jungle.

The sun was downing fast. I checked the progress of elephant proof trench (EPT) work. It was time to return. We looked down from the tip of the outcrop of a huge rock. The thick thorny and scrubby forest growth threw us a challenge to cross over while descending. There was not a sign of life. We shouted and whooped as we entered thicket, so that just in case, any elephant lurking in the vicinity would be warned of our approach.

Normally, under the jungle law, with hardly any exception, big animals will make way for noisy *Homo sapiens*. We kept talking loudly, when we were more than half-way across the danger zone, lulled into a sense of security by the absence of any response.

Srinivasa had only been stayed behind for a minute for easing himself, when we heard wild, piercing shriek. He dashed racing; his trousers clutched at half-mast and called out, "*Aane*, the elephant, run for it"! We simply darted round its head off the path. Out of the corner of my eye, I saw a young bull turn after me trumpeting and growling I ran for my life. Twisting and dodging round the bushes, I could not shake it off. Every time, I looked round, it was within a few steps and closing in. It was ridiculous. Thorny bushes were tearing at my clothes and skin, as I searched for a way through. I must have covered about hundred fathoms, when bushes formed a green blank wall. By then the thing, "monster of the bush", wheeled about and back tracked with squeaking and followed by rumblings from members of the herd who had rushed to the rescue of the young male.

It was a near death experience and it took a pretty long time for me to recover from the shock and realisation, exactly what had happened. By the time Srinivasa accompanied by his staff arrived at the scene, where I was throbbing to recover, I felt my body and limbs looked a kind of mosaic. I was attacked by millions of "little beggars", the scrub ticks, while racing through thorny bushes. These "skin-snatchers" were in plague proportion in that dry season of the year. They had dug themselves into my skin, not sparing even pits and secret places. They had been busy in sucking my blood. While they torn skin and sucked blood and became engorged, they injected a neurotoxin into my body. Every forestry professional knows ticks are at their worst in winter and summer. Even animals and birds are not spared from their attack.

Incidentally, I was cautioned by one of the tribal guard few days ago about the activities of this dreadful "ticks politics", in the jungle. He had warned me to get smeared with a mixture of 1 part Neem oil, 1 part Citronella oil and 25 parts coconut oil and mixed with Dettol, an antiseptic, over the body whenever I entered the forest. Unfortunately, this preventive treatment (=anti-ticks therapy) was ignored by me that day, only to suffer from unbearable itchy and pain in the coming weeks. The mixture is also said to be an effective (preventive) treatment against other skin snatchers and blood suckers of the jungles, like leaches, dog flies and mosquitoes.

6.9 Elephant Images in the Wild

There are two popular images of Indian elephants in the wild; first, is of beasts peacefully living in social family groups and second, the subject of many adventure stories – as the loner/individual wanderer, said to be the 'rogue' or killer elephant and bad-tempered, threatening or vengeful.

In fact, the lone female elephant is something of a rarity in the wild. Only under exceptional circumstances will an individual cow breaks away from the herd and leads a solitary life. The factors contributing to this exclusive behaviour can be varied. The decay of the molar teeth forces them to remain close to lush vegetation, while the other elephants wander off to feed more freely elsewhere. Old age may leave an elephant crippled with arthritis or limping due to internal/external injuries, unable to maintain the speed required to keep up with the rest of the herd. Interestingly, the animals that are forced to break away from the herd, traditionally, are always sub-adult males. These are, rather driven away by the matriarch to prevent inbreeding.

However, female elephants are crucial to the welfare of group-structure, particularly, where the young are concerned and the movements of the herds may well be adapted to the condition of an aging cow, despite her advanced age and possible deteriorating health and she still has an important role to play in the elephant society, as matriarch.

Males, by contrast, take little or no responsibility in educating or protecting the youngsters and when they are afflicted by the crippling characteristics of senility, they may simply be left to fend for themselves. Without social ties to hold them back to encourage concessions to be made on their behalf the males may depart at any time, more or less according to their personal whims.

6.10 Lone Bull

The 'lone bull' never sticks to one particular herd. He wanders far and wide visiting herds found within his home range. Being a siring male, he remains with the herd, as long as a female remains in oestrus. Once his responsibility of servicing is over, he moves on to next herd in search of females in season. Sanderson doubts if there are any such an animal as a true 'lone bull' and dismiss the theory of an adult bull being driven away from the herd by a stronger bull. While it is true that few bulls are truly solitary and are undisputed monarchs of the Indian jungles, there are records of bulls having been seen for years on and standing by themselves or sometimes in close association with another bull, since such animals do not wander far as elephants in herds do in their seasonal quest for food. Their movements are well known to the forest dwelling tribes of the area. Sanderson is correct in declaring that there are no 'lone bulls'. The loneliest of them will, on occasions, seek the company of a cow in season or even associate with another bull for a brief while. However, the term 'lone bull' is applied, much more properly, to an adult male that is solitary. As a rule, it does not join a herd except as a transient association. On the contrary, 'lone bulls' are those which remain solitary due to personal reasons or due to conditions leading to aberration. It may have been undergoing agony or pain from injuries or bullet wounds. It does not show any interest in joining the herd or breeding activities.

A tusker with his peculiarities of build that proclaimed his identity was well known as 'true lone bull' in the Periyar sanctuary for over a decade and was never seen in the company of other elephants, though elephants were seasonally common in the area. Forest dwelling tribes and elephant-men make the distinction between a truly 'solitary bull' and a 'bull of herds'.

In the field, the term '*Onti* – the lone bull' has been used loosely to mean 'solitary bulls', but the context will make it clear which kind was meant. True lone bulls may, on occasions, drink with a herd or stay close by a herd, but may not copulate with females, due to its old age. But, bull of a herd may be referred to a sub-adult bull, normally retained as a protector against possible threats by enemies. It may not be permitted to copulate with females by the matriarch.

G.P.Sanderson argues that a true lone bull is never an animal driven out of a herd but one that has chosen a solitary life of its own volition. A solitary bull cannot just walk into a herd and be accepted, even if he is prepared to accord priority to a larger breeding bull already in the herd, as a matter of course. Even among animals moving in a herd, there may be sharp antagonism among adult bulls.

6.11 'Rogues'- Are They Born or Created?

The problems of exploding human population growth and food supply in a nation always collide. Similarly, in respect of social life of elephants, when man and his livestock compete for the same source of food and the same forest space, conflicts may take a serious turn and elephants have to fight a loosing battle. Man attempts to protect his property and crops by fencing the encroached forests which, once belonged to elephants. When such a situation is created by a thoughtless act of man, initially, the elephants respect the electric fence and other man- made barriers and move away. Elephants are not, by nature, savage animals to break through barricades. The fact that an elephant when captured can be tamed easily is in itself, an evidence of its gentleness. However, when the elephants are constantly persecuted and driven to starvation, they have nowhere to go. They will naturally, turn around and retaliate. At first, the charges and attacks will not be severe or dangerous. With depleted sources of natural food, due to over grazing by livestock, the elephants turn to crop raiding.

During their seasonal movements within their home range, when they come upon crops raised by encroachers, the pachyderms get flabbergasted; in panic, they do more damage by trampling than eating. When shouts, bursting of crackers, air shots are not sufficient to repel these animals, then fire arms will necessarily be used by farmers. Guns in inexpert hands will not kill as intended, but only maim and injure these poor animals. No doubt, they will be repelled temporarily, but the animals will come back again. Meanwhile, the gun-shot wounds will fester and irritate the animal which will be maddened by chronic pain and sufferings. This situation turns even worse; a sober animal may turn into a 'rogue'. Rogues, as already branded are lone elephants which do not behave as normal elephants do, but attack human beings, livestock and cause destruction to property. This retaliation against man is as a first step to take revenge, as the victim realises that the cause of his agony is man and man alone.

These animals tend to live out their remaining days in a solitary uproar, whatever the reasons for these apparent banishments. Occasionally, they become so bad-tempered and aggressive that they will attack any intruder on sight or even terrorize farm lands, causing extensive damage to crops that have been cultivated by man. It is to these, particularly, unfriendly and potentially dangerous individuals that the tag, 'rogue' is applied. It may be surprising to learn that not only very few individuals worthy of such a label in the country, but it is also a condition more commonly found in the African elephant.

The term, 'rogue' should not be applied casually to every lone bull that is almost certainly suffering in some way. It may be that old age has sent it slightly unbalanced or may be that it has incurred an injury which causes continued aggravation, keeping the poor creature in a constant state of pain and nervous tension which is released only by furious assaults on any obstacle, human being or farm animal – that catch his eye. Unlike tiger, leopard, lion or grey langur monkey, such elephants are not found to be antisocial to the members of their own community. In his book, Thirteen Years among the Beasts of India (1878), George Sanderson tells story of an Indian elephant, which patrolled several miles of jungle roads near Mysore. Its initial mock-charges at travellers suddenly turned into fully determined assaults which could end up fatally. Sanderson took it upon himself to free terror-stricken people from the menace, which was so violently disrupting their lives. When he finally tracked down and killed his quarry, he found that the victim had somehow lost most of its tail and that the remaining portion was festering so badly that it was obviously the cause of his madness with which the unfortunate animal suffered.

This kind of changed behaviour forced upon in males, is described as an aberration, the phenomenon of which persists for some time. It is possible to bring about relief to their agony, provided early attempts are made to tackle the miseries. To deal with the problem, first locate the victim by tracking and find out causes of its sufferings; provide immediate medical treatment by tranquillising. If situation warrants, and could be rehabilitated, such an unfortunate victim be trans-located to a safer habitat. All that it needs are the safe habitat and human compassion.

In the extreme case, for a wounded animal in the wild, death is the only means of escape. The wounded elephant, therefore, be relieved of its miseries by involuntary mercy killing, though it is considered inhumane. (Mercy killing or Euthanasia refers to the practice of ending life in order to relieve endless pain and intractable suffering). Sooner is it performed, better it is for the agonising victim. The approach of all concerned should be to prevent elephants becoming rogues and thus avoid decimation of the species. No elephant has become a rogue of its own volition; it becomes rogue by circumstantial association with humans. These associations or confrontations should, therefore, be avoided because, both man and the elephant stand to loose.

6.12 Mother's Love

Babes demand immediate feeding, the moment they are born; they are hungry because they are born after a hard work, while coming out of mother's womb. In the first few weeks of its life, the calf rarely strays more than a few steps from its mother's side. I followed the herd after two days to find that the young had stretched its legs by running up and down and kept up with the family's continuous ambling. Their routine takes them into grasslands, swamps, thick forests and up the steep slopes, swimming across rivers and lakes in their rendezvous sojourn. When wallowing, its mother and elder sister or aunts take great care not to tread on him and whenever the going became tough, mother would reach down with her trunk and push or pull the baby over the obstacles. Cows are extraordinarily tolerant of their babies. Mothers protect their young to protect the fertility of the species. The family with a baby moves in slow-pace and normally covers about 5 km a day.

To begin with, the baby is nourished exclusively by its mother's milk. It takes about 3 days for the baby to learn to suckle at the proper place, between mother's front legs. Cow's breasts hung down amazingly as in the shape of humans, but baby has to stretch to reach them. When suckling, calf's pink mouth with triangular hairy lower lip is firmly fastened on the nipple and his trunk lay limply to one side or is held back in 'S' bend above his head. Mom, occasionally, touches its forehead with the tip of her trunk, as to assure safety and show affection. Like all new born calves it suckles little but often, probably consuming two-and-a-half gallons of milk a day. At times, calf's trunk hung down straight or was brandished like an uncoordinated, whip-cord or rubber hose-pipe like. Some times it sits down and puts the tip of delicate trunk in his mouth and suckles it like human child suckling its thumb. Perhaps, it served the same function of reassurance as in human. The cow, some times, permits her older calf to suckle and on occasions, both mouths are simultaneously fastened to a nipple each. Calf soon learns that it could also get a free drink from its grand mother and some times aunts. The young always accompanies the mother, totally relying on her for protection and training. Mom provides a practice session at forest pools, while drinking and bathing. Thus, the family life is considered great for babies, extending love and affection by all family members.

Calf's survival depends upon certain appreciation of the world around it. The calf's natural curiosity for exploring and testing its surroundings must be carefully held in check primarily by its mother, followed by more experienced and knowledgeable elders around it. The bond between the mother and her offspring is very strong. A more placid approach to child care is generally exhibited by the mature and experienced females. Protection of young ones in the herd is every one's concern; hence the importance of herding.

The Park Warden of Masai Mara Reserve in Kenya narrated an instance of an elephant, whose relationship with her baby was so strong that even after the premature death of her infant, she carried decaying corpse around for several days before finally abandoning it.

It is the dictum of natural selection that by protecting their young the fertility of the species is passed on to the next generation. But for the devotion of cows towards their young the species may have, by now, vanished from the face of the earth planet".

That kind of devotion is a common feature in female elephants until such time – about six months – which the youngsters begin to stray from their sides. Indeed, the mother may enjoy the relaxation of her duties to such an extent that the little calf is sometimes in danger of being left behind when the family unit moves on to fresh feeding grounds. Usually, one or more of the younger females will be keeping a wary eye open for the juvenile. I have seen a panic stricken herd that left behind a six month-old calf, on seeing our approaching vehicle at the steep slope of Gopalswamy hills. A four year old female, followed by an older brother returned and helped the calf in escorting, then clambered up the steep slope.

Between one and two years of age, the little calf is well and truly embarked upon a long trail of learning. His first preoccupation, once he has less access to the supply of milk, is to learn to feed for himself. At what stage the calf begins to rely on the vegetation he can collect on his own is still something of a mystery because of the length of time that so many calves continue to suckle milk. While close to his mother's side he will have played with such food items dropped from her mouth and may even have tasted them by himself. But his inquisitive trunk will have given him ample opportunity to practice picking leaves from bushes and a blade of grass from the ground as well. Grasses make up the bulk of the diet, although a great many different types of vegetation are readily consumed according to their availability and the season of the year. Calves of about a year and more engage in trials of strength and tests of each other's characters and moods. It is important that these individual attributes are known by all those with who many years of adult life is to be shared. The young males seem to be the most vigorous in these contests and indeed it is this trait, which 10 years later, eventually leads the matriarch to take the firm but necessary steps to expel them from the company of their close relatives.

At this stage, however, their exuberance is tolerated because they still have much to weather out and learn about survival. Their prepubescent sisters will be busy helping with any new arrivals to the unit and generally, easing the material burden of the older females. Much of the learning of all the young, regardless of their age, is done by watching and imitating.

Asian and African elephants are good swimmers and both help their calves across fast flowing rivers by swimming downstream, so that the force of the current keeps the youngster pressed against its mother's side. The elephant may seem one of the more unlikely land creatures to be good at swimming, but in fact, it takes to the water willingly and expertly.

There is, obviously, a long term value in calves being allowed to explore for themselves within the boundaries of safety. The young ones take a long time to mature and are able to learn a great deal from adults, which increases their chances of survival in later life.

6.13   Bonding and Bickering

A young cow had given birth to a baby for the first time near Moolehole forest of Bandipur reserve. The calf after a long time of search where to reach for the breast of his mother tried to suckle. His attempt for the first time was unsuccessful. Again he tried once or twice to suckle from his mom, when pushed out; he tottered over to a large cow. What followed after that amazed me. Another cow elephant paid absolutely no attention until he was right under her stomach and then suddenly kicked him by her hind leg three times, sending him sprawling. The baby bowled over in the dust, picked up and staggered back towards his mother.

The sub adult female who had been following his movements intently, opened her forelegs and pulling the baby under her belly, straddled him protectively. He swayed gently under the sub-adult female for few minutes and then tried once again to approach his mother. He was sent flying with another kick. The sub-adult female this time stood over him and rubbed his back. Painfully and slowly, they made their way down the steep rocky hill, the newborn collapsing every few paces. The whole group of the family stood disturbed until the mother went down to rescue the baby.

When, I saw this calf again after few days, he was progressing well and had filled out, having lost his crumpled baggy appearance. It seemed to me that elephants were, at times, strangely unpredictable in their attributes. I never saw such an intolerance again, as shown by an adult cow elephant to the baby, although reading through the literature on elephants, I found that such behaviour was not, as rare as, I had thought. However, as a rule, the cows' behaviour towards their young calves is well known to be one of tolerance and gentle, with every member of the family unit taking part in caring for them.

6.14   Weaning of Calf

The calf is a valuable long term investment in elephant society. Weaning in elephants is a gradual process and may take two and a half years or even more. By the end of the first month calf starts tasting from what his mom eats. He may try to bite grass and pulling out clumps with his mouth, not knowing how to use his trunk. Although some of such green material may have been swallowed, his activity seemed to be essentially exploratory. Within the family unit, calves continue to suckle for as long as they were allowed and long after they had switched over to a predominantly, vegetarian diet. One of the male calves, I noticed was still suckling at the age of about seven. When he thrust and tugged to get at the nipple, his six-inch long tusks poked the old matriarch in her breasts, until often she pulled away or detached him with a shove of her trunk.

6.15   Calf Behaviour and Play

The young male calf is very playful, often aggressively, attacking his elder brother or sister, ramming them with the front of his mouth where the tusks would appear later. Elders put up with him in a good-natured way and being the youngest of all he enjoyed a blissful period of being allowed to do whatever he wished with no discipline.

Throughout the first year of his life mother keenly absorbs of the movements of her calf. Any attempt by the baby to run farther than fifteen to twenty steps away, usually, causes her to go and retrieve him. Much of the time they are in actual physical contact. There are few minutes which may pass without some form of tactile contact, whether it is the rubbing of flanks, a touch of the trunk or of suckling.

At five months the calf becomes very bumptious, shoving against his elders and climbing on top of them when they lie down in the middle of the day to have nap. He seems to be activated by a never-ending supply of energy that makes him chase falling leaves or scatter the egrets, mynah that come to catch insects around the herd. Often he runs about at random pretending to charge furiously at some imaginary objects, trumpeting in treble. This kind of play also helps him to stretch his limbs.

By six months the calf loses his baby looks. The red hair fall out and replaced by stiff black bristles. His body grew fatter and assumed the elephant proportions, which keep changing with age. Only the tusks were missing. His skin was the colour of mud, the shade depending on which wallow he had in his last visit, except when rain drummed hard on his back and he becomes a dull bluish grey. His penis looked surrounded by loose wrinkled skin until it was difficult to distinguish his sex at first glimpse.

His male character, on the other hand, developed very obviously and before his first year was out he was mounting other calves in infantile sex play, becoming sufficiently excited for his male organ to regain temporarily its former prominence. Never did I see a female calf mount a male this way. It was the earliest fundamental difference in behaviour between the two sexes, occurring some thirteen years before any possibility of true sexual conjugation.

6.16   Musth in Male Calf?

Whatever it's mysterious function, *musth* does not seem to occur in very young age. I have not seen any occurrence of dark fluid from temporal glands in calves either in Bandipur, Nagarahole or in adjoining sanctuaries.

6.17   Dreaded and Daring

While the male calf grows, he keeps learning. His movements are experimental and often comic; he adopts dozens of postures that adults seldom use. Slowly he learns to sprawl on his tummy, rolls on his back, drags his hind leg like a wounded buck and sits up like a dog with his ears hanging down, picking up stones and clods throwing on his body and kicking dust and so on. This type of mixed personality is good in cases of crises. Boldest and courageous ones are the defenders of challenges in the wild. They come face to face with unfamiliar situation.

6.18   Calf's Trunk

Calf's trunk causes him great problems. Even drinking with it is a mystery and during the first year he kneels at the edge of water, holding the tip of his trunk out of the water and tries to drink with his mouth, as do all very young calves. Gradually, fiddling with his trunk in the water and sucking the tip, by trial and error, he learns how to suck up water, hold it in his trunk as he raises it and then pours it down his trunk, where it seems to irritate him so that he shook the tip and wiggled it in knots. He learns to hang, swing and twirl his trunk and slowly exploring every possibility he becomes more adept in its uses.

All these activities do not appear in young male's behavioural repertoire, many were only learned with the passage of time. Sometimes it looks, as if he were watching his mother and deliberately imitating her motions. Occasionally, he puts his trunk up into her mouth and samples what she was eating, demanding and pulling some of it out and then chewing and swallowing it. This is probably the way, calves learn what to eat.

6.19   Fear in Young

The young ones also learn to fear. When they are young, especially, males rush up to strange things, like vehicles and other animals and venture to threaten with their little ears cocked wide apart, head raised and piggy eyes squinting aggressively. They are not afraid until they notice that they are alone. Mothers watching their daring performance, signal them twirling their trunk anxiously to backtrack. Then suddenly young lose heart and rush back to their mothers' side with their tail hoisted in the air and squealing in their nervousness. Such calves never again venture singly.

Inquisitiveness to know about strange things like vehicles and humans also induces them to behave in similar manner. On such occasions, their moms seem to appease their fear, by touching with their trunk, in what appears to be a gesture of reassurance until they calm down.

6.20 Pseudo Tusks

At two years the pearly tips of milk tusks, called 'pseudo tusks' appear briefly before dropping out to reveal the permanent tusks behind them. This moment varies considerably from one calf to another and unfortunately, cannot be used as an aging criterion. Naturally, like all things calves are eager to try out a new found capacity and try to participate, rather ineffectively, in the scraping of bark when the family stripped Bende *Kydia calycina* tree. The calf also butts his elder brother or sister or cousins and the new sharp points give them a serious weapon and an ability to inflict pain, but at the same time social inhibition seemed to grow against all-out use of these weapons.

6.21 Social Education

Social education in calves is an important survival tool that is needed to be learnt from their young age. The calves are required to be equipped with knowledge, as how to react quickly against actions from adversaries and fight back, when circumvented with challenges. I have never seen any nursery in elephant family groups to teach survival techniques. Most of the time babies remain attached to their mothers. It is the individual mother that teaches primary lessons along with discipline. For social animals like elephants, survival strategy is very much a family affair and acquired through mock fights and exercises.

These social encounters usually begin with two little elephants wrapping their trunks around each other in an embrace, followed by a pushing match, although often the calves are of such uneven ages that the result is a forgone conclusion. But rather than shoving the smaller one roughly the bigger will use the minimum force necessary to achieve his objectives. The younger the calf the gentler is the procedure. Younger calves are, eventually, taught social education through tuition by the sub-adult.

As months pass by, calves come to know their little world and all the elephants that lived in it. Their family group pushes these youngsters on a never-ending cycle of quartering the home range of the forest to eat fruits, pods, delicious vegetation of the swamps that survived the vagaries of dry season. They are also introduced to important land marks of the area, like springs, water holes, rivers, *nallas*, grazing grounds and salt-licks.

At two-and-a-half years of age calves attain full of health and energy, but still very much dependent on their mothers. The older calves that I have observed, remain for at least the first ten years of their life, called juveniles continue to be nurtured by the love and protection of their family group. Even when next siblings are born, the older calves still receive plenty of attention from their mothers, which goes on until they reach adolescence and in some cases long beyond.

6.23 Juveniles Play – Fights

This was a time of great excitement for the youngsters and they would race around in play groups, hopeless by mix up, so that one could no longer distinguish to which female each of the calves belonged. In their rough and tumbling plays, they resembled puppies and take on all sorts of elaborate three, four or five cornered combinations. If the level of aggression ever threatened to get out of hand there was usually nearby mother or an adolescent female who would rush to sidle effortlessly into their midst and single out a calf to be eased away.

The calves continue to play and fight improving in their skill all the time. They learn to use higher side of a slope to their advantage, so that each can press down more effectively on his opponent. Occasionally, the play becomes so serious and jerky that the weight of the body behind each thrust, but their encounters are normally characterised by gentleness and the vanquished merely receives a slight prod in his flank as he turns away.

However, should an obstacle such as a fallen tree comes between the two contestants during their play – fights then they will suddenly threaten with redoubled fury, each knowing that, in fact, it cannot get to grips with the other. Their behaviour is rather like that of dogs barking at each other across the fence.

Play-fighting must be of functional significance to an elephant; probably it teaches an animal its exact strength relative to the other that inhabits the same area. In this way, through friendly contests in which animals do not get hurt, a hierarchy originates in which each individual knows its place. The experience gained in the techniques of manoeuvring and thrusting may also help an individual to win if it does get into serious fight. In later life, when competitive situations arise over water or food and even sex, the dispute is usually settled by a mere threat display, which may be no more than the extension of the ears or simply, the wave of a trunk in the direction of the opponent. Serious fighting in tuskers is extremely rare in the wild. Threat display in elephants, as in many other species, appears to protect from actually being attacked.

As adolescence approaches, at about the age of eleven to thirteen years, males indulge in vigorous play-fighting, interspersed with bouts of mounting each other and the females of their age. This is the last burst of activity before they become totally independent and forced to leave the family units for ever.

6.24 Juveniles, Their Platonic Friendship

Life is not quite straight forward for the developing males. Until now males strove to keep their relationship 'virginal', as it were, with other members of the family, under the prowess of the matriarch. On attaining puberty males' restless antics of the past few years culminate in their making sexual advances toward females of their own family unit. Hence onwards, males and females no longer remain simply friends. The platonic friendship between two animals of opposite sex grown up together is an oxymoron and has to end like, when 'Harry met Sally'. The world can't be wrong that males and females do not get drawn towards one another, simply because they have interlocking accessories and raging hormones. It is very rarely that 'platonic friendships' between two animals of opposite sex happen, when they have grown up together and are like siblings. The corollary to this is that for a male and a female playing on attaining puberty, a platonic relationship is next to impossibility. Before the friendship turns into sexual act, the adolescent male is driven out of the herd by the matriarch.

Now is the time for him to go in pursuit elsewhere. The matriarch, who may be his mother or grandma, is increasingly agitated by his disruptive elements within the family group. She interrupts his advances and forces him to the fringes of the herd. When he tries to return, she pushes him out again and again, taking little heed either of his reluctance to be separated from his close relatives or of her own strong ties with him. Her responsibility lies with the family unit and she will welcome only the advances of breeding males who are not too closely related with the females around her. Incest is as much a taboo among elephants, apparently, as it is among humans. Inbreeding is not, generally, successful in the natural selection and in evolutionary terms and her behaviour is, genetically, controlled to prevent it from happening.

The adolescent male soon realizes that his presence within the family unit will no longer be tolerated and that to avoid being attacked, he must distance himself. The extended larynx – rumblings of the females keep him informed of their position in the jungle and he will follow them around, as a satellite, taking care not to be seen too close. It must be a difficult time for the sub-adult not yet established as a mature individual and banished from the sides of the elephants with whom he has shared every moment of the last dozen or so years of life. Eventually, he meets similarly placed sub-adult bulls excluded from their families. After all, 'boys are boys' and they can now engage in their trials of strength without being castigated and as more of them meet up and wrestle playfully and form a loose hierarchy of dominance. Adolescent males have to keep wandering far and wide, until they prove their winning streak before they turn 25 years of age.

6.25 Adolescence

The onset of sexual maturity is the change that relinquishes them from the feminine care that had been lavished upon them for so many years. The strong ties between the individuals remain, of course, but there is a new generation of elephants growing up and it is on these inexperienced and vulnerable calves that the family unit must focus attention.

The former juveniles are now adolescents taking their places in the structure of elephant society. The female, her maternal instincts with the family unit still developing, now awaits her first relationship with a visiting breeding male and her first pregnancy. She will teach her first calf all the rules that brought her up so successfully, through her first dozen or so years.

Female calves at puberty become increasingly reluctant to fight with their brothers and male cousins and become more and more maternal to the younger calves. Mothers, sometimes, resented the attitude of these teenage 'nannies'. This was, particularly, the case in younger mothers with their first calf, but the nannies were undoubtedly useful. Simultaneously, they probably gain valuable experience by the time they would become mothers. If social causes were to limit the population, then it was not through maltreatment of young calves. In the older age groups, however, aggression was more readily seen. The aggression towards young was, perhaps, to give rough treatment, so that they would readily face the harshness of the nature.

6.26 Bachelor Group/Coalition Party

Sub-adult males approaching sexual maturity have no place in matriarchal society. The matriarch attempts to put away the scandal of seductive males. Small group of sub-adult formed when they are driven out by matriarchs of different herds. They may not travel too long a distance from the parent herds. They will be continuing their feeding as satellites. They are now capable of fending for themselves against natural enemies like tigers and humans. After some time, bachelors may break up and rejoin their respective parent herds and remain there for a short period. While they are with the herd they act like protectors of the family from possible threats of predators.

These sub-adult bull-groups, on rare occasions may number 4 to 5 individuals and naturally comprised members of different ages. Their biological function, as they attain maturity is simply reproduction, when a group of 5 or so meets with a unit of females, their preceding trials of strength and the consequent respect for the differences between them will have established who has immediate access to the cows and who must wait his turn. The largest bull is the eldest and he has the privilege of siring the female in season. The matriarch is fully aware of their presence and she knows, instinctively, that when she or one of her cows is in heat, the close proximity of the breeding males must be tolerated.

Batchelor group with *makhna*; note large head and power loaded trunk aompared to young tusker. Large head and powerful trunk help to compensate absence of tusks while fighting when they attain adulthood.

Throughout their bachelor wanderings, in female dominant society, the bulls harbour deep respect and affection for their females that is equalled by few animals in the wild. Obviously, the close ties of their youth are never really broken. Once, they are given the rare opportunity to resume contact with the opposite sex, they indulge in a reunion of courtship, love play and sexual act, typical of partners.

The males begin to form a loose association with the family units, before any of the cows comes to heat. The matriarch is, usually, aware of the significance of their movements and she is, largely, tolerant of their awakening interests. It is, after all, in her interest to have a strong male escort in the vicinity, in case any danger requiring a show of strength.

6.27   Unity in Elephants

For elephants, the unity in a family is one of the important factors of survival strategy. I was deeply moved by the constant affection and care which they showed every day within the families; mothers, daughters, sisters, brothers, babies all touching and communicating with each other in a very loving and affectionate way. Communication among the family members seemed to be the key factor to their security and successful living. Unlike humans they do not have male parent or bull companion living with them; but perhaps, for elephants this is an advantage because they have to deal solely with female problems. They admit the males only when they need them for mating, which is after all the purpose of survival and carry on the genes to next generations. No male, not even wounded tuskers showed any kind of tension with the herd, when they entered a herd. When the bulls arrived, the same greeting and touching ceremony took place. The matriarchs not only perform the usual maternal tasks, but also the roles which we tend to think of as male-leading and defending the family units with extreme efficiency. Whatever the reason, these female-led families remain united and truly stable. But then, I came to know that stability is not an absolute necessity and that large family units might split, especially, during prolonged summer and when signs of stress surfaced, especially when food and water became scarce or threatened security.

During the days I stayed with these herds, I was able to get glimpses of incredible complexity and sophistication that elephants showed in their social activities. I came to understand their relationships and at the same time to respect them; longed and pledged to protect them. I could not bear to watch someone lift a gun at an elephant's head and blow its brain out, for sport or for man's greed. What a waste of life, the gift of nature? Days of my spending time with and observing social cult of these criminals, taught me something that no text books or any university could ever do. And as a result I felt a good deal more civilized.

Chapter VII

Why Do They Do What They Do?

The fierce attacks of elephants are uncanny on occasions. The lack of hesitation contrasted strongly with the normal threat behaviour of elephants. It is, however, a theory of ethologists that threat displays evolve from behaviour that originates in conflict situations. In case of such elephants, swaying, swinging, kicking dust, throwing dirt over head or at the object of aggression, twiddling the trunk and tossing the head about are the indicators of intolerance of an intruder. It is interesting to see, how they develop into threat displays from infancy to adulthood. This is their survival strategy. But for their steadfast and power driven threat displays followed by trumpet and charge against potential enemies, they would have been vanished from the face of the earth like prehistoric ancestors.

As the dry season wore on, mud wallows thickened and cracked and *nallas* dwindled to a trickle and sank into the silts at their base. Creepers hanging on the bushes shrivelled into curly brown shreds, grasslands and bushes started burning for which park management was blamed to have allowed such vandalism in the reserve. The wild fires were set by some miscreants and disgruntled tribesmen, who could not be appointed as 'Fire Watchers'. Forests were also set ablaze by graziers from adjoining villages, in order to rid of tall woody grass and to hasten sprouts of flush grass for their livestock to graze on. Food and water for the elephants became scarcer. With the scarcity of food and water, came the competition among the elephant herds other herbivores. Cracks and stresses appeared within elephant family unit's solidarity, splitting into smaller groups. The year 1982 had a prolonged summer ending with worst drought.

Family units within kinship groups, as witnessed during my visits, were almost always within earshot of each other and would swiftly combine to beat off any danger lurking around. Their usual place of conferences used to be water holes.

7.1 Tackling Drought Situation

Bandipur reserve and adjoining Madumalai, Wayanad and Nagarahole wildlife reserves had the experience of freak drought during 1982, in their recorded history. Forest fires were seen in every corner of the reserves. Regular water holes were shrinking day by day. The situation was so bad that peace and tranquillity of the park were disturbed. The resident animals faced acute shortage of drinking water. The elephants and gaur, however, migrated to places, where they could find some water and browse. For resident animals water was the crucial factor. Water from bore wells was pumped out to impound in man made troughs, specially constructed for the purpose. Temporary storage facilities were created, the bottom of which were sealed by spreading leak proof thick plastic sheets. Water was transported by truck tankers and stored, as also in pits dug out in dried up water holes. Water was also stored in cement and stone troughs, spread over the park. But deaths among elephants, especially, young, weak and the aged did occur in large number during those summer months.

The health of entire ecosystem of Bandipur was found shaky. I could see signs of increased stress in elephants. Many of the matriarchs and next in the order of hierarchy showed flow of dark oily liquid, a sign of stress and insecurity. Kinship groups broke out into smaller herds. Interaction with elephants was found difficult for me. Health loss in elephants was a great concern in the management of the reserve. Kabini reservoir in the western sector of the park almost emptied leaving behind mud-flats. Few elephants that ventured to approach the river course for a drink got bogged into quagmire. Death of aged and weak elephants, including starving calves led to a compelling investigation. Post-mortem investigations of some aged cows gave us shocking clues of heavy accumulation of mud into their alimentary canal and digestive system. However, causes of death, according to post-mortem reports, as concluded by the Vets, were due to dehydration, exhaustion and starvation. At the Bandipur reserve alone, I was able to locate nearly thirty elephant corpses in various stages of decomposition. Some, I spotted by following the descent of vultures, others from the reports by Rangers. Unfortunately, many of the corpses were too disintegrated, for me, to be able to find out the cause of death or who they were, but in other cases the causes were obvious. Accidents took their toll. If an elephant survives of old age the ultimate terminator may be tooth-wear and decay. With the sixth set of molars having ground to stumps, that died of old age on the bank of Kabini, the mastication of certain rough, but necessary types of food had become impossible, resulting in slow death.

Fighting in nature is rarely fatal though, I knew many working males apparently, gored to death by wild bulls, with tusks that pierced into the bodies. The Mysore Palace Tuskers-Biligiriranga and Rajendra were the victims of such attacks; they were gored by wild bulls, when they were let out in to the forest at Kakankote elephant camp, where they were enjoying their old age pension. Both of them succumbed to severe injuries.

Predation by tigers was an important risk for calves. At the time of severe drought, death of aged and young proportionately increased. Starvation, the ultimate controlling factor for many elephant populations, had raised its dirty head in Bandipur Reserve, during 1980s as well. Very few animals were out of condition or suffering from mal-nutrition during summer months. By and large, the elephants of the reserve were remarkably healthy. A matriarch and a cow next in command in the herd showed a flow of dark liquid from their temporal glands at Hulikatte pond. I photographed them. This condition, I could relate to stress and strain, these animals underwent in sourcing food and water. Another cow elephant that I shot by my camera, near Erekatte had hundreds of wart-like small abscesses or bubbles like out-growth, the exact cause of which, I could not immediately make out. I once saw an old cow, may be a matriarch of a big herd at Kabini reservoir bed, had her left rear flank pushed in, might be due to some kind of accidental fall. However, thighs, back, shoulders and forelimbs of almost every elephant, in general, were well padded with flesh. Considering overall killings and natural deaths, the Bandipur reserve has been loosing at 6 elephants a year, on an average.

7.2 Population Trend

Even prolonged summer or drought had to end one day. Fortunately, 1983 was a good year for the reserve. The forest bursts out with new life after early rains. The landscape took the colourful extravaganza. As rains nursed grass, grasses nursed ungulates; the ungulates put on fat, they in turn, fed by predators. Wheel of life continued ever after in the reserve, amidst struggle for survival under the law of nature. Deadly games between prey and predators were witnessed every moment. Rains had triggered the mass migration of elephants and gaur into the reserve. Their home-ranges of different herds covered contiguous forests and grass lands of Madumalai sanctuary of Tamilnadu, south Wayanad sanctuary of Kerala and Biligirirangan Hills Sanctuary and tiger reserve, including adjoining Nagarahole national park of Karnataka, covering an area of about 2,500 sq km. But it was not known which of the herds used habitats of above reserves and their extents. At this time of the year, say between May and October the Bandipur reserve becomes a tapestry of teaming wildlife. The reserve once again transforms making it a paradise pretty – the place of peace and harmony. By now, majority of elephant cows in herds had kids at their heels. During elephant census of the rainy season, it was confirmed that one thirds of each herd consisted of babies of less than one year of age. Elephant families are like gypsy tribes, always on the move. They never confine to any particular habitat; if they do so, there is no way they overcome starvation.

A steady growth of elephant population was recorded over a period of 1973 to 1986. It was also the case with other wildlife populations, such as ungulates and carnivores. These increases had been registered with the improvement in habitat, because of total protection afforded to the park over more than a decade. The latest census of elephant along with tigers and other animals carried out during November 1992, recorded an upward trend. Improved habitat conditions, assured water supply, supported by ensured security were responsible in the increased population of prey species.

The population of elephants remained almost steady over the years. The density of elephants was maintained at 0.8 to 1.0 per sq km, which is considered as reasonably a healthy population in such a habitat. The comfortable density in a given ecosystem, however, remains @0.2 to 0.5 km^{-2}. Other prey species also indicated steady increase thus providing required prey biomass for increased population of carnivores. The census data, however, should be taken as an indicative, rather than actual, in view of various field problems, like thick undercover and human error. The health of the habitat does not depend on the presence of excessive populations of elephants/ungulates. Unlike African Savannah, Indian jungles have to bear jumbled maize of biodiversity- plant and animal kingdoms. The vegetative biomass is higher, while the animal biomass being low in Indian forests, as compared to African savannah. However, it is assumed that the bearing capabilities per unit area of Indian soils, as well as African soils are said to be almost similar. This assumption, however, requires detail study.

7.3 Behaviour of Members in Herds

The boundaries of home range of kinship groups of elephants varied depending on the ecological niche at their disposal, say, any where between 300 to 500 square km. Home ranges elephant herds and those of tuskers did overlap. If not disturbed, elephants follow the same daily pattern of feeding and seasonal movements throughout their lifetime. Elephants are faithful to their home ranges and are quite adaptable too. They are good swimmers and can endure extreme climatic conditions. They are also adaptable to treacherous mountain ranges.

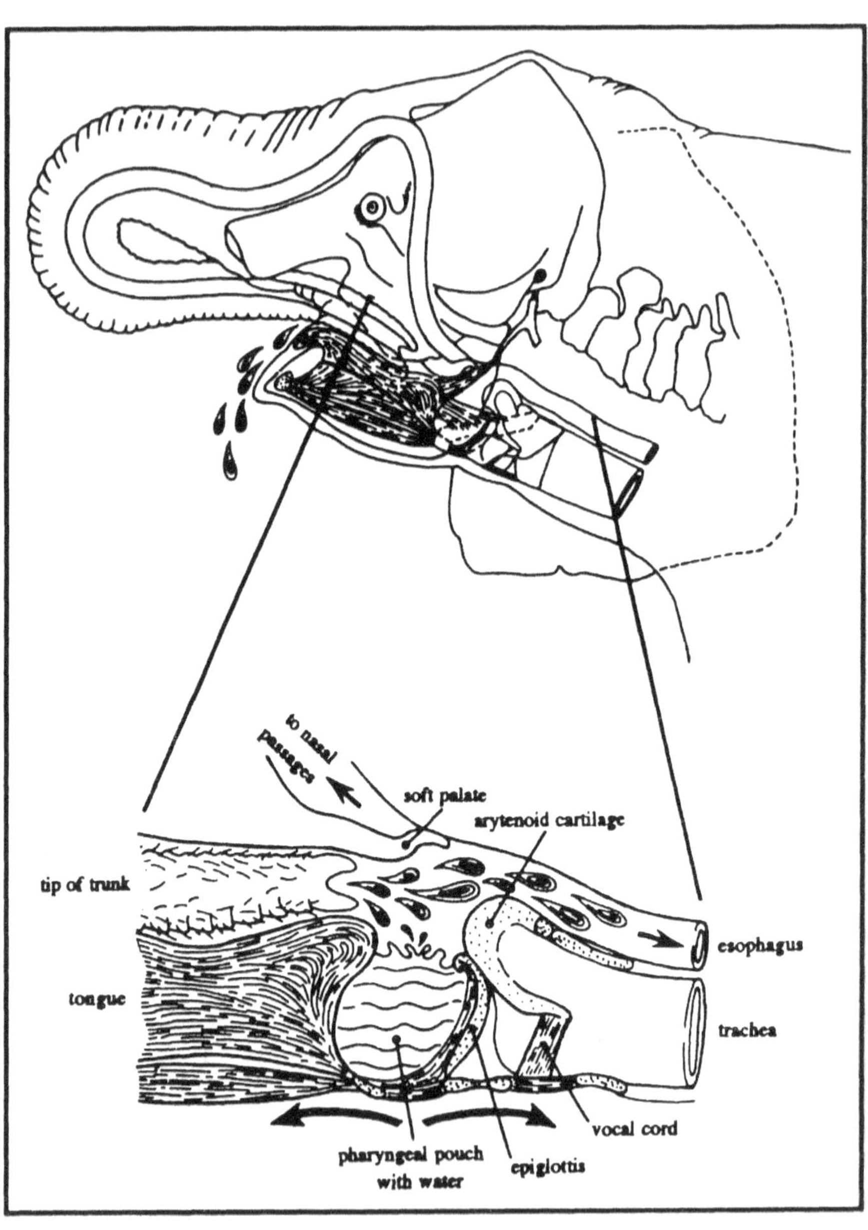
to nasal
passages
soft palate
arytenoid cartilage
tip of trunk
esophagus
tongue
trachea
vocal cord
pharyngeal pouch
with water
epiglottis

Elephants are diurnal or crepuscular in nature; they spend two-third of their life-span or even more in sourcing food and water. Rest of the time is devoted to other activities, such as bathing, wallowing, dusting, playing, resting and love making. Wild elephants have been seen resting their heads on slopes, mounds or ant hills. Interestingly enough, some observers report that an elephant's heart beats considerably faster when it is asleep than when it is awake, the phenomenon opposite of human race.

Thermoregulatory mechanism in elephants involves as with all other mammals, physical, chemical and behavioural regulations. However, the huge bulk and the lower ratio between its body surface and body mass as compared to smaller animalsit is easier for an elephant to keep its body warm. The reverse is also true, when the elephant finds it hard to keep its body cool.

On warm days elephants limit their activities to cool hours, seeking shade, bathing, mud wallowing or spray water from naturally occurring water sources. If such water is not immediately available they suck sweat collected in 'Pharyngeal pouch' located in their gullet and spray to their ears and body. Some writers believe that elephants siphon out 'retrieved/ regurgitated water' from inside the stomach. This is is not true. Being herbivorous, the elephants can't retrieve or regurgitate water or food, unlike carnivores. Moreover, it is believed that elephants lack in vomiting centres in the brain. The overall body temperature of working or riding elephants during hot sun might be very high. Incidentally, as already narrated in earlier chapter, the absence of sweat glands on the body surface makes them, all the more intolerant of heat. The sweat is thus collected in the gullet. This is drawn by the trunk and sprayed, which serves as a coolant. Place here image No.Parangeal pouch tif :a line sketch on lef side.

Drinking of water daily is vital for all species of ungulates and the elephants are no exception. During dry season, elephants often dig out water holes in river beds called 'elephant wells', where the water ceases to exist above the surface but continues to seep through underneath the silt. When elephants finish their drink, other animals, including tigers and leopards drink from these wells. Thus, 'elephant-wells' play an important role in the survival of many other species, especially during prolonged summer. The elephants are thus reckoned as nature's efficient 'water diviners'.

Despite their massive size, the elephants can be extremely docile and tractable. On the other hand, they are subject to excitation and alarm on the very slightest provocation. At times, male elephants can be extremely dangerous reacting belligerently, even attacking passers by. This is, particularly, true of an Asian male elephant in *musth*, the physiological functioning of the body and a phenomenon that might be associated with sexual activity. It is, generally, believed among captives that no animal on earth is so dangerous than a tusker in *musth*. But in the wild nursing mothers are no less dangerous, especially, when their babies are threatened.

Altruism is a behavioural attribute often associated with elephants. No one really knows whether or not a particular behaviour can be interpreted as a maternal or sisterly instinct or a self centred as the doctrine of natural selection could largely be in perpetuation of the species. A cow elephant has been observed endangering herself to rescue her calf from a storming river; another was observed carrying her dead calf in her trunk until it rotted. Yet another was observed a baby sitting over her sleeping brother to make sure he was not left behind; she woke him up with a hard kick to join the family. Bull elephants are also known to help each other in times of distress and misery. They do not desert their wounded or dazed companion, but would stay and support him physically, by ranging themselves alongside and boosting him to his feet.

These are just a few examples that make elephant behaviour so unique and fascinating. It should be pointed out that because of the long bond between the mother and her offspring and the strong family ties; a great deal of elephant behaviour is believed to be learned or acquired and not inborn. This type of benevolent behaviour is not found in any other wild animals. This is how the elephant is described as 'intelligent gentle giant'.

7.4 Swimming and Bathing

Water is no obstacle to elephants, which are amazingly home; to those who have not seen them, let me tell you they are the superb swimmers. They can cross island after island swimming across water bodies, over 2 km and more, holding the trunk above the water level like a snorkel, but they have to do enormous 'leg-work'.

Elephants, both Asian and African, are good swimmers. They can swim at the rate of about a mile an hour. Elephants keep their bodies totally immersed while swimming, showing their tips of their trunk above the water. Babies assisted by mothers keeping them close heir body or by lifting and holding them by trunks can keep pace with the herd while swimming across rivers and lakes. Such rendezvous are a common sight at Kabini reservoir of Karnataka and Periyar reservoir of Kerala. The photographs of elephants, shot immediately after their emerging out of water at mid-day, present the most fascinating pictures, as if, carved in ebony.

CARVED IN EBONY ? MARCH-PAST OF A FAMILY OF PACHIDERMS IN THE HIGH-NOON

A consequence of their great bodily bulk is that the elephants are virtually unsinkable as they have natural buoyancy. After a certain depth it is difficult to make them walk, for they would rather prefer to swim; but they do not ride high in the water. They swim almost submerged or just below the surface of water and the advantage of this is, when the surface currents are strong it is obvious that they can overcome from being drifted away.

7.5 Rituals at Water Holes

As already narrated earlier, the very young calves, when taken to water body by their moms for the first time are reluctant to enter; they are pushed in by their mothers or sisters or 'aunts', using trunks or by kicking lightly. While in the water, young calves are helped and guided by the trunks of their mothers or sisters. I have observed the young calves, some times, scramble on to the shoulder of their mothers during a dip shower in deep water.

For an invigorating bathing ritual, elephants enter the forest pools and rivers carefully, fanning out and then rolling over in the water, frequently submerging themselves. The elephant's body keeps buoying when it tries to dive in the forest pool. They are not found in places where there is no source of drinking water, for they drink every day though they may not bathe every day. They are also getting indulged in bathing and mud plastering/pasting, even while it rains during monsoon.

Water heals, revitalises, soothes and it can make elephants' skin more dewy and luscious, a nature's way of cosmetic treatment. Ancient Indian *Rishis*, the, Romans and the Greeks all knew the curative powers of water. Retreating to the water pool has a tantalising effect on their body and mind.

7.6 Mud Slinging?

Hardly any other animal in the wild, expends so much a time and energy in health care than the elephant, towards its skin wash or bathing, massaging, mud-packing and even dust blowing. Though the thick skin appears to be very insensitive to human eye and touch, it requires constant attention, actually being very sensitive to the animal. The numerous skin folds and crevices often harbour all sorts of ecto-parasites. There are even elephant lice (*Haematomy zus*), but these can be controlled by well developed skin muscles, either by shaking off the pests or by smashing them by rubbing against a tree-trunk. Forest flies, dog-flies and mosquitoes bother them the most while in the depth of the forest. They are the daily monsters. Intermittently, elephants engage themselves in "flies driving business", holding a green twig in their trunk.

Elephants mix mud with water to convert into slurry and draw through their trunks and spray it over the entire body. It is interesting to watch elephants muddying the water kicking with a forefoot or by churning action of the trunk. It is an elaborate ritual in elephants. A tusker was undergoing this kind of ritual for nearly 45 minutes at K. M. Katte water hole of Bandipur, while I was watching from a tree-top *machan*. Semi-solid mire that was freely available picked up in lumps in the crook of the tip of the trunk and flung over the back, head and flanks. The tusker even packed mud at the joints, in between front legs, the entire head behind the ears and face and wherever its trunk could reach.

Elephants also indulge in a mud-wallowing, when it is dry and too hot, as in summer or on an overcast day or even when it is raining. Dusting is usually done soon after climbing ashore from water; the dust is collected by the trunk and blown over the head, flanks and back. Dust is also sprayed over wounds to seal them. Earth is kicked up by the forefoot using toe-nails and then gathered. There appears to be a tendency among gravid cows to eat earth mixed with salt or in natural salt-licks.

Apparently, all these mire-smearing, followed by dusting, etc., believed to relieve cutaneous irritations or to provide some cutaneous gratifications; the way elephants eleborate, in bathing, dusting, wallowing and mud-slinging does suggest such a purpose. Plausibly, this worldly process works as an effective "naturopathy" – curative, preventive and soothing. Mud-therapy is described as an anti-parasite therapy that serves keep insects and parasites off from pestering.

Elephants also rub their body both when their bodies covered with wet mud and their skin dry and clean, against tree-trunks. For this purpose, a tree stump or a branch is chosen, often with slightly leaning and rub themselves. Such trees are often found, covered with mud from about 3 ft to 9 ft up their trunk, in the neighbourhood of forest pools.

I, once witnessed sitting on a tree *machan*, a tusker after having a mire-application, detached a dry twig from a nearby tree-branch, held it by his trunk, scratched himself over the flanks and back where his trunk could not reach. Another tusker, suffering from a gunshot wounds and maggot-infested rubbed himself against a Teak tree to get rid off maggots. Yet another tusker picked up a flat stone near a salt-lick placed it over his neck and shook himself to ward off itching.

7.7 Bull's Charge

A series of distant trumpeting by an elephant came piercing through the forest canopy, as I was driving through. This time, I was accompanied by one Miss. Elizabeth, a writer from England. I was taking her to show an over view of the "valley of green canopy", within the Bandipur park. As soon as we approached a rivulet, the Waggoner in which we were travelling brought to a halt on my signal to the driver, vociferous shrills of trumpet echoed, followed by swishy whiffs through the bushes; then silence reigned the atmosphere, but the situation became tense. Behind a tall dark *Terminalia* tree stood a big bull, head high, tip of his trunk sniffing the air around, peering in our direction, one foot swinging to and fro, almost ready to charge. We were only a few steps away from the beast. We watched the bull excitedly, as he kept policing on us, with his pendulous penis dangling, his eyes burning with fury and hatred. A young lady stood behind him, partially covered by a bamboo clump. She looked shy and submissive in the presence of the bull. I soon realised, the cow was in season.

"Shyness in that teenager manifested charm and sexy; she communicated to her male partner how personal and special the occasion was. Courtship and sex in elephants is a private affair, you know", I whispered to Miss. Elizabeth.

"Since reticence limits intimacy, the shy cow should try to break out a little. What needed was a little romance and a little tenderness", expressed Miss Elizabeth.

"Both male and female were together in their courtship sojourn", I whispered again, as I kept watching the couple having moved away from the main herd.

The cow reached the bull in an attempt to push him away from our view.

"Yes, sex there seemed an exclusive and a private affair", avowed Elizabeth, as sex therapist.

When sex seemed perfuming the air the cow portended as if she liked his body smell. While the bull remained absolutely silent, his penis twitching with spasm, the cow raced her tender tip of the trunk all over his body and planted a kiss at his pendulous genital organ, expressing her commitment, while he shrugged with low bleat.

We began to wonder, if she was trying to please him or simply attempting to distract him from our sight. She looked at the bull, so inquisitively, as if to ask him, "Show me how to please you". The bull remained reserved.

The cow gracefully nagged him to move further, the bull caught her up, moving sideways with his trunk around her curved body.

"It is a quiet sex; it is like watching a great movie with the sound switched off", quipped Elizabeth. "The scene is a pleasant and entertaining isn't it?" she whispered shuffling closer to me.

"Since the rules of Love-*Sutra* are constantly being rewritten, here's a look at love in its new hybrid form and what you need to look out for the panoramic inscription", I remarked.

When the bull touched her clitoris, she got excited and squawked and spluttered; she giggled maliciously as if to say, "Cool off and join the party my lord".

But the bull seemed crazy for love sounds, looked deep into her eyes to say "Let it go sweetie, I may listen to you later".

As the bull raised his trunk and rested it on her back, ready to mount, the cow whisked away giving out vibrant sounds from sexy whisper to soulful shouts, as saying, "Are we going to check out the wonderful cacophonous words of noisy sex?"

Both male and female touched each other's genitals. She then turned to face the bull as to beg of him to kiss in French, touch in Turkish and ravish in Portuguese techniques!

The young lady stared and touched his penis as if asking him innocently, "What are you going to do with that to me?" Her response was a turning point and the *Kama Sutra* came alive!

"I can go all day babies", raised his head as to boast himself. The bull placed his trunk in her mouth and seduced her softly, "I want to take you higher and higher, my lady".

The cow then submitted and offered herself, while the bull fixed her up and copulated placing himself in a perfect alignment resting his trunk promiscuously over her neck. The act lasted for nearly thirty seconds. The bull took time off and seemed to enjoy each layer that he went through, while the cow caressed her body against his.

Finally, when the heavens had merged with the earth in the resounding shrieks of thunder, both of them emerged from their respective exertions, tired and yet satisfied. She perhaps, did not know the sex could be so good!

He gave her a gentle back-massage, cuddling her up warmly and quietly listening to her, as part of post-play rituals.

Elizabeth, in an outrage, lent a spicy whiff in the air and said, "Alas, I had been to Khajuraho, before I landed at Bandipur, did you know what happened there?"

Obviously, she wanted to distract my focus from the scene and move away from there.

"It is a sleepy, small town, feeling lonely till I hit the erotic temples, where every god had his day. I must confess that I did not quite look up (I was alone and the guide was too graphic), but I could imagine what Khajuraho did stand for and continue to do to tourists? So yes, I guess, I could call Khajuraho a romantic place of history", she concluded her narration.

As the situation shifted to 'the vertical expression of a horizontal desire', I signalled the driver to move.

The driver attempted to start the vehicle, but it produced creaking sound, refusing to start at the first attempt. The metallic piercing noise manifested itself, it seemed, an annoyance to the love-loran pair of elephants. As the cow whisked away, the bull in his fury gave out piping trumpet and charged at us, his pulpy penis held in 'S' shape jerking up and down. The lady in her sixties, sitting next to me, covered her face tightly with her hands and screamed at the driver "move, move faster and still faster .....!"

As the vehicle started off at the second attempt, the bull chased us at full speed, his head held high, trunk coiled and ears spread wide. He must have persuaded his chase for nearly a hundred metres, his eyes fixed on us. As we drove past he swerved off the road, trumpeting and thrashing the bush, throwing up branches and dust, a demonstration of what he, probably, intended to do to us. Oh, it was a terrifying sight.

I realised then how easily this gigantic bull could have squashed us all into pulp, should the vehicle be stalled. I could see the breeding bull behaving in this outlandish manner for the first time! It was very frightening. The old lady, who had crouched on the seat of the Waggoner, was petrified. I had a camera in my hand, ready to click, but the circumstances were so overwhelming that I missed to shoot that charging bull.

For the next two days or so, whenever elephants were sighted even at long distances, Elizabeth closed her eyes and shouted at the driver, "Drive fast and faster".

At the end of her visit to the reserve the unmarried woman at her sixty or so, came to me to express her gratitude for all she had enjoyed, rather experienced. Presenting a complimentary copy of English book, "Rendezvous of the Himalayas by Solo", authored by her, she whispered sitting next to me, "Please take care of your elephants including that 'charger', though I could not stomach the sight of horny male".

7.8 A Tale of Bull Fights

Serious fights between adult bulls in the wild were never seen by me during my many years of association with elephants in the reserve and elsewhere. However, I once witnessed a scuffle between two bulls, while, watching from a tree *machan* at K.M. Katte water hole. The skirmish was brief and decisive; it was over within few minutes with a loud shattering sound of tusks. Disputes, if any, between tuskers are resolved by exhibiting one's superiority; rarely by bloodshed. Eventually, sex is the nature's most powerful drive for the rivals to fight against, but not over home range. In the bye-gone era, when tuskers were hunted by licensed hunters, there used to be more bulls to compete for sex, when battle could have been the decisive factor to win over the female in heat. In recent years, ever since guns changed over from hunters to poachers, the near wiping out of bulls is looming large. To mince matter worse, farmers are taking heavy toll, thus reducing the number of magnificent bulls. Under the situation, one hardly comes across fierce "bull fights" in the wild.

As a rule, adult bulls appeared to have understood the hierarchal system based on their size and height, a mild threat gestures were usually enough to resolve any conflict and to establish superiority. Tolerance between bulls declined only at times when a female came into oestrus, but even then smaller bulls moved away rapidly out of the fray, though with wild commotion, when threatened by the one larger.

In their interaction with cows and calves, the breeding bulls, rarely, exhibit aggression. A large bull approaching a family unit might project his ears half forward in mild threat and sometimes the young cows and calves run away. More often than not, they turned to greet him by extending their trunks towards him and gracefully, touching or placing the trunk in his mouth, possibly in appeasement. Bull's intolerance towards females and young is however, typically hierarchal and their behaviour is usually gentle.

Fierce fights between wild bulls and camp males, on occasions, may lead to deaths of the latter. But in the wild, more often they are only skirmishes. I don't subscribe to a statement made by some writers that the fights between bulls might sustain over a period of time, with breaks for feeding and drinking. Obviously, sexual rivalry may be the cause for them to fight and earn sexual favours of a cow in heat. But it is not always true that two bulls in the same area engage in such combats that last days in and days out. Even where a measure of hostility is apparent between the two males, the one next below in hierarchy may avoid the fight and make way in favour of the dominant male. Considering the fact that males are wandering over a wide range of distribution and that several parties or individuals, usually, feed in the same expanse without any dispute, such fights do not appear to be motivated by territorial rights. Eventually, they may clash in assertion of dominance, when the paths of two bulls happen to cross. In such a situation, "tallest animal wins just as the fastest wins".

Elephants, in general and bulls in particular, are not born enemies to continue their battle either to take revenge or fight until death or do they compete over the same source of food. On the other hand, bulls may be considered as adversaries that compete to establish claim over a female in oestrus, but not as potential enemies. If the combats are inevitable, the looser will move away or if the dominance of the stronger is accepted, they may continue to feed together. I once photographed a single-tusked male that was found feeding in the company of two other males – one a tusker and another a *makhna*, both of whom seemed to have accepted the dominance of the earlier one in Nagarahole reserve. Dominance was established amongst them by rituals of skirmishes for fairly a long time.

An interesting thing I experienced in the company of these trios was that a single tusked male, was found pinning down an elephant near a water hole. My arrival at the spot at that high noon did not disturb their skirmishes. It was a rare occasion for me and I waited for an opportunity, so that I could get some close up shots of the rituals of mating. By keeping the camera ready to click, I expected the male to mount the cow any moment. Suddenly I noticed, to my astonishment, a dangling penis, almost touching the ground under the belly of that animal that was held pinned by single tusked male. It took fairly a long time for me to realise that it was a *makhna*.

7.9 Threat Charge

Gradually, I learnt that threat charges were usually not as much in an earnest attempts as they looked to be. The cow elephants had the most impressive displays, but I got the impression that at times, when I delayed my retreat to the last minute cows/males seemed to hesitate to drive home their charges. After few days, whenever I came across the same ladies, I decided to call them bluff and remained rooted to the spots, determined as I was. I was greatly thrilled to see them skid to a halt in a cloud of dust ten paces from the van or hides. These demonstrations became no more than a mock-charge. By far the most readily upset in elephant family groups, was a lady that showed her anger and annoyance at my presence. I pushed forward my open palm with fingers raised upwards. The lady remained stately and unruffled, lowering her head, She remained composed, letting loose her trunk, indicating that she accepted me as her well wisher. It seemed to me, we had a perfect understanding and secretly loved each other. The behavioural attributes of this lady, further encouraged me to evince interest in making friendly gestures of 'palming' with matriarchs of different family groups visiting the park. It worked.

Paste here Image No. Exhibit 73.tif : caption matriarch coming to a jerking halt at my palm drive against her crashing attack! I often wondered what terrible experience this cow must have suffered in the hands of man for her to hate and fear as so much!!

7.10   Putting Trunk in One's Mouth

One afternoon, I was passing by Wesley road, when a matriarch, accompanied by a younger cow started dumping dried lantana across the road on seeing approaching vehicle. This was, perhaps, to put an obstacle to prevent our vehicle, so that her family could feed peacefully. I asked the driver to stop the van and told an official colleague of mine, who was travelling with me, to keep a constant watch, because within about few minutes she might charge. The younger cow fiddled her trunk and then turned to the matriarch, followed by putting the tip of the trunk in her mouth. In turn, the matriarch placed her trunk on the face younger cow. This seemed to reassure the younger cow, constantly keeping an eye on our vehicle. We stayed put watching her next reaction. Almost after five minutes she delivered an impressive threat charge, kicking cloud of dust behind her. Our vehicle didn't stir, though I could reassured my friend, who was terribly stricken. She returned diagonally with curved flanks to join the herd, exhibiting anger through her red eyes. After few moments, she repeated her charge with similar intensity, when the driver switched on the starter. She stopped with a skidding jerk. "Enough is enough, let us bid good-bye to your dreaded elephants", cried my friend, who was shivering with sweat all over.

I thanked her for a spectacular show and sped off.

7.11   Redirected Aggression?

A cow elephant launched one of her perfected threat charge against me near Moyar Gorge. I remained stationery in the van. She swept past closer to me and discharged her aggression on an innocent bush, with such fury that a shower of leaves fluttered over her body. This was an example of 'redirected aggression'. That was the example of aggression of the lady, stimulated against me, but redirected at another object, the bush.

It is said a redirected aggression is usually elicited by an object that simultaneously evokes fear. This seemed to be true with this cow elephant, who for all her threats never dared to press her charge home. I often wondered what terrible experience this cow must have suffered in the hands of man for her to hate and fear as so much. Similar behaviour we find even in human beings. In a fury of anger we redirect our abuses on some innocent or weak person, before we realise our shortcomings.

Another distinct pattern of behaviour of practical as well as theoretical interest was the twiddling of the trunk, the swinging of one of the front legs to and fore and rocking from side to side almost crossing the other leg, which I saw when an elephant appeared to be deciding between attack and retreat. These were typical "displacement activities" in elephants. Such attributes were a great help to me in predicting charging elephant's next move. Larger the marked activities, lesser is the chances of elephant charge. Very often the most impressive threat displays emanated from the most frightened elephants, were unlikely to make a serious attack.

7.12   Reaction to Tiger Roars

This time, I was sitting in a hide built on ground at the edge of Karigoudanakatte tank. I waited for the leopard to revisit partially devoured chital kill made the previous night. The remains of the kill were dragged nearer to the hide, so that I could get close up shots of the predator. An elephant proof trench was provided around the hide as a safety against possible attack by elephants. I saw a small herd of elephants, numbering some twelve, emerging out of the jungle, raised their trunks, obviously, to grasp the wind from the remains of the kill. Instead of entering the water hole for a drink, the matriarch accompanied by two other cows, hesitantly, approached the carcass, sniffing the air around. I wanted to take photographs of a really charging elephants. Keeping my camera ready to shoot, I cupped my hands and with a heave of my diaphragm gave an excellent imitation of tiger's roar. Immediately, pandemonium erupted among the members of the family group. The remaining members of the family also joined their elders and all heads swung around in my direction.

They staged a magnificent assault on a broad front. Imposing angry giants with their trunks raised like radars and ears cocked, while I clicked my camera. They swept up to five metres of the hide, then stopped and peered around as if the target they had found was not the one they had been looking for. The eldest cow elephant waving its head and foot swinging in her highly agitated temperament, did not dare to come any closure, but found a thick bush on which to redirect her aggression. She picked up heaps of soil in her trunk by kicking the ground and threw over her back. She repeated this act until her anger subsided. The movements of my camera lens and metallic "click-click" sounds aroused her suspicion and enraged further. I could see the stress response on her person. The perceptions in elephants being faster, she might have hoisted a danger signal. Suddenly, all the members of the family dashed in the thicket from where they had emerged few minutes ago, while the lady stood sentry. I felt it was a survival strategy amongst the elephants. She exhibited her mixed personality-anger, protest and let-go against the audacity from an intruder like me in her domain. The combined response was typical of elephants society challenging their enemy, whether a tiger or a man. Annoyed by unceremonious treatment meted out to her, she retreated and joined the herd without even caring for water.

7.13 Keeping Tigers at Bay

I have seen a herd of elephants dramatically reacting to the presence of mating tigers in the vicinity. Mating tigers are a real threat to elephant society, in particular, the baby elephants. So, elephants always try to keep such tigers at bay.

While, I was watching those lovelorn tigers for nearly two days, sitting on a *machan*, at Nagarahole reserve, a herd of elephants arrived at the sight. My watch showed four O'clock in the afternoon. After a drink, the herd of eighteen elephants arrived in front of the *machan*. Some of them visited salt-licks and were busy in picking up pinch of mineral-earth, while others were engaged in feeding on browse, towering above the roof of bush canopy. Suddenly, I saw a commotion among the members of the herd. Elephants had reacted quickly either on getting scent or listening to growls of copulating tigers from the nearby forest. I knew that those tigers were inside the jungle as I had seen both male and female crossing the view line at mid-day. I was expecting them to appear, any time at the water hole for a drink and cool their body, but in vain.

The entire herd seemed agitated giving out muffled grunts and I could see unrest and commotion in the herd. With one danger signal by the matriarch, all the mothers with rumblings pushed their babies under their bellies and entered the thicket. Simultaneously, juvenile males – three of them in the herd started challenging with offensive growls and trumpets, against the presence of predators in the vicinity. Tigers from the opposite end of the forest started hurling defensive roars and grunts in reply to threatening calls of juvenile males. The entire forest reverberated. The *machan*, where I was sitting, not only vibrated vigorously, but also reverberated by the hitting waves of shattering shrills. I sat dumb-stricken, shivering and not knowing what to do. What was to happen next, I could not guess in that hi-drama, between two of the most powerful and mighty beasts and staunch adversaries of the Indian jungles.

Two of the three sub-adult males from the herd dashed helter-skelter towards the *nalla*, trumpeting continuously and kicking cloud of dust behind them. Sub-adult males had, it seemed to me, dashed to deal with the impending danger from tiger-mates, at the command the matriarch. This they did so, I guessed, with a view to block the way of approaching tigers along the *nalla* and in the direction of water hole. While all cow elephants maintained calm and continued their browsing activities, while the third sub-adult male kept on trumpeting as if to send a strong message of warning, "we are the mighty rulers of our home land, sooner you keep away safer it is for you". While the tiger duo from the other end kept thundering through their intermittent roars, as if to assert, "this is our territory as much as yours, better leave us alone".

Expecting some interesting events and thrilling moments to come by, I waited with my camera ready to click. After a while trumpeting and growling subsided; silence reined the jungle, but tensed up. The entire scene around me looked like a movie set. Every living creature there including me anxiously waited for the next event to appear in view.

Cow elephants with their young at heels, slowly emerged into the open at the view lines one after another, indicating that the things had returned to normalcy. Every member of the family looked relaxed and resumed normal feeding activities, but babies still stuck to their mothers' bellies. I kept watching for some memorable moments of the day, looking alternatively, at the camera and in the direction of male elephants that had entered the forest. I could then slowly raise my body temperature and relaxed, while waiting for some thing to come about, some great moments of my life.

Nothing happened until the golden rays over the forest valley disappeared. Just when moon appeared over the eastern horizon above the tree canopy, the emissaries of the matriarch appeared on the far end of a view line. They returned to join the herd as valorous knights after their successful mission. Eventually, they had driven away the enemies. Heroes were greeted by family members, who were anxiously waiting for their arrival. While elders proudly blessed the males congratulating them by caressing gently with their trunks over their heads, the youngsters kissed them graciously touching their trunks and placing their tips of trunk in their mouth. The kaleidoscope of heroic welcome to sub-adults – a typical to elephant society was truly heart rending, which none other than this writer alone could witness.

Having experienced the magnificent panorama of "sight and sound" of the jungle, which passed on, as if on a silver screen, I returned to the forest lodge. Though happy to claim to be the luckiest person to enjoy some of the rarest of rare events of nature, I felt disappointed in not getting an opportunity to capture that amazing 'jungle sight' on the film nor to record those astonishing 'jungle sounds' on the audio tape.

7.14 Reaction at The Sight of Vehicles

Normal reaction of a matriarch or a cow next in hierarchy is the blind charge on approaching or moving away vehicle in the jungle. But this particular cow elephant that stood next to the forest pool, irresolutely swinging her trunk and swaying her head from side to side, on seeing our approaching vehicle. Her calf by her side held his head up, waiving his trunk to sample the air of suspicious smell, was preparing for an assault at our vehicle. But he was prevented from doing so, by his mother obstructing him by placing her trunk at his chest. The cow seemed to be in conflicting scrutiny, whether to come head on and investigate the vehicle or to follow a prudent retreat. Eventually, she made up her mind and slowly advanced towards the metallic monster. Her ears were cocked half spread out, her trunk snaking inquiringly, then back and forth in a rhythmic swing.

I was entranced by her determined advance so close, as my nostrils could inhale her body smell. Never before had I been able to see the hairiness around the jaw, nor smell the warmth of wild elephant, which now wafted over me in concentrated waves. Her steps were deliberate and slow and finally she stood within two elephant paces.

Her daring advance was a great contrast to other elephants' impassioned threat charges. This cow gave the impression of being intensely curious about this metal manifestation, which intruded into her world. I wondered how far her tolerance could be developed and if after all, the centuries of men killing of elephants, she would ever accept my presence.

7.15 Defensive Behaviour

Elephant herds, generally, do not flee in panic at the first sign of danger. The lead cow slaps her ears, a signal to which other members of the family respond instantly by crowding together. Under her guidance adults and sub-adults form a closed or semi-circular defensive outwork of fortification with the calves pushed between them. When the danger is confirmed and imminent, young cows with infants attempt to break out of the group and enter the thicket, leaving behind the leader to deal with the situation.

The elephant is not fitted with mobility, to negotiate downhill side with ease. It becomes clumsy and handicapped in its fast movements along down slopes. If the terrain is hilly, it is recommended that one should flee downhill and escape. For, elephant's pace is slower downhill, while he can run comparatively faster uphill, besides it can reach up its target with trunk easily. While fleeing downhill it is advisable to choose a course covered with boulders and stones. Man can easily hop and skip over the stones, but not elephants. The animal will find it difficult to maintain balance. The elephant is believed to take utmost care while negotiating hilly terrain. It does not believe in taking risk and getting hurt. If the animal looses its balance by slightest slip, means death is inescapable.

7.16 Mother Mourning Over Death of Her Baby

An extreme attachment of an African cow to the dead baby was witnessed by the warden of the Aberdare N.P in Kenya. He narrated the heartrending observations to me during my visit in 1982; that calf was shot dead while mother defended her young. The body of the young was carried for three days after it had been shot. Even more bizarre was that the cow that refused to abandon the decomposing corpse of her calf carried it round for days resting on her tusks. The only other animals, I have seen caring so much of their young in Bandipur reserve and elsewhere are the Gray langur mothers, who may carry a dead babies for three days or more before abandoning them. I have never seen an Indian elephant carrying a dead baby, but I have seen mothers keeping in wait over their dead babies, trying desperately to lift them stand or with hopes of their revival. Such responsiveness to inert bodies is of obvious value in attempting to save a member of the family, who has temporarily collapsed. The helper may also later benefit from the sick animal's recovery when it resumes its role in the family unit's life. It may participate in the communal rearing and defence of the calves or if it is the matriarch herself, may continue to lead in times of stress and misery for the benefit of the family unit, by relying on her accumulated store of experiences and wisdom.

A Zoologist brought up a theory of natural selection must always try to explain such, apparently an altruistic behaviour in terms of the helper's own advantage or in cases, where one animal sacrifices itself to save another. Such behaviour must statistically tend to perpetuate the genes which prompted it, by increasing the chances of survival in a closely related member that carried same genes. What is far harder to explain in these rational terms, is the value of the extra-ordinary interest which elephants, sometimes, show in corpses of their clans by way of mourning, even when they are decomposed and bones scattered? What might be working in their mind, we do not know? The family should, however move on to feed in order to continue its progeny.

7.17 Why do Elephants Kill Humans?

There are innumerable recorded accounts of elephants – both bulls and cows killing human beings. More than 300 humans are killed by elephants each year in India. The most shocking among many accounts is killing of one Mr. Nair, Instructor, Wildlife Management Studies, Dehradun, in Bandipur reserve during 1979, as witnessed by Johnsingh, a research fellow. According to him, "on that fatal morning, Nair escorted by him went into Bandipur reserve on foot for a shoot with camera. Nair approached a magnificent bull on foot with his camera, despite the warning by Johnsigh that the wind was blowing towards the bull and it was risky for him to approach the bull on foot, that too, when the forest floor was unfavourable".

"Nair persisted in his enthusiasm to get some close shots of the bull. While he clicked and clicked, the bull developed suspicion against that metallic sound of the camera and got enraged. The beast charged provokingly. Unfortunately, Nair had a hefty body with bulging tummy, unbecoming of a Forester and was not quick enough to retreat and escape. He was swiftly overtaken by the bull and smacked him down with a kick. He was dead before hitting the ground. To make sure, the elephant knelt over his body and drove a tusk through the shoulder blade", narrated Johnsingh, woefully.

"Later it was discovered that bull's bad temperament was due to a deep ulcerated wound on his head, full of maggots, obviously, caused by a gun-shot", blurted Johnsingh.

Pestering wounds, such as this, inevitably, are a death warrant in wild animals. Animals go mad due to pain and agony. So, one must take all precautionary measures while approaching wounded animals in the wild. They become unpredictably dangerous and revengeful against humans, having come to know, man alone is responsible for their sufferings.

7.18 Predation on Elephants

In the fabric of creatures that form food chain on the earth planet, elephants are excluded, though occasionally, calves are mangled by a territorial tiger or by a tigress with dependent cubs. This predation, I feel, might be out of their brutal superiority or an open challenge towards an adversary, but not necessarily out of inevitable menu under the food chain.

Some observers have been astonished by the timidity of elephants, but perhaps the creatures have sufficient historical cause for fear. Not only man hunted them for at least twenty thousand years, but predators were more formidable than man, until he invented fire arms that were pushing elephants to the brink of extinction.

Amongst those were the Sabre-toothed Tiger of America and the Scimitar Cat of Europe and Africa, which preyed on elephants in the Pleistocene era. They were heavy duty carnivores with strong paws and huge stabbing canines, the remains of which have been found in caves surrounded by the bones and teeth of young mammoths, which seemed to have been their principal prey base. European elephants had also to fear the cave lions and cave bears, which were certainly larger than the predators of today. Probably, the heavy armament and thick skin of contemporary elephants had been developed by natural selection. Only the more strongly armoured and possibly also, the most timid matriarchs survived to pass on their attributes to their descendants. Man too, might have played a part in the elephant's evolution.

Even the stone-age man was a great hunter. Evidence of this comes from the discovery made in the nineteenth century by a palaeontologist by name Maska of a camp of mammoth hunters in Czechoslovakia. The camp lay between two mountain ranges, where herds of mammoths, probably concentrated during their annual north to south migration. The success of those hunters could be measured by the fact that bones of 900 mammoths were uncovered at one site; killing on such a massive scale might well have hastened retreat of the mammoths to Siberia, where their extinction might have occurred.

The fossil evidences have come mostly from Europe and North America, but there is little doubt that the ancestors of the Asian elephant suffered similar attacks, first from dangerous predators and later from the 'Stone-age' man.

Even today, there are many dubious hunting techniques, which probably dominated in the 'Iron-age' as well. Those included were: the stampeding of elephants from steep hill sides until they tumbled down to death, driving them into marshes where they got bogged in, burning them to death when they entered tall grass savannah and digging pit-falls within which sharp bamboo spikes and spears were installed and so on.

7.19 Home Range

The Bandipur Tiger Reserve is in no way an isolated expanse, but self contained ecosystem. The ranges of elephant herds overlapped extensively with one another. There was no question of the elephants carving out the available area into mutually exclusive niche, called home range, as other territorial animals like tiger or leopards do. Yet there was no completely homogeneous mixing either. Each family unit did not roam equally throughout the whole park. Most of them preferred certain favoured areas. Their day's march depended on availability of food and water. Each matriarch knew when and where to take her family and what to look out for. On rare occasions, when I did see a family in the company with other herds, there were no territorial disputes or hostility. During their movements of their forays, they seemed to coexist comfortably with sociable family units, they met on the way. Elephants pass straight through a concourse of other family units without any trumpeting or menacing noise on either side. They get tagged on to the slow movements of this large feeding assemblage and it seemed from this and other examples that when a strange elephant or family unit or orphan baby comes to a new area, it simply joins temporarily with exchange of greetings and gestures, whatever groups of other elephants happen to be there, without any territorial manifestations.

It appears, therefore, that elephants influence the movements of other herds by mere attraction than repulsion. Some of the family groups may have self-imposed restrictions, so as to move in their limited home range. If they were not avoiding other elephants, then why did they always stay in their little pocket-handkerchief of forests? The answer possibly may be that elephants are very conservative creatures with a strong attachment and respect to their home range, though the areas that only recently have become village limits with extensive cultivation. Certainly they persistently raid the crops like sugarcane, paddy, millets, coconut and banana after dark and enjoy the alien fruit which they find within their erstwhile home range. Standing crops turn out to be malls/provision stores where they do much damage by trampling rather than eating in shear confusion during their nocturnal excursions, when they are branded as 'crop raiders'.

7.20 Habitat Modification

Asiatic Elephant Group had organised a seminar at Bandipur reserve during 1985. In the course of field visits, when I mentioned about damages inflicted to the trees in the tourism zone by elephants, one of the delegates muttered, "It is not damage, but a process of habitat modification".

"Yes", accepting his corrected version, I continued my deliberations, "the elephants are an essential part of nature's scheme. By opening up rank grass and thick bush growth, they also open a way for other animals which would not otherwise, be able to penetrate into these areas. I believe and advocate that the best way to manage the habitat of the reserve is to interfere as little as possible with natural cycles. Wild animals feel at home, where there is safe habitat with enough to feed and drink".

"Wildlife managers, generally, advocate fire as a management tool in the development of habitat. By adopting rigid fire control we are allowing grasses to grow woody and the forest to grow thick. Denied of palatable grasses, grazers like elephants, gaur and deer move away in search of greener pastures. To encourage evenly distribution of grazers over the entire habitat, it is advisable to advocate 'control burning or even singeing in mosaic pattern' every alternate year", continued my appraisal.

"Fires in the wildlife reserves and national parks are accepted as an important tool of management practices. Forest fires are levellers and keep the weeds under check and help open up new grounds for grasses to grow", I concluded my briefing.

But some hard core conservationists present there did not approve of the prescription of use of fire as a management tool and on the other hand, they went on to argue in favour of thinning teak plantations and removal of dead and drying trees from the reserves, the ideas of which I disapproved, stating that they are contrary to the conceptual approach to biodiversity conservation.

7.21 Seasonal Grouping and Herd Movements

Bandipur elephants, like elsewhere in south India, formed large herds in the wet season, when food availability was found to be plentiful and competition was presumably low. Large groups were also found on the periphery of the reserve during cropping season, where the elephants came in conflict with humans. In contrast, under the conditions of extreme drought, when food availability became critical, signs of stress among the elephants were observed, leading to breaking away of family into smaller units. Signs of stress among the herds were also seen in times of mounting pressure by predators in the vicinity and when poaching activities increased. After the drought, however, when the bare earth was once more covered by green sprouts and browse species plentiful, the elephant families bonded together.

7.22 Adaptability to Different Habitat Conditions

As regards home ranges of Asian elephant herds and bulls, very little work is done in India. A limited work on the home ranges and habitat utility of herds and bulls have been carried out at Madumalai-Bandipur complex extends over 450-500 sq km, the home range of a bull varies from 150-300 sq km. This gives an idea of the adaptability of elephant behaviour to different habitat conditions.

There is no doubt that if it were not for man's pressure on the boundaries, the home ranges of elephants in Bandipur would have been much larger; although for the present food is abundant and they don't yet need to wander far beyond the park boundaries. The greatest threat to their future lies in the ever-tightening circle of settlements, cutting off any possibilities of dispersal, should the ecological cycle turn to an unfavourable phase. If ever elephants dared to venture back into their former range, as it is presently in vogue, conflict with man would be inevitable. It is time to take necessary preventive measures right from day one, anticipating increasing trouble in the coming days ahead.

7.23   Hunger-The Stronger Instinct Than Fear

Lone bulls and herds are in the habit of raiding crops during harvest-season and get injured or killed by country explosives that are planted concealed in tubers, fruits, jaggery or other eatables. The palatable crops grown by farmers adjoining the national parks draw the attention of elephants to cross the boundaries and cause extensive damage to crops. The compensation paid during the decade 1981-82 to 1991-92. On an average Rs.560,000 (US$16,000) are spent each year by Karnataka Government, while the Indian Government is spending almost equal amount each year, under the 'Project Elephant'. It is so enormous that the same money could have been sufficient to provide permanent solution to keep elephants at bay from agricultural fields, by creating hundreds of km stretch of barricades using rejected rail-lines, in addition to elephant-proof trench combined with solar electric fence and dry-rubble walls. It could have thus helped creating a permanent asset and also help mitigate human-elephant conflicts to a great extent. Even now, wisdom should prevail in our planning process to find a lasting solution.

7.24   How Should be Your Conduct With Elephants While in Jungle?

While meeting elephants face to face in their domain, I conducted myself, as a well wisher and affectionate; approached cautiously in their broad sight, but still, made no noise and looked around for any strange intruder. Then I moved very slowly towards them, so that they accepted me as harmless creature on two legs. I did not venture to cross critical line. However, always maintained a safe distance of about 50 metres and had my safety and security at the back of my mind. Safety in elephant dominated jungle is the top-most priority than other considerations. With these prerequisites, I experienced a feeling of completeness and serenity.

The stability and security between elephant tribe and me had taken a new dimension, instead of hating me, they embraced me. They gave me an opportunity in indulgence and developing confidence in my activities.

My conduct with matriarchs and tuskers, though, I considered safe, might have tempted others to think, they also could do the same with other elephants. Such an assumption could have proved them suicidal. Several photographers who have injudiciously approached elephants on foot have been thrown out or killed. For this reason, I must, emphatically, warn any visitor to Bandipur or any other reserve inhabited by elephants, not to walk up to wild elephants on foot. I'm not trying to make an issue or exaggerate the situation, but a word of caution to my visiting friends. I do not want any fatal accidents, provokingly or un-provokingly taking place in or out of protected areas and blame some wild elephants have reacted in an understandably hostile way against humans, their age-old enemy.

Chapter VIII

Musth - the Desire That Chases

It is often difficult to determine the sex of an elephant in the wild, when they are not facing you. The male has no scrotum externally and the testes are placed abdominally (close to the kidneys). It is, particularly, difficult to differentiate the sex when a *Makhna* – the tuskless male is in the company of a herd. A *Makhna* can be identified by the presence of vertical bulge at the rump, underneath the tail/anus. The bulge supposedly part of the male genital organ is commonly seen both in *makhna* and tusker. A massive head and a strong trunk in *makhna* compensate the absence of tusks in their skirmishes, or a serious battle against rivals, particularly over a female in oestrus.

Studies on the Asian elephants have not been as comprehensive, as in case of its African cousins. My own study in Bandipur reserve showed that female elephants first gave birth between 13 and 15 years of age, but they continued to reproduce every 4.7 years, a rate that was comparable to the productive trend of African populations. However, the elephant population of Bandipur also showed large fluctuations in births, similar to those observed in Africa. Over all, a steady population trend seemed to exist through the years in Bandipur, with slight fluctuations during summer between March-May. In Tropical Mixed Deciduous Forests of Bandipur, the interaction between vegetation and elephants tended to exist at near equilibrium in a normal year.

I could not categorically say there was a 'population explosion', when we counted more than 1,000 elephants during rainy season or did we conclude that for some reason, the numbers had decreased, when they were counted at less than 700 elephants during summer. Neither was it the result of a rise in the birth rate, nor a decrease in the death rate. However, the population density of elephants was worked out @0.5 and 0.8 per sq km, depending on the seasonal variations and habitat conditions. Elephants moved in and out of the reserve during their periodical shifts between adjoining sanctuaries, such as Madumalai, Wayanad, BRT Hills and Nagarahole, the extent of which was spread over 2,500 sq km. In the profit and loss account, no appreciable variations were noticed in respect of elephant populations, between rainy season and summer. In the overall assessment, it could be reckoned that a steady population trend existed in the Bandipur reserve.

If elephant populations and the habitat conditions were indeed undergoing cycles of changes, it would be very difficult to prove the process of evolution playing over with few years' observations. Elephant populations are usually well buffered against the vicissitudes of the environment. A long-lived mammal, such as the elephant, has very low mortality rate. Between the ages of 5 and 40 years the annual death rate may be less than 7 per cent in most populations. Even juvenile mortality is relatively low and normally does not exceed 10 per cent a year. Elephants also breed very slowly, with a gestation period of 20-22 months, followed by one and a half or two years of anoestrus. It is evident that the elephant does not breed as rapidly as most other mammals do. The rate of recruitment of the young in Bandipur was found to be 8.1 per cent, according to my study.

In a normal situation, the elephant is adapted to breed slowly and maintain a population density level of 0.5 per km^2. An animal with such longevity usually lives nearer to the carrying capacity of the habitat. The population dynamics of a long lived elephant species can be understood only if long-term studies are carried out. Poaching amongst Indian elephants is restricted to only to males for their ivory. In a way, this is far safer situation with regard to Asian species, in that the females, which are more important in contributing to progeny, are immune from ivory poachers, as compared to African species, where even females are targeted by poachers because females to possess ivory as in males. In Bandipur reserve my own studies have shown the sex ratio of 1:10, i.e. one adult male for every 10 adult females, seems to have positive effect on elephant fertility.

In certain regions of the country, the sex ratio in elephant populations has since been reported to be disproportionate, thereby jeopardising the normal breeding phenomenon. In such a situation, it remains to be seen how these populations are going to respond in future. One possibility is that *makhnas*, the tuskless bulls, which are relatively few in numbers, could increase in relation to tusked males in the near future. The elephant populations of these regions could then begin to resemble predominantly dominated by *makhnas*. The regions already affected are: the elephant populations of Periyar in Kerala and the North-eastern India, representing West Bengal, Assam, Arunachal Pradesh, including Meghalaya, where majority of them are *makhnas*, since majority of tuskers have been shot out. If poaching continues to be severe, then the situation may resemble Sri Lankan elephant populations, where over 90 per cent of the males are tuskless i.e. *makhnas*.

In case of Bandipur, the elephants, in particular, some kind of haemostatic or self-regulatory mechanism was found to be at work, as population density was steadily growing. There was a regular rate of reproduction, as almost one third the matured cows in any herd had babies at their heels, as recorded during census operations.

8.1 Reproductive Organs

The reproductive system in elephants is quite complicated. The genital organs, both in male and female elephants are located ventrally that pose bit of a problem in differentiating, their sex at a very first sight. The relative positions of the female reproductive organ and male reproductive organ are shown in fig.

Reporductive organs

8.1.1   In Female

The two ovaries are situated close to the kidneys. The fallopian tubes are about 30 cm long and are quite difficult to see, as their junction with the uterine horn is fairly deep in muscular tissues. The uterus has two horns and a common middle but partly divided lumen which leads into a long uro-genital passage. This, in turn, opens externally at the vulva. There is a well-developed clitoris. The two mammary glands are situated between the front legs and are known as breasts (not udder as some Vets, erroneously call it)

Elephant gestation period is 20 to 22 months – a fact established from a range of observations that wade back over many years. Towards the 16th month of pregnancy the female's mammary glands begin to swell visibly. I must emphasize that 22 months is the average duration within a recorded range between 19 to 23 months. Many of the older books and journals will tell us that the duration of pregnancy in elephants varies according to the sex of the foetus, being longer in males than in females, but I am not aware of any scientific evidence to support this.

Normally, the change in the elephant's dietary system from dry grass with its low crude protein content during the dry season, to that of fresh green grass and browse with high protein content at the height of rainy season, stimulated ovulation and fertile mating. On the contrary, in case of very few elephants, according to my study, it was revealed, that ovulation was influenced in the dry season. The mean age of first ovulation is about 12 years.

In all the mammals, the period from late pregnancy through birth to lactation is the time when mother and offspring are the most vulnerable to extremes of environmental crises and the elephant is no exception. In the Bandipur reserve, the peak conceptions in the rainy season meant that the majority of births took place 22 months later at the start of the rains, which without doubt, is the best time of the year from the nutritional point of view.

8.1.2   In Male

The position of testes in the male foetus or pre-pubertal or adult elephant, they are located within the body cavity and embedded on dorsal side of the body-wall and very close to the kidneys. Production of sperms: in all other mammals, the scrotum with testes is suspended ventrally, so as to maintain below body temperature, when in the scrotal sac and spermatozoa are stored in a discrete epididymis immediately on top of each testis. But the elephant cannot cool his testes in the absence of sweat glands on the body, as already illustrated in preceding chapter. The mean body temperature of the elephant is between 36-37°C. This suggests that the whole process of spermatozoa production in the elephant must be, particularly temperature – resistant. Furthermore, the elephant has no epididymis. In its place, a long and highly convoluted duct connects each testis to the opening of the seminal vesicle and this duct performs the main function of the epididymis of the scrotal namely transport, concentration, maturation and storage of the spermatozoa.

The figure illustrates, why the male elephant requires such a proportionately long and unusually pendulous penis? The vagina of the female is ventrally situated, unlike other mammals, where it is placed just below the anus under the base of the tail. The male has to hook the end of his penis into it. To do this sexual act, the penis has two dorsally situated elevator penis muscles, which unite to form a thick common tendon, and in turn, inserts on the top of the penis near the tip. These muscles account for the characteristic 'S' – shaped flexor of the penis at erection and enables the male to hook the tip of his penis, snake hood like, in the vagina. The length of the penis that enters the vagina is rather limited and if spermatozoa are to reach the uterus, which is still about 60 cm away, a large volume of ejaculate is required. This in turn, accounts for a very well developed accessory organ of the male. There may be as much as 850 ml to one litre of fluid injected in the seminal vesicles.

It must be emphasized that although an animal may be classified as mature on the basis of the production of spermatozoa, it does not necessarily follow that the same animal will mate with females, as the older males tend to keep the younger males away.

The mean age of the start of spermatozoa production is about 15, when the combined testes mass reaches 650 to 700 grams. Recent comparative studies have indicated that in most elephant populations – male and female elephants reach maturity at about the same age. In other words, when females ovulate for the first time, males of about the same age have just started the production of spermatozoa and at this age they leave the family units to wander as satellites or join to form bachelor group.

Although, it is quite clear that females are seasonal breeders, there is yet no positive evidence for cyclical reproductive activity in the male. The testes continue to grow throughout the life and in normal bulls over 40 years of age; each testis will weigh over 3000 grams.

Mating takes place less than one minute on each occasion. The length of oestrous cycle in females is about 3 weeks. The ovaries provide a fascinating study in themselves, because of amazing variation in the number of ovulations that occur in the elephant before each pregnancy. Elephant can be either monovular or polyovular and that ovulation is spontaneous.

8.2 Sexual Maturity

Before attaining adulthood, the males wander away, rather more appropriately, driven away from the herd by the matriarch. This phenomenon is the nature's way of avoiding inbreeding. By wandering far and wide male has to prove his winning streak. Sometimes, in the absence of the breeding bull, a female may be found flirting with a sub-adult male. 'Flirting' in elephants is a form of communication that she is in oestrus. More she articulates, the more exciting she gets. It is just another form of 'social grace', like 'thank you' and 'please'.

'Flirtation' in animals, as in humans, could be described as "a behaviour leading another to believe that sexual intimacy is possible, while preventing that possibility from becoming a certainty". Flirting and intimacy in one breath are very akin to the first phase of stimulation of sexual behaviour. Flirtation takes advantage of a situation, where an animal can't have sex, but she can have sexual behaviour, partially, availability of the male adding pep and fire. It is an excitement without sex; it reaffirms the sexuality of both male and female. But such attempts are soon made abortive by the matriarch, supported by other members of the family, which gather around amidst abyss. Such a rare sequence was witnessed by me on one morning at Madumalai Sanctuary. A perfect flirt is one who can achieve a balance between arousal and deflection, which means to say, 'attention without intention'.

There is a belief that when a bull is in a state of *musth* is incapable of mating. This is not true. Mating or copulation is a private affair in elephants. While bull becomes horny almost instantly without comparable stimulation, cow especially, a teenager may take longer to get warmed up. She can only be aroused by a gentle stimulation by partner. She may not like to be 'bull-handled' or moved around like a piece of bamboo shoot.

She may like to make love on a clear sheet with a tender, sensitive and subtle bull. For, her sex is not just an appetite to be filled but an intensely personal celebration. A male stays with the female in heat for two to three days, guaranteeing that he must be the father of her offspring. The bull in *musth*, which I photographed at Bandipur was in the company of a cow inheat for two to three days. The dark liquid was flowing down the cheeks profusely from his temporal region.

While, I was talking to a group of trainees from Rangers' Training College, Coimbatore, about the behaviour of a bull in the elephant herd, as observed by me in the wild, an instructor, with fairly good knowledge on wildlife management, vehemently argued that even a school boy from his village knew that elephants would not copulate except in water. But in nature, given the chance, I asserted, elephants can try those ground tested techniques, guaranteed to make the earth move in synchronization; they may mate both in water as well as on land. Even in water they have to position themselves correctly. The missionary position limits her clitoris stimulation as well as her ability to move around beneath his body. The female has to stand erect on level ground at knee deep water when the bull can copulate, but not while swimming. Yet others claiming to possess knowledge of elephant lore, consider it a bad omen to witness elephants mating. They say, "It forebodes disaster". This remained a gossip: after all, copulation in elephant is a natural phenomenon, just as in other mammals.

Pliny (23-79 A.D), the Roman author, believed that elephants mated in privacy. The belief is current in India as well. And it is not only laymen who hold this view; even those elephant keepers maintain the view. They say that elephants engaged in love making or on a honey-moon trip, will not tolerate the presence of other elephants nearby. Some writers, who ought to know more on sexology even go so far, to assert that the mating behaviour in elephants resembles that of human, trying different positions, by keeping the discussion light. The chief reason adduced for this might be the bull on top and rear entry position allows plenty of room to get a good buzz going.

I have seen a large cow in heat with two and a half year old calf that remained at her heel moved away, occasionally, rejoining the herd; the bull constantly chased her during their foreplay. They remained together for 2-3 days. While the bull sampled her vagina, the 'peaking exercise' by stroking bull's penis with the tip of her trunk, until the rate of arousal of orgasm raised. The principle being, perhaps, to bring him to several peaks and back down again without his climaxing and breathe until arousal subsided a bit. Next rev him up to a heart pounding level. Finally, she could take him all the way. Later the bull could apply that technique successfully during copulation.

I have also seen a cow elephant coming to season for the first time, found non-cooperative with the suitor. She was force-confined to a spot by other females in the herd, amidst whom, the cow watched him looking at his tips of trunk and penis only to think what they would be doing to her later. The law of nature dictates that only the strongest male will sire the cow in heat to pass on the genes to next progeny. In such a situation, the cows in the herd tend to cooperate in the performance of successful conjugal acts. The belief that only a rutting bull will mate is erroneous. A profuse flow of rut fluid is certainly an indication of maturity in bull. However, males who show no symptoms of being in a state of rut have also been found copulating successfully.

As in most other mammals, the condition of the cow is advertised by scent. But the elephant is unique, in that visually fragrant signs of her being in season are not manifested (*mahouts* know that their wards have come into season mainly by circumstantial evidence, such as the interest shown in the cow by the bulls), but the cow swings in her tail between hind legs sharply so as to slap the vagina with the brush like tip and swings back; tail is held aloft in the air and waved about as a scent-flag. A belief by some naturalists that the cow in oestrus stamps its leg in order to attract males is erroneous. The leg-pads in elephant are cushioned and function as shock absorber; it can't stamp to produce vibration on the ground like hoofed animals.

8.3   Musth – The Desire that Chases

Musth (Hindi, *musth* = intoxicated or ruttish; Kannada, *mada*) is aphenomenon known to occur both in African and Asian elephants. It is associated with a secretion from the *musth* or temporal glands, located subcutaneously, midway between the eye and the ear, on either side of the elephant's head. The exact nature and functions of this gland and the associated behaviour is not scientifically known. However, it is generally agreed that the pattern of which *musth* appears in the Asian elephant is quite different from that of the African. The African elephant exhibits, perhaps, a "general condition", while the Asian elephant a "specific function".

In case of African elephant *Loxodonta africana*, both male and female secrete *musth* pre – and post-puberty. When the female is in heat, the male secretes a different type of *musth* liquid than usual. This secretion may function as an individual and group's recognition, as well as communication system. It may indicate reproductive state as well.

In respect of Asian elephant *Elephas maximus*, only the male secretes *musth* post-puberty (15-55 years), depending on physiological functioning of the body and nutrient status. Secretion lasts 1-4 months, averaging 3 months. There is reported to be a correlation between secretion and level of testosterone. When in *musth* the level of testosterone is reported to rise by 60%. The *musth*, possibly functions to communicate sexual status of an individual to other males and females. *Musth* flow is also observed in females, particularly in the matriarch and the female next in hierarchy, when they are believed to be under stress, say during drought when food and water become scarce or under threat by increased poaching.

The following order of events take place prior to and during secretion of *musth*:

1.   **The orifice of the temporal gland dilates.**

2.   **For the first few days, the secretion is clear and often is mistaken for tears.**

3.   **The *musth* flow becomes dark and sticky and this is associated with sluggishness in wild tuskers, while increased aggression in camp males.**

The periodic occurrence of *musth* in adult elephants, marked by a dark, oily exudation from temporal glands with a tender swelling of the temples and forehead, is something peculiar to Asiatic elephants and its full significance is not yet known. Little that is an original, in addition to what G.P. Sanderson wrote about *musth* a century ago, available in the literature on *Elephas maximus*. Based on the behavioural patterns with the camp males, *musth* does seem to have some sexual significance, though it is not, as popularly supposed, merely an expression of abundant virility. *Musth* afflicts old elephants as well and some animals in *musth* are in very poor condition due to heavy logging work. The manifestation and consequences of *musth* in the captive elephants have been left out of reckoning as so many artificially imposed conditions supervene. It is not safe to draw any conclusion from the behaviour of captive elephants in that condition. Almost invariably, it is an adult bull that gets into *musth*, but in rare cases a cow may do so. G.P. Sanderson records two instances of cows in *musth*, 'in newly-caught females in the prime of life, and in very distressed condition'.

The *musth* fluid is a thick, oily substance, dark brownish in colour and has a pungent smell also. In the case of middle aged and old elephants, it is almost black (like that of tar) in colour; in young elephants it is usually brown. The discharge is scanty or profuse according to the age and health of the elephant.

The flow may occur for the first time in males at the age of fifteen years. But it is so small in quantity that the trickle does not reach farther than 2 inches. Up to the age of 35 the flow is not abundant and the behaviour of the animal also not very much affected. Between the age of 35 and 55 the discharge becomes so profuse that the male's face is wet all the way down the cheek on both sides and sometimes, I have seen it dripping to the ground. This is when the state of *musth* would have reached climax. Such a condition in tuskers exhibits true masculinity.

POLISHED TUSKS ENHANCE THE PERSONALITY OF THE BULL

Tusker in *musth*, the desire that chases for female in heat.

When the animal is in rage, the flow tends to increase. The smell exuded by this fluid is very pungent and acrid. Some elephant tamers find the odour too strong for them. In Sanskrit texts, however, it is not considered malodorous. In 'Kiratarjuneya' it is likened to the scent of 'Saptaparna' (*Alstonia scholaris)* or Cardamom flowers. According to biologists, the temporal glands become enlarged and present a somewhat inflamed and swollen appearance, when an elephant is in *musth*. My observations, followed by photographic evidences also confirm this state.

The flow in bulls goes on for about forty days. For the first few days it exudes in minute quantities, then gradually increases and having reached the maximum towards the middle of this period, the flow begins to decline, drying up altogether at the end of 40 days. This particular period is marked by lethargic, as if in sleepwalk with frequent urination. Indeed, the animal appears to be urinating all the time. The urine at this time is deep yellow in colour and has a pungent smell not quite unlike that of the *musth* fluid.

Along with these changes in the physiology, some other changes also occur in the animal's temperament and behaviour. Sometimes, there may be more serious consequences. The elephant's behaviour begins to change gradually forty days before the *musth* secretion starts to flow and continues for forty days after it has ceased, thus, the state of *musth* covers nearly 120 days. Some keepers place the duration of the *musth* period at anything from a few weeks to five months, depending upon the animal's age and state of health.

I was not generally critical in my observations of *musth* in females, while watching them or photographing them. Of the two cows in *musth* observed during the annual census, in one of them was heavy. It was the matriarch of the family. I could take series of photographs of it along with other animals of the herd while they had a drink in waist-deep water before they had dip shower. It could be that the rare incidence of *musth* in cow elephants is in some way related to pregnancy or stress.

There is a great deal of confusion surrounding the phenomenon of *musth*. Among camp elephants, the adult bulls become aggressive and very dangerous – they may even try to kill their *mahouts*. Recent studies by Jainudeen and others show that *musth* occurs once a year in all adult male elephants at a time when the male hormone testosterone is at a very high level. R.C.Sharma, Field Director, Pench Project Tiger, Madhya Pradesh informed this author that a male in *musth* pierced his tusk into the gullet of a female, which did not yield to fulfil his desire.

In the wild almost all males that have been photographed by me, were at different stages of *musth* state, in some cases dripping profusely. But they were never found aggressive, towards me. They were as close as 30 ft. from my vehicle, some even I faced eye-ball to eye-ball.

Some bulls in *musth*, often exhibited a marked lethargy, as remarked by Sanderson. This lethargy does not manifest itself in immobility or slowness of movements. I subscribe to this statement that the animal would exhibit a marked indifference to the surroundings and that the bull in *musth* often appeared to be in a state of somnambulation, though its stride was not shortened. But in the wild no animal, big or small, can afford to be complacent, howsoever powerful an animal be, it has got to be alert and guard himself from its natural enemies in the jungle, like tigers and above all against man, the most dangerous animal on earth. I would rather describe the state of *musth* in tuskers as comparable to drunken state in men. Just as drinking provokes desire in humans, *musth* in tuskers provokes desire. To fulfil his desire the tusker wanders far and wide in search of company of females in heat.

Valmiki, in his Ramayana, refers to the elephants of superior breeds, describing them as "enormous like mountains, intoxicated by *musth* and strong with *musth* fluid constantly flowing down their cheeks/temples. To see tuskers without the *musth* fluid was considered inauspicious in those days.

Kalidasa describes the state prior to the flow of *musth* fluid as *antharmadavastha*, the state of sub-nascent. In the writings of King Dilipa,he says, "although he had given up all the royal trappings, his well-built body and his face conveyed 'regal majesty', just as an elephant conveys his state of sub-nascent *musth* even though no *musth* fluid is streaming from his temples".

In a party of elephants it was noticed that the cows were attentive and considerate to the tusker in *musth*. Bulls in *musth*, even females in *musth*, frequently squirt water over their swollen *musth* glands and forehead and apparently, the ravage serves to unclog the *musth* pores by flaking. I have seen a bull wandering aimlessly near about a water hole at Nagarahole. It even passed by the side of my jeep that was parked in the middle of the road near the *machan*, where from I was watching the animal. Its body was smeared with thick clay and *musth* was found flowing profusely. It was, in fact, frantically in search of a female in season. This was evidenced from the fact that it soon joined the herd that arrived at the water hole from the opposite direction for a drink and then found flirting with a female.

A peculiarity noticed in tuskers in *musth* is that they often carry tight-packed clay on their tusks, so closely adherent that even a swim in fast-flowing water fails to wash it. This adherent clay is acquired when the tusker gores earth at river banks and even the clay-bottoms of forest pools while in *musth*; this goring is not something done in frenzy, but evidently, indulgedto force outflow of *musth* from the temporal glands by the pressure exerted on the swollen glands. The period of occurrence and affliction of *musth* flow varies with individuals and even from one bout to another in the same individual. I have witnessed a big bull with short tusks, goring hard into the clay bed at the edge of water at K.M. Katte of Bandipur, presumably, to force open the flow of *musth* from its temporal glands. I could shoot it with my camera sitting on a tree *machan*.

Some elephant-tamers of bygone era, preferred to call this discharge as *maile* (body waste) rather than *mada* (*musth*). But the odour from body waste is unpleasant and can be smelt from a distance, while in the case of *musth* fluid the smell is rather pleasant. Elephant-cows have not been known to become erratic in behaviour while they discharge dark liquid. But bulls may become imbalanced and at times, dangerous, as experienced by many *mahouts* of camp elephants.

Experienced *mahouts* can foretell the coming of the state of *musth* in a male long before the fluid begins to flow. The eyes of the animal become altered. Male displays defiant temper. His behaviour becomes erratic; responses and actions disorganised from those in the normal state.

Experiences with working elephants have also shown *mahouts* do provide the company of one or two cows with males approaching the state of *musth*. It is just to provide fair sex for the sake of company to prevent possible erratic behaviour that cows are kept with the males during festivities, processions, in work-camps and zoos.

When the animal is in the state of *musth*, he may obey commands, but not very willingly and some times disobey also. He tends to act by impulse. Even the most obedient and docile elephants have been known to defy *mahouts.* And though the *musth* male need not necessarily be aggressive and dangerous, occasionally he may become so, if annoyed or hurt. When a male in *musth* turns unmanageable and runs amuck he can prove a potential danger to human life and property, as witnessed in many cases.

After all these are the cases of aberration. As in human beings, remedial measures should immediately be provided to appease the animal. It is customary for people to treat every rutting elephant as a 'mad' elephant. This is wrong. Madness in elephants is altogether different physiological disorder. They may become mad if they are bitten by rabid dogs or rabid big cats. Some people might consider the rutting state, a cause of madness in camp elephants. I have seen camp males may become frenzied from being ill-treated by man, in majority of cases. Man can turn healthy bulls into 'killer animal' through ill-treatment, such as starvation, stealing ration, beating madly and so on. And if the mahout is sensible and well trained he can handle his charge with humanitarian touch and maintain healthy relationship.

As the intensity of *musth* increases, the elephant tends to become more peevish and aggressive. He resents everyone, even those who were nearest to him and on whom he was dependent the most. The first to loose favour are the attendants responsible for grooming and giving him a wash and food.

We have the technical knowledge in the modern scientific world. Any animal showing signs of running amuck should immediately be confined to stationary confinement and soothing treatment be meted out. In extreme cases, by tranquillising the animal, it could be chained and brought under control. The animal needs proper management just as in humans in their old age problems. A man who handles such an animal needs to have utmost patience, compassion and suitable knowledge. *Mahout* in such circumstances should serve as friend, philosopher and guide.

Experienced *mahouts* tie up elephants before they become uncontrollable. They are kept at the crawls. Sumptuous quantity of food and water are given to keep the animal calm rather than starving. On the contrary starving enrages the animal. They are also given some soporific substance mixed with food. In yesteryears *mahouts* used to feed a dose of opium inside a ball of kneaded flour or jaggery. In modern times, according to advice of Vets, they rely more on bromide, which is given in fairly large doses. Tobacco is also supposed to help. About half a kilo of snuff fed everyday may help keep the animal from making nuisance of himself.

As long as distemper caused by *musth* is not wholly subsided, the animal has to be fed from a distance. No work is taken from such an animal for three or four months, though some light works can be extracted in the initial stages of *musth*.

The exact mechanism of *musth* state and its connection with maturity of the animals, reproductive organs and sex impulse, in general, are yet to be studied fully. In case of African elephants some extensive work has been done by Synthia Moss and others. But the same findings cannot be applied in case of Asian elephants.

The problem of *musth* and its consequential developments in elephant-bulls shall remain unsolved, principally because they can not be castrated or vasectomy done, in view of the fact that testes are located deep inside the body, unlike in other domesticated animals, whose testes are located in scrotum suspended ventrally.

Sudden change in weather conditions, especially, when the males are shifted to a distant places may cause physiological changes, unless they are acclimatized to the wholly new climatic conditions. The state of *musth* in changed conditions may aggravate. In some of the tuskers from Kerala which were transported to Delhi to take part in Asiad 1982 sports, the state of *musth* in few tuskers was aggravated on account of change in weather (winter cold) conditions; the condition of one of the tuskers manifested severely and that it was not permitted to take part in the Asiad show, but kept chained. He was detained at Delhi for more than a month until the chronic state of *musth* was diminished.

A typical instance of an elephant having run amuck, following an onset of rut, was that of Udayagiri. This tusker was part of the Presidential stables in New Delhi and used to participate in national festivities. He had first been captured when eight years old in the Assam jungles and was carefully, trained on the lines of Akbar, the famous elephant of Kaziranga. Udayagiri attacked and trampled to death an attendant, who was attempting to put him to chains. Immediately afterwards he calmed down after getting food which was accepted readily by him. After recovery from *musth* he was freed from chains. One day when he was being taken for a walk, he suddenly ran amuck. He attacked a passing by military vehicle and then chased a man who narrowly escaped. The mahout with great courage held on for about three hours and did his best to control the elephant. When all his attempts proved futile, he jumped down and made for the nearest roof top. Consequently, the dreaded beast was shot dead.

The bull in *musth* may show incredible strength, when in frenzy. When they are annoyed from hooting and bustling noise of passing vehicles they simply pick up a motorcar and toss it into the air, very much in the manner of a child playing with a toy. Many such instances of running amuck of temple elephants of Guruvayur in Kerala state were narrated by Dr. Cheeran, Vet, in charge, when he was invited to visit Bandipur as a resource person to train our local Vets, in tranquillising technique and treatments.

During the first week of March 1998 a young tusker strayed out of Bhadra Sanctuary, near about Koppa, as in earlier years. He continued to remain there for more than three months, causing damage to crops and property, according to Mr. Sanjay Mohan, then Deputy Conservator of Forests, Koppa. Local people were enraged and agitated. The situation forced the Forest officials to capture it when all efforts failed to drive it back to Bhadra forest. All required preparations were made for its capture as a last recourse: *kumkies* – the camp elephants were brought in sufficient numbers, heavyduty trucks arranged and tranquillising equipment with drugs stored in sufficient quantities. Surprisingly, the belligerent tusker de-camped on the previous day of proposed "operation capture" and back-tracked at an unimaginable speed; it was found within its home range of Bhadra Sanctuary within two days, having traversed a distance of about 40 km.

What could have made the belligerent tusker to sudden retreat at such a speed? Was it a danger signal hoisted by the camp elephants through 'ultrasound' or a message of threat warning sent? These were the series of inquiries made by the DCF and his assistants at Koppa, during my visit there. At the spur of the moment, I had no tested answers with me to satisfy their inquisitive minds. These sensitive perceptions needed detail study. However, I made out an inquisitive questionnaire to DCF and his deputies present there, "Was there any captive male in *musth*?"

"The answer was, yes".

"Sure enough, the *musth* from an elderly or superior male in the vicinity, must have acted as a threat signal conveyed through infrasonic waves to that cantankerous tusker to flee from the region", I concluded.

8.4 Infatuated Sexual Act and Love-play

As among most herbivores, the wild passion or infatuated sexual act occupies frequently while playing. But sexual act in adults occupies only a very short time, less than a minute. But the foreplay in elephant preceding the sexual act is elaborate. Coition is usually repeated many times during two or three days of their togetherness; the bull and the cow may move out of the herd or even amidst the herd, they pair.

While it is true, unlike most other animals, the male in elephants cannot copulate unless the female is co-operative. The peculiar anatomy of the elephant and its courtship habits make it, all the more, necessary for the bull to have the co-operation of the cow for a successful coition. The pre-copulate play is gentle in elephant; the bull cannot, by aggression force the cow for copulation, the situation that may arise in some other animals, where there is little or no courtship. Here the bull caresses the cow with tender movements of his trunk and they are repeated by gentle bodily contacts.

A caress at just the right moment makes the cow in oestrous feel loved, touched and desire fulfilled. She must be feeling 'physical hunger', her skin an appetite. It needs to be stimulated or else, she may feel deprived. 'Skin hunger' can cause not only blues, but also acute depression, restlessness. Getting a dose of touch from a male is as important biologically as taking a stimulant.

Females have greater appetites for touch than males, because they come in physical contact with a bull once every three to three-and-a-half years. Females' ravenous epidermis needs more sexual foreplay than their male partners. As juveniles, they were more socialised among the family members to express affection physically. They had greater license than their brothers to caress and greet each other with a kiss. As adults they expect more touching in their lives by males and when they don't get it, they might feel deprived.

Physical expressions of affection also send a strong message to the world of courtship. As the relationship progresses a male's touch reassures that he be the father of her progeny.

How emotionally gratifying caress is in all the right places! The best part of sex comes from caressing and tender stroking. Body touch by members of the family or fellow cows may not be able to make her heart sing like a lover's touch does. Touching by a lover can put her at ease and more responsive.

While the bull is peculiar in his genital anatomy, except that the testes are not discrete in a scrotum but located within the body (a feature shared by some other animals, such as the whales and dolphins, shrews and sloth), the cow has the widest perineum known among the mammals. Cow's vagina is situated lower down in between hind legs with a vertical slit; this renders it quite necessary for the cow and the bull to be precisely aligned before copulation can be effective. The bull lays his trunk along the cow's back from behind and manoeuvres her into position before attempting to mount her, a move dependent entirely on the willingness of the cow.

8.5 Copulation/Conjugation

The pair may be seen together with increasing frequency, getting to know each other and testing each other's moods and emotions. For a few moments, every now and then they continuously investigate each other with their trunks; caress each other, while two great bony heads press. The twosome would see their growing intimacy through to the end. Consequent to this pairing, her mild responses become more urgent as the effect of hormones which previously circulated in her blood at only low levels, is felt. Now she goads her male into action, looking for the right approach that will spur him into sexual act. She touches him with her trunk and smells his penis, then retreats and advances once more trumpeting in excitement. He attempts to mount her from behind, but she slides from under him and moves away. He hesitates, again perhaps, reminded of his youthful rejection, but she turns and signals her approval by fluttering her ears and coiling her trunk with his. He approaches from behind and samples her genital organ as she stands still. He then attempts to mount her once more. This time she does not move away and as he positions himself, forelegs lying along her back, trunk touching her neck, he fixes her and his penis penetrates her vagina. The union is short, perhaps, half a minute or so, until the transfer of genetic material is completed. He dismounts and moves aside. The result of *Kama sutra* must have been the great feelings of orgasm'. Her excitement soon aroused further and she is quick to respond to his next move.

Already their association has grown so intense, but short is at the ebb. They browse together and may even copulate again and again. By being together for a while after the 'climax', it can relieve the performance pressure, they may both be feeling exhausted. At the end of post-play and completion of his mission, he is off to lead a lonely life or perhaps in search of another mate. He is thus nick-named, *Salaga*, the 'sire-bull' or breeding bull of the herds.

8.6 The Pregnancy

Elephant births in the wild have seldom been observed, as they generally occur at night-between dusk and dawn. In contrast to other mammals, pregnant elephants show almost no visible body swelling.

The mammary glands of a young elephant pregnant for the first time swell up from her flat chest in preparation for lactation, but older cows may continue to lactate from one birth to the next and the size of their breasts cannot be used as a clue. I never actually, witnessed the momentous of a birth of a young in the wild, although, I came close to it on half a dozen occasions. As such observations in the wild are rare, I have drawn fairly fully from my field notes to describe the first hours of life of babies.

Number of offspring per birth is usually one, rarely twins are born. They get covered with hair after few months of their birth; the density of hair reduces with age. New born calves may consume two-and-a half gallons of milk a day. Weaning is a very gradual process beginning at the first year of life and may continue till 7th year. Termination of suckling may be initiated either by the ability of the calf to use its trunk to pull grass and leaves or by its growing tusks that poke its mother's chest while the calf is attempting to nurse.

8.7 Twins and Triplets

Occasional births of twins and triplets are seen both in the wild and in captivity.

In Siam on Oct. 27, 1913 an elephant had given birth to triplets; all were males; one was still-born, the second was too small, while, the third was normal. The latter two died on Nov. 8 and 9 of the same year, as the mother neglected them despite every effort made to bring them up. The mother refused to suckle them.

In Burma on Oct. 26, 1961 an elephant cow gave birth to twins. The first was male and was born at 6.30 in the morning, the other, born after an interval of 3.5 hours, was a female. The male's height at the shoulder was 2 ft. 9 in. and that of female 2 ft. 8 in.

Twins were born to a female elephant, Alka at the Orang National Park, about 150 km from Guwahati in Assam on 15th December 2010. The elephant calves, both of them female, were reported to be hale and healthy. It was Alka's fifth delivery. It is said Alka has scripted history in the Orang National Park.

Paste here :Image No. Scan 0010.tif twins born in captivity –Orang Nationa Park, Assam.

8.8 Rate of Growth in Calf

Cows suckle their young for a minimum period of two years. The calves continue to suckle milk till the next calving. I have seen and photographed four and a half year elder calf and a year old younger calf suckling together simultaneously in Bandipur reserve.

Gee (1964) used to measure every year the circumference of foot print and height at shoulder of a female baby elephant which was born on Feb. 6, 1950. His studies confirmed the "thumb rule" that the height of an Asian elephant is approximately twice the circumference of the front foot print. Here are recordings of height at various ages:

At the age of one year, the height: 4 ft. 1 in.

At the age of three years: 5 ft. 1 in.

At the age of seven years: 6 ft. 1 1/2 in.

At the age of eleven years: 7 ft.

At the age of thirteen years: 7 ft. 2 in.

At 13, she was only 4 inches shorter than her mother.

8.9   The Longevity

A number of factors govern the life-span of an elephant. The captive elephants put on strenuous work are bound to wear out sooner. Again, if they are not given enough work, they will become sluggish and consequently, their health suffers. In the wild, an elephant gets just the right amount of exercise and enough food, so as to be healthy and agile.

Then again, in captivity, elephants miss that variety in their diet available to wild cousins. They are also denied those clear flowing streams and ponds where they can bathe and sport in freedom, in addition to water and mud therapy to keep the skin supple. It is a pleasing sight to see members of the herd playing in a lake. Dip shower for an elephant family is a private affair. It is a romance to see tusker, the monarch of the jungle, roaming majestically in the jungle. It is the epitome of royalty, power and grace. Cows are sleek and lumpy and not bony as most of them become in captivity. The youngsters in the company of wild herds get disciplined by their mothers to be a successful members to lead the family, which otherwise denied to zoo born babies. Zoo born babies tend to become erratic in their behaviour, as they are pampered by keepers and soon get weaned at the age of two. And then, they have none to fear, in contrast to the wild ones, who are scared of tigers and man, the master predator.

8.10   Age – the Guess Estimation in the Wild

A rough estimate of the elephant age can be obtained from its ears. In a very young elephant of 6-7 years of age, the pinnae, the top edge of the ear is not turned round as in human; but with advancing age it twirls over. In old elephants of 35 to 45 years, the curling round of the upper edge of the pinnae is very prominent, say up to 1 inch. In some old elephants, the ear lobes are usually ragged and torn especially along the lower edge.

A real elephant-tamer carefully watches the growth of elephants from birth through various stages and can guess more or less accurately the age of an elephant by looking at him. While the calves are yet growing, the degree of accuracy is very great. With grown up elephants in the wild it is rather approximate. An elephant keeps on growing physically up to the age of about 55 years and his age can be guessed from his height at any time before he has reached sixty years. In estimating the age of a grown-up elephant, one has to take into account, whether temples on the face are flat or caved in; depression on both sides of cheeks; the upper part of the ear erect or folded; the lobe flaccid; the degree of pallor or pigmentation on the face, ear-tips and base and tip of the trunk; shrinking of legs; depression on both sides of the tail root; protracted gait and slow movements; the general shape of the body almost shrinking. On examination of the dung reveals declining of grinding in association with digestive power of the animal. If there are heavy undigested matters, it indicates the old age. The state of the tusks also gives fairly good indication of the age of the male elephant. The foot prints may give an indication of pads having worn out, in case of old age. As already discussed in the preceding chapter, age of an elephant could be estimated based on number of replacements of sets of teeth.

These external signs, individually and collectively, can be related to their corresponding age, by an experienced observer, for it is seldom that a birth certificate of wild elephant is available for inspection.

A final useful field guide is provided by elephants over about 50 years of age. In these animals the temporal region of the skull (just above the eye), is sunken in relation to the rest of the skull. This is simply a sign of old age and is not connected with poor physical condition. The cheeks also get sunken as the age advances.

8.11 Age Determination

For the sake of comparison six molars that are fully developed and erupted (but not worn down) at the following age:

Tooth	Age in year/s
M-1	1
M-2	2

M-3	6
M-4	15
M-5	28
M-6	47

Eventually, M-6, the last molar is worn out at an estimated age of about 60 years, when just a fragment of the tooth remains. An elephant with a few remaining fragments of M-6 soon dies of starvation, as it is unable to chew its food. In other words the final wearing down of M6 places an absolute upper limit of about 60 years to an elephant's life span.

8.12   The Dentition

There is, however, a lot more in an elephant's teeth than its tusks. Those housed within the small mouth are themselves the wondrous theory of evolution, not so much for what they are and for how they function, but more for the manner in which they appear and for the consequences this has for the elephant's ultimate survival. In both Asian and African elephants, the more usual mammalian tooth pattern is discarded. Gone are the nipping frontal incisors and the adjacent tearing canines. The upper incisors remain as tusks, which play only a minor role in food gathering and no role at all in preparing the food and in swallowing. The tusks are not elongated canine teeth; they are actually modified upper incisors and they grow continuously. In the mouth itself, only the molars remain. So, one must note that elephants are inefficient at digesting their food. Something like 45% of their vegetation intake passes straight through the digestive system. They need to eat for 16-18 hours, and often longer, every day to take in several quintals of greenery from which they will extract enough nutrients to satisfy their bulky needs. An elephant needs to digest, it is estimated, about 50 tonnes of feed each year.

This method of obtaining nutrition, of course, places a special burden on the teeth and it is clear that if an elephant were equipped with a full set of permanent teeth early in life, the teeth would very soon be worn down to the gums. With regard to the teeth, the evolution has provided a formula which enables the elephant to chew its way through several decades of its life.

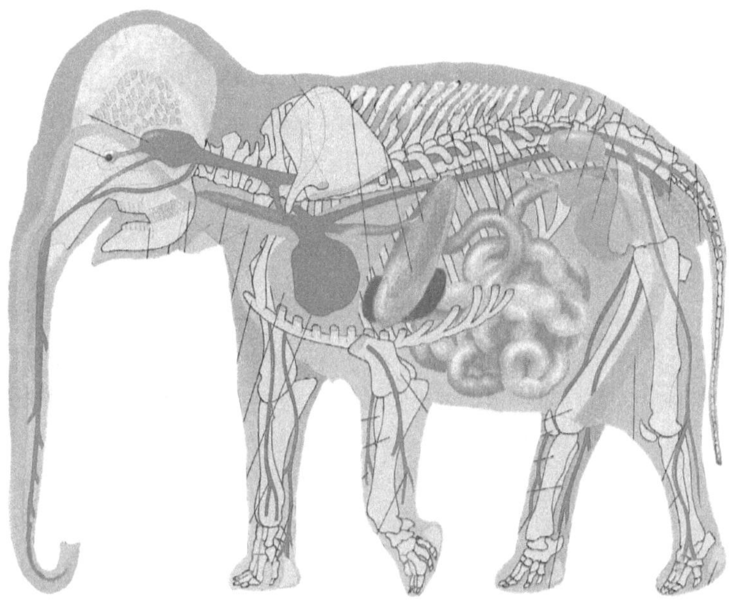

The system works as follows: the elephant is equipped with broad, flat molars which occupy the left and right sides of both upper and lower jaws. Each of these four areas will accommodate six molars, giving a total of 24 in all. They do not appear altogether, but replace each other in a series. Each set of teeth lasts for few years and as they wear out, they are replaced pushing from behind by the next set. The following teeth are always larger than the ones from which they take over, so that tooth size keeps pace with the expanding jaw.

The new born elephant has eight teeth, for the first and second molars are already in place at the time of its birth. The first of these is nearly two inches long and the second, immediately behind it, is twice the size. After three or four years, the first molar set has not only been ground down, but has moved forward into contact with the jaw bone. It now flakes off in distinct layers (lamellae). The second molar continues to move forward until it assumes a dominant role, which will last for coming three or four years. By this time, at about seven years of age, the third molar set is growing in each of the four places on the jaws. They become fully functional at 13 years of age and remain so until the fourth molar set is in complete use by the time the elephant reaches its twenty-fifth year. The over lapping growth and wearing down process means that at this stage the fifth molar set has already erupted, although it will not be in a full working position until at least another 15 or 20 years have passed. At this point, elephant will be in its mid-forties and in its prime of life, by which time it should have made its vital contribution to the next generations.

Now, it has only one more set of teeth to come in place. Before the fifth molar set is fully functional, the sixth and final molar set, which measures up to 10 inches along its grinding surface is well underway. An animal in its fiftieth year will be on its last set of molar teeth. Thus, its days of healthy feeding are coming to an end. As the teeth wear down and flake away leaving an empty space behind it, the elephant becomes less and less efficient at feeding. Eventually, bark and other fibrous material eaten will pass through its stomach without being broken down completely. Gradually, the food eaten must consist of more lush and capable of being easily chewed. Such food is not abundant generally and as the elephant begins to suffer from malnutrition, it wanders in search of succulent plants and may break away from the herd. Death is not too far away for such aged animals. Once the teeth have gone, the animal is irreversibly left to a process of degeneration. Most die around the age of 60; others may live until they are well into their seventies and few even eighties.

Dental formula:------------total 26 (24 molars + 2 incisors)

8.13 Stress Factors in Breeding

The cows take care of the pregnant female for the next 22 months. After delivery, she will not conceive again for at least a year and a half after that. Her days will be spent with other females, producing a calf every three and a half to four and a half years throughout her life. The young females will remain with the herd and the young males will be banished once again to the bush.

My long standing field observation has made it possible to know far more details about the Indian elephant. The existing discovery that the elephant has a kind of built-in birth control mechanism adds a new dimension to the elephant study. Comparative observations recorded by me in different parts of India have revealed that as the elephant population density increases and food becomes scarce, they breed less frequently and produce fewer calves. In an un-crowded condition with an abundance of food, female elephants reach puberty at about ten years of age and can continue their reproductive activity until they die of old age at about 60. Within these 50 years they may produce one calf every three and a half to four and a half years. But in an overcrowded condition, when food is in short supply, the picture can change dramatically. Puberty may be reached at anywhere between 12 and 20 years of age, while females may stop breeding at about 50, before they reach old age. In other words, their effective reproductive life can be reduced by 20 years. But that is not all. Within this period the frequency with which they give birth can also be reduced, from a calf every three and a half to four and a half years to one every eight to nine years, thus, bringing up only 5 calves in their life time, on an average.

8.14   Death in Elephants

Death of an elephant is one of the saddest sights on earth. The only significance of death is in its effects on population dynamics and the causes of death are analysed for their relative importance. For human beings and for elephants, the death of a family member remains a significant factor in the behaviour of the survivors. In life, the individuals of both species are tied by strong family bonds and emotion. Frantic efforts are made to save a sick or dying relative, whereas, other herbivores and even carnivores, don't take notice of the dying or dead. "Death is a passage, not only for the departed soul, but also for those who continue to live.

They have to learn to cope with the changed situation and understand altered relationships. One can't hold on to any thing for ever; nothing lasts to eternity."

Loosing some one you love, makes you vulnerable and raw. Death is some thing most of the elephants keep in the periphery of their vision while they are alive. "Healing begins with acceptance and surrender, the only way out of the pain. Tears, hysteria or even dozed numbing grief come naturally at a time like this. Weeping, wailing and futile remonstrance only hinder the departing spirit from its onward journey."

Many great Zoologists, including Charles Darwin, have thought that elephants possess strong emotions towards a member of the family. I have little doubt, that when one of their member dies and the bonds of lifetime severed, elephants have a similar feeling to the one we call 'grief'. Unfortunately, science as yet has no means of measuring or describing emotion even for human beings, let alone for elephants.

The relative importance of different causes of death in elephants was also very much in my mind. This has hardly been studied in the wild. The figures which exist are mainly concerned with shooting of elephants for sport, ivory, meat or against crop damage. Nothing exists on record as to the numbers that die from diseases, misery and old age. Anthrax, rabies and *Arterio sclerosis* have all been diagnosed and manuals are printed about how to care for domestic elephants by Indian authors. They also list so many diseases that elephants may be prone to that one is left with the impression that for all their size, they appear to be exceedingly delicate and sensitive creatures.

Deaths among elephants are quite common in nature: skidding while negotiating steep slopes, fall from heights, premature births, fight among wild bulls, buck shot injuries, electrocuting from high-tension lines passing through forests, fall in the abandoned elephant capture pit, while capturing elephants either by pit method or by tranquillising or at the time of *Khedda,* diseases and from poachers, accidents caused by speeding railways, speeding vehicular traffic on highways passing through national parks and sanctuaries and so on. Because of their huge size severe injuries to elephants due to mishaps are not uncommon in the wild. I have come across many deaths on account of mishaps and accidents.

8.15   Ruthless Killing of Elephants By Humans

Almost every alternate day, we read with dismay in the print media that large numbers of elephants are killed ruthlessly by farmers, estate owners, who are in the habit of passing live current in electric fence around their lands. Anti-elephant communities poison the elephants, which stray out in search of food. This is a deliberate act of terrorism by man to take revenge against poor pachyderms. I had come across such offences committed by estate owners around Bannerghatta National Park limits during 1973, when two magnificent tuskers were found electrocuted. Again during November 1982 two cow elephants became victim to similar type of electrocution. Their calves, however, became orphans. Poachers/ivory hunters take a heavy toll of tuskers.

Deaths by accidental fires in the wild are rare. But camp elephants, some times, get severely injured or killed from man-made fires: A foolhardiness of man was exhibited, when a 'sequence of running of elephants' was to be shot for a Kannada film, titled *"Huliya Halina Mevu"*, meaning feeding with tiger's milk? This shoot was permitted by the Divisional Forest Officer, just inside the Nagarahole National Park in the year 1974. Three sides of an arena were covered by heaps of brush-wood, leaving a narrow passage in one direction for the elephants to escape. All the elephants numbering about sixteen in an enclosure were expected to run in the intended direction of the opening, the moment the heaps of brush-wood were fired. But events of sequence did not happen as planned. On seeing the blaze around, panic-stricken elephants as they were, ran helter-skelter in an utter confusion under a thick cloud of smoke. Instead of running to escape in the intended direction, the pachyderms got stuck in the blaze. The film shooting, using camp elephants as stage performers, thus culminated in the greatest ever tragedy of 20th century where six elephants died on the spot and many others suffered serious burn injuries.

Occasionally, nature's fury also works against the welfare of wild elephants. A hungry tiger/tigress with cubs at heel, some times, snatches away a kid from its mother. The strategy adopted by tigers varies from animal to animal and the topography. Firstly, tiger maims to cripple the baby. The victim's mother tries to persuade the calf to rise and follow the herd. When the victim fails to do so, mother finally abandons it in favour of the marauder. The law of the jungle dictates that it is better to lose a crippled one and be ready to deliver a healthy baby next season.

Elephant babies are occasionally found dragged under water and killed by crocodiles when they visit rivers and lakes for a drink, followed by a dip shower. Angry rhinos also, kill male juveniles, when they wander about in Manas and Kazhiranga national parks of Assam.

A tusker which was wounded by buck-shots found suffering from traumatic pain at Begur forest of Bandipur reserve. It was reported to be in the habit of raiding crops at nights. The animal was unable to walk long distances and kept to shades solitary trees at the edge of the forest. The Begur Ranger, Prabhakar(Jr) sent wireless communication, about precarious condition of the unfortunate tusker. I wanted to examine the animal, personally, before making my next move. On my arrival at Begur Reserve Forest, I saw the tusker moaning, while taking support of tree-trunk of Palas *Butea frondosa* tree. The tusker aged between 45 and 50 years, was found infested with maggots. I could see the animal undergoing almost pre-death agony.

I asked the Ranger to keep a constant vigil, lest it might fall prey to a bullet of some unscrupulous poachers. Meanwhile, I approached the Chief Wildlife Warden, Bangalore, seeking an official green signal to end its miseries by involuntary euthanasia. (Euthanasia, more commonly known as 'mercy killing', refers to the practice of ending life in order to relieve endless pain and intractable suffering). While, I waited for an order from Chief Wildlife Warden, the victim succumbed to injuries inside the reserve forest after two weeks. His tusks measured 4'-9" each and weighed both put together at 56 kilograms, the value of which worked out at Rs. 675,000 or US $15,000.

Wild elephants often get trapped in marshes and quagmires from which they find impossible to wriggle out; more they struggle, deeper they sink, unable to extricate themselves. They soon get exhausted and meet an agonizing death. A cow which was stuck in a deep quagmire at Kabini reservoir during 1981 summer was extricated with the help of a 'living crane of the wild' – the massive Bharath, the camp male elephant.

Elephants, both lone bull/group of young bulls and herds, are attracted by palatable crops grown around the park boundaries. When they visit farmers' fields, they serve them as departmental store; not only they browse crops, but also do lot of damage by trampling out of shear confusion. Enraged farmers take law into their hand and inflict injuries or kill them by buck-shots or by electrocution or by poisoning. Elephants, being highly social, emotional and intelligent, they resort to attacking humans to take revenge against humans, who ruthlessly kill their relatives. Such ongoing conflicts between the two, poor and innocent people become victims of their grief.

During harvest season, farmers are busy winnowing grains at threshing yards. While guarding their hard earned annual harvest, keep vigil even at nights. Some of the farmers are in the habit of covering themselves with hay to keep out the winter cold. Elephants, especially during their rendezvous chance upon people sleeping covered under hay, the latter get killed. These are common occurrences along the fringes of forests.

High way accidents are quite frequent; elephants, in particular, the calves are hit by speeding vehicular traffic, especially, along the high ways passing through national parks and sanctuaries. Such an accident made a headline news, when a two month old male calf in the herd was run over by a speeding vehicle on the state high way near Kolikere village, about 10 km. from Yellapur of Uttara Kannada district in the early hours of the night of 14th December 1997. Enraged mother of the victim, supported by six animals of the herd literally blocked the traffic. The traffic on the high way was thrown out of gear for more than 14 hours. The grief stricken mother reported to have attacked a truck driver. Elephants also damaged window panes of a public transport vehicle, the driver of which ventured to surpass. A two-wheeler was also trampled by the sobbing pachyderm after its rider made a futile bid to cross the accident site. These dramatic episodes showed highly emotional and strong bond between mother and her baby.

Occasionally, elephants get carried away by flood waters despite their buoyancy and proficiency in swimming. On 31st May, 1998 a body of wild bull was found washed down by flood waters of Tunga River. The bull might have been caught unaware while crossing the river on the upstream of Sacrebyle elephant camp, near Shimoga. Efforts to save the animal were found futile, according to an eye witness. It was suspected that the bull got killed by forced-fall across the dam at Gajnur. He was between 35-40 years old.

Shocking headline news appeared in the print media on September 24, 2010 that a goods train mowed seven elephants on the night of 22nd near Binnaguri in North Bengal's Dooars Elephant Reserve of Jalpaiguri district. Of the seven four were adults and three babies. While four died on the spot, three succumbed to their injuries next day morning. This was the biggest toll of elephants ever in a single day. There have been repeated incidents in this district in the past as well.

Most annoying sight, I witnessed in the visual media that 2-3 year old elephant calf that was separated from its herd was found harrowed and beaten to agonising death by a group of senseless goons in a village of West Bengal on October 26, 2010.

In the early part of 2010, a mass murder of elephants numbering six reported in Simlipal Tiger Reserve of Orissa, suspected to be a handiwork of organised poaching gangsters. The Simlipal reserve had been under seize of Naxallites for nearly three years, keeping the protective staff at bay. This is really heart-rending incident.

There are number of instances when elephants, particularly, males go amuck during festivities, processions and religious functions, resulting in killing passers-by, some times, their own *mahouts* and in the end fall victims to bullets. The ongoing conflicts between humans and elephants are on the increase, both in Asian and African countries, principally, because elephant ranges are shrinking pushing them to remote and hilly regions.

These are only few incidents that are illustrated here. Such tragic deaths and disgraceful killings will continue as long as increasing human populations and their ever changing lifestyle continue. India is loosing, on an average 350 elephants a year by way of killings by man. These killings are in addition to natural and unnatural causes, such as, diseases, and injuries that account for nearly 100-150 elephants. Under the cloud of human-elephant conflicts, the poor elephant is the loser. It has to fight single handed with its back to the wall. In view of above increasing signs of grief and loss, it shall be the sole responsibility of Foresters and Wild-lifers to protect their right to live, by providing them safe habitats. A total protection to elephants including other wild animals need be ensured by fighting against anti-elephant communities. In the ultimate analysis, we the human beings should learn to live, the way elephants live.

8.16 Emotional Intelligence

The tragic deaths of elephants and signs of grief and loss meted out to elephant society in the hands of humans are a clear indication of "emotional intelligence". Emotional intelligence is a form of social intelligence, which involves ability to monitor one's own and others' feelings and emotions and to use this knowledge to guide their way of life. While doing so, one must remember that the elephants are highly social, highly emotional and intelligent with fantastic memory.

The elephant is also considered as "Keystone species" of the Indian jungles, because of its overall influence over other animals and the ecosystem. A keystone species is a pivotal mammalian species responsible to maintain the bio-ecological health of the ecosystem. In tropical forests of India, among others, the elephants are the only species large enough to eat and disperse the seeds of some of the important plant species. Other animals in the jungle also stand to benefit in obtaining food, water and shelter. Studies have shown that 30% of the gigantic tree species and 40% of the tall tree species in the forests depend on elephants for seed dispersal and their germination. The elephant is also considered as the natural gardener, responsible in shaping the landscape, pollination, germination of hard-coated seeds and even improving fertility of the forest floor with heaps of dung. The elephants foster forest ecosystems and help maintain healthy environment most essential for human survival. The elephant, therefore, assumes global significance in so far as biodiversity conservation is concerned. Biodiversity conservation, as we know, is reckoned as an antidote to regulate climate change, which is causing concern to all citizens, including scientists and governments, the world over. The Indian elephant, which stands tall, is facing threat of extinction. Hence the judicial activism has come forward to rescue the country's biodiversity and her environment and of course, to rescue the wildlife, in particular, elephants and their habitats in the *suo motu* proceedings.

8.17 Judicial Activism

Interestingly, the Chief Justice of Karnataka High Court, initiated *suo motu* public interest litigation (PIL-14029/2008) against tragic killing of elephants by farmers and dumping them in irrigation channels around Bandipur tiger reserve, during November 2008. Some six elephants were reported poisoned by farmers, when they were strayed out in search of food. This was a welcome step and could be termed as judicial activism. Such a step showed inability and failure of the legislature and the executive wings of the government. Though the farmers and politicians of our

Constitution make a legitimate distinction between three wings of the public, the involvement of judiciary was found readily available, as the last recourse, in saving country's biodiversity.

This author was asked by Hon'ble Chief Justice to assist the High Court proceedings and desired to submit a Comprehensive Action Plan Report, dovetailing with proposal of the Chief Wildlife Warden. After detail discussion, 'Green Bench' of the H.C of Karnataka was pleased to direct the government of Karnataka, including the government of India to implement short term and long term programmes in protecting the elephants. Consequently, a special monitoring committee, to oversee "Action Taken Reports" was also appointed, in which this author was one of the members. Under the same directions, the members of the Monitoring Committee were also appointed as Members of the 'Wildlife Advisory Board' of Karnataka state.

The "Comprehensive Action Plan to Mitigate Human-Elephant Conflict" as directed by the High Court of Karnataka, comprising short term and long term measures, were as under:

1. **Elephant Conservation is synonym to Biodiversity Conservation reckoned, as an antidote to resolve global warming and climate change. Hence, elephant conservation assumes a 'global significance'.**

2. **Wildlife management is a multifaceted and specialised scientific discipline; all possible preventive and protective measures need to be taken to mitigate conflicting factors than attempting to search for remedial measures after disasters are struck.**

3. **Need to bring in total ban on growing palatable crops, including tobacco cultivation in eco-fragile area upto a distance of about 10 km around the parks, by encouraging alternate cropping pattern: castor, cotton, Niger, etc. which are non-palatable should gradually replace palatable ones. There is an**

urgent need to put in place science and technological inputs to prevent elephants raiding crops.

4. Make crop insurance, a mandatory in eco-fragile areas around the reserves, with the participation of Department of Agriculture and Insurance Department, followed by timely settlement of compensation/claims.

5. Need to provide Coal for tobacco curing barns at subsidised price by Tobacco Board to wean farmers away from entering forests for firewood.

6. Need to specify time limit for settlement of compensations/ claims towards crop damage, human injury/human deaths, by the Forest/Wildlife departments.

7. Money generated from eco-tourism need be used to make park self sufficient to manage, improve tourist facilities & share at least 1/3 of it to better the living conditions of local communities, so as to muster their participation in conservation programme.

8. Tourist outfits located just adjoining national park boundaries need to be uprooted and relocated beyond 5 km from borders, as per dictum of Indian Board for Wildlife Preservation and Project Tiger Consultative Committee. This helps facilitate free movements of elephants and other animals.

9. Ensure placement of trained anti-poaching squads in modern weaponry, through State Police Academies to deal with hard core criminals. Squad personnel are provided with special hardship perks and other facilities.

10. Appoint trained personnel in wildlife Management and Wildlife related laws to deal with crimes, followed by prosecution in court of law, in addition to manage wildlife

and their habitats in a professional way. They need to improve personnel capabilities and bring in accountability.

11. Forest, Wildlife and Police officials are needed to be empowered with more legal teeth to deal against hard core offenders and to pronounce summary punishment. Although ban on trade in wildlife skins, ivory and body parts of big cats are imposed, black marketing still thrives, with penalties too small and rewards too high.

12. Farmers having squatted in encroached forest lands without *patta* need to learn to live with elephants in harmony (just as tribals have learnt to live with wildlife for ages). Encourage farmers switch over to improved breeds of milch cows & other livestock with stall feeding facilities.

13. Encourage applied research involving Universities and Research Institutes by providing fellowships/scholarships, set aside for the purpose. This is one field requiring big investment, because in the absence of research data, wildlife management becomes truncated.

14. Need to boost funding by the centre and state governments to preserve invaluable biodiversity resource, in particular the elephant and the tiger. The country/state is in a position to foot the bill of conservation.

15. There is urgent need to relocate tribal communities out of protected areas (PAs), so as to keep the habitats free from anti-elephant communities & to bring tribes on main stream of human society as per approved scheme of the Government of India.

16. Field staff patrolling to protect forests wealth and wildlife and so also officials managing national parks and sanctuaries,

along with their vehicles shall be exempted from general/local election duties.

17. Ensure state-wise inter-connectivity of island-like potential elephant habitats by insular corridors that help socialise with distant elephant populations and maintain healthy gene pool. Also bring in potential reserve forests under the fold of elephant/tiger country as additional PAs.

18. Need for region-wise inter-connectivity of potential elephant protected areas with insulated corridors to facilitate elephants from island like areas to socialise with distant herds. This could be done to start with interconnecting elephant corridors in respect of southern states, such as, Maharashtra, Goa, Karnataka, Kerala, Tamilnadu and Andhra Pradesh, coordinated by the Ministry of Environment and Forests, Government of India, New Delhi.

19. Need to have Region-wise Elephant Corridor Inter – connectivity Committees for other elephant regions of the country, like Central India, North-west India and North-east India, led by Ministry of Environment and Forests to identify and prepare blueprint, including upkeep of interstate frontier lines. The committees will also keep track of welfare of elephant populations that may spill over to break new grounds of neighbouring states. The concerned states should welcome such elephants as revered guests since they are known to bring good luck and rains.

20. Field staff managing wildlife need be covered by insurance against accidents, injuries and deaths, while on duty apart from providing 'risk-to-life' allowances, as they are required to perform duties in hostile environment and during odd hours.

21. There is urgent need to declare biodiversity milieu – Forest and Wildlife, as priority sectors, so as to give total protection.

22. Huge stock-piles of Ivory are in the custody of state forest departments. There is an apprehension among the public that ivory pieces are likely to be pilfered and many may go unaccounted for over a period, while changing hands of officials. So, the entire stock in the country needs to be destroyed/burnt/buried, since domestic and international trade in ivory is banned. This ban is likely to continue in perpetuity. By doing so it would send a powerful message to the world community that we do not attach any value to so called white gold. Nearly 12 tonnes of African ivory valued at US $ millions was burnt by former President, Daniel Arap Moi of Kenya on 18th July 1989 sending a powerful message to the world ivory traders, smugglers and users too. Moi's dramatic action was part of a sustained campaign by conservationists' world over.

23. State High Level Statutory Body – "State Wildlife Board" need to advise to appoint Monitoring Committee for elephant and tiger conservation to oversee action taken there on, as per the directions of the Supreme Court of India.

24. Last, but not the least, efficient wildlife conservation management requires effective "Management Plan" for each of the protected areas, incorporating latest scientific & technological inputs, previewed by specialists/scientists before it is sanctioned by the government.

8.19   Regional Elephant Reserves Net-working

In accordance with the directions of High Court of Karnataka in *SuoMotu* W.P. No. 14029/2008 (GM-RES_PIL) for implementing 'ActionPlan to Mitigate Increasing Human-Elephant Conflict', there is an urgent need for constituting regional committees, called "Regional Elephant Reserves Networking (RERN) by Insular Corridors". These committees comprising of respective state governments in coordination with the Ministry of Environment and Forests, Government of India, New Delhi, need be formed. Consequently, the RERN Committees for South India, Central India, North-western India and North-eastern India, including international borders of Nepal, Bhutan and Myanmar, need to be put in place. These potential elephant ranges with insulated corridors will be in tune with the nature, as against, much talked of inter connectivity of country's river-system that is likely to harm the environment. The following steps need be initiated by the Ministry of Environment and Forests, Government of India:

8.19.1 Need to Identify Potential Elephant Corridors

Any animal species, need four basic necessities namely, food, water, shelter and mates for their long term survival. The survival of the Asian elephant *Elephas maximus* L. in particular, in addition to being dependent on largeforest tracts, is also intimately linked with conservation of biodiversity.

Continuity of healthy gene-pool is another important factor to prevent inbreeding in elephant for its continued evolutionary process. Ancient literature and historical evidences show that elephants were distributed over the Indian sub-continent including Rajasthan, Punjab, Gujarat, Madhya Pradesh, where they are now extinct. According to IUCN/SSC Asian Elephant Specialist Group, out of 35,000 – 50,000 Asian elephant populations, there are estimated to be 25,000 – 30,000 elephants roam the Indian jungles. Considering the past ranges of distribution, the elephant conservation programme cannot be restricted to a few island-like national parks and sanctuaries alone. The forests outside protected areas (PAs) would often serve as vital ecological corridor links and they must be protected to prevent isolation or fragmentation of elephant populations. Region-wise inter connectivity of potential elephant reserves of India by insular corridors can play an important role in the dispersal of biota as well as facilitating healthy gene flow amongst distant populations, thus increasing the heterozygosity within taxa of the region. The habitats linkage is, therefore, crucial for large ranging animals, like elephants to spill over using these corridors during their seasonal movements and to socialise with distant populations.

8.19.2   Elephant Population Trend

The elephant populations in India have been gradually on the increase since 1980s, when the first census was conducted by the Asian Elephant Specialist Group. According to elephant census of 2007 the population trend in south Indian protected areas, however, varies with density between 0.2 and 1.2 per sq km. The increase in elephant population, however, has not been uniform throughout the country. There is a negative trend in the elephant populations in the north-eastern parts of India and Orissa, while it is positive trend in the south. The population in Assam was reported to have gone up from 5246 in 2002 to 5281 in 2007; in Arunachal Pradesh from 1607 in 2002 to 1690 in 2007, while in Meghalaya population has gone down from 1868 in 2002 to 1811 in 2007. in Nagaland it is increased from 145 in 2002 to 152 in 2007 and in Orissa from 1841 in 2002 to 1862 in 2007 and in West Bengal there is marginal increase from 292 in 2002 to 300-350 in 2007. In Uttarakhand, there is a decrease from 1582 to 1346 and in Uttar Pradesh there is an increase from 85 in 2002 to 380 in 2007. In south India, Karnataka recorded a decline from 5838 in 2002 to 4035, while Tamilnadu recorded an increase from 3052 in 2002 to 3867 in 2007 and Kerala too registered an increase from 3850 in 2002 to 6068.

8.19.3   Need for Conflict Resolution than Conflict Management

Human-elephant conflict, often leads to injury and deaths on both sides due to increased anthropocentric pressure on the elephant habitats. Formerly, impenetrable forests are now accessible by logging roads, infrastructure development projects and human settlements. Today, elephant distribution is mainly restricted to remote and hilly regions, termed as island like populations. These isolated elephant populations are unable to socialise with larger populations, as ancient migratory routes are cut off due to human invasion. In view of the grim situation the proposed "Regional Elephant Reserves Networking" (RERN) will help interconnect ecologically potential areas by insular corridors, so as to reduce the risks of human-elephant collusion.

In this context, it should be noted that there is no such a thing as total solution to end human-elephant conflict for technical, financial, political and sociological rationale. The problem can be highly emotional too, as crops and properties are destroyed, apart from loss of human life. The elephants are, generally, perceived by people as the property of the states and concerned governments alone are responsible for the protection of elephants and obviously, prevention of elephants from their onslaughts and safety to human life and property rests on the governments. Government machinery is, generally, unable to rise to the occasion, in the pretext that it is ill-equipped to tackle such challenges. The present RERN proposal, however, aims at protecting elephant and other wildlife populations, whose conservation would help maintain biological diversity and ecological integrity of the regions.

8.19.4   Use of Advanced Science and Technology

The advent of space technology has revolutionised the study of features of the earth surface and in particular, vegetation cover which is the major biological expression. Satellite remote sensing, by direct application, will be considerably beneficial in terms of accuracy and speed. Realising the capabilities of satellite remote sensing for better scientific forestry and wildlife management, the satellite data of regional elephant ranges coming under the proposed project would be of great help for survey and demarcation of potential elephant corridors. Regional elephant habitats will then be considered for inter connectivity, duly identifying and demarcating them. The region-wise satellite data could be obtained from Regional Remote Sensing Service Centres (RRSSC) of Indian Space Research Organisation (ISRO). All these data help determine biologically and ecologically sustainable elephant corridors.

Simultaneously, research undertaken, among others, will be directed towards conflict resolution than conflict management, apart from helping conservation management of elephants and their habitats. This book will also endeavour in evolving a system by dove-tailing modern technology with traditional practices, in finding workable solutions to ever escalating human-elephant conflict. The ultimate outcome of this project will be a search for compromise and a step forward in the "conservation resolution" blue-print of endangered elephant tribe.

8.19.5 Networking of Elephant Reserves-as Conservation Strategy

In view of the fact that Asian elephant in India is stated to be endangered throughout its range of distribution, a widely applicable conservation strategy and management practices are urgently required to be put in place, so that the mistakes that happened in the past shall not recur. Unfortunately, the quantitative and qualitative information on the patterns of biological diversity, ecological conditions and extent of threats, the Asian elephant is facing are inadequate. The implementation of conservation strategy and protective measures, in particular, are also inadequate. The region-wise survey and identification of ecologically potential corridors will facilitate to interconnect island like elephant habitats, so as to redress the problems facing the management. Execution of linkage of elephant reserves by such potential corridors shall help to suit ecological requirements of elephant habitats and to insulate them from escalated anthropic interventions. The elephants, since ancient times, have enjoyed strong bond with people of India, both as religious and cultural symbols. Luckily for the elephant; the Government of India have declared it as "National Heritage Animal". Developing country like ours essentially requires resolving human-elephant conflict and fortunately, the country is in a position to foot the bill of conservation of elephants and their habitats. It is for Indian citizens to take advantage of the opportunity and participate in the conservation of country's biodiversity, in which elephant is the part.

8.19.6 Elephant Ranges of Distribution in India

There are more than 64 protected areas in India covering an area of more than 24,580 km^2 of forests, which harbour between 25,000 to 30,000 wild elephants in the country. In fact, exclusive elephant habitats represent less than 23% of the above protected areas. The Task Force for 'Project Elephant' has identified 11 viable elephant ranges of distribution in the country, of which 3 are in south India, involving inter-states in their spread, with elephant populations ranging between 9,250 and 11,200. They are required to be constituted as exclusive "Mega Elephant Reserves", according to the Director of Project Elephant, New Delhi. The isolation of elephant species due to fragmentation of habitats has rendered the populations to non-viable levels leading to local extinction. Although optimum carrying capacity of Indian jungles is found to be 0.2-0.5 elephant per km^2, physically 3-5 km^2 of forests are required to support an elephant, without upsetting the nature's balance. Going by this logic, the existing national parks and nature reserves alone cannot ensure long term survival of the elephant species. Expansion of existing elephant habitats needs to be done by adding adjoining ecologically viable woodlands. Private holdings, where possible, need to be acquired and constituted to serve as effective corridors in networking of elephant habitats. Such corridors need to be insulated against anthropic interventions. If their natural ranges of distribution are large enough and stable enough to sustain growing elephant populations, crop raiding proclivity is likely to be minimised. Simlipal Biosphere Reserve, in Orissa State, may be quoted as an example. Here, the resident elephant population of about 500 are spread over an area of 2,750 km^2, the density of which accounts for 0.2/ km^2. The low density of resident elephants supported by enough food and water through the year are believed to be the reasons for the absence of crop raiding proclivity. Resultant human-elephant conflict in the park does not exist, though number of villages/ enclosures exist within the boundaries of biodiversity reserve (Sadly enough, for 3 years, the reserve was under seize by Naxlites, impairing the developmental activities and losing many heads of elephants). Efforts are needed for similar healthy environment to be created in other elephant reserves, through inter connectivity of additional neighbouring forests by establishing insular corridors.

8.19.7   Net-working – Steps to Initiate

The following steps – under short term and long term action plan need to be initiated for Regional Elephant Reserves Networking led by the Ministry of Environment and Forests, New Delhi:

Phase: I Region-wise survey to identify and demarcate ecologically potential elephant corridors and preparation of blue prints.

Phase: II The respective governments will execute and declare corridor linkages with existing elephant habitats.

Phase: III Consolidation of such areas by constituting them as 'add on' RFs and develop them as ecologically viable entities to serve as insular corridors for free ranging of elephants.

8.19.8   Conceptual Approach

The concept that single large elephant reserve is better than a number of fragmented reserves or islands like protected areas for a long living and large ranging elephant is generally accepted by scientific and wild-lifers communities for efficient conservation management. It is desirable, therefore, to bring ecologically potential, but fragmented elephant reserves or island-like forests, closure together, including private holdings, if any, inter connecting them by corridors. Such corridors shall be constituted as Reserve Forests (RFs) or protected areas (PAs), under Wildlife (Protection) Act, 1972, so as to insulate them against anthropic disturbances.

8.20   Regional Elephant Reserves Networking (RERN) – Southern India

Out of 25,000-30,000 wild elephants in the country, there are reported to be 9,250 – 11,200 elephants that range the forests of southern India.

Having almost 35% of India's elephant population, this region assumes significance in elephant conservation programme. The Regional Elephant Reserves Networking (RERN) – Southen India, comprises the PAs of Kerala, Tamilnadu, Karnataka, Andhra Pradesh, Goa and Maharashtra states. The project proposal would help conserve elephants over mega habitats

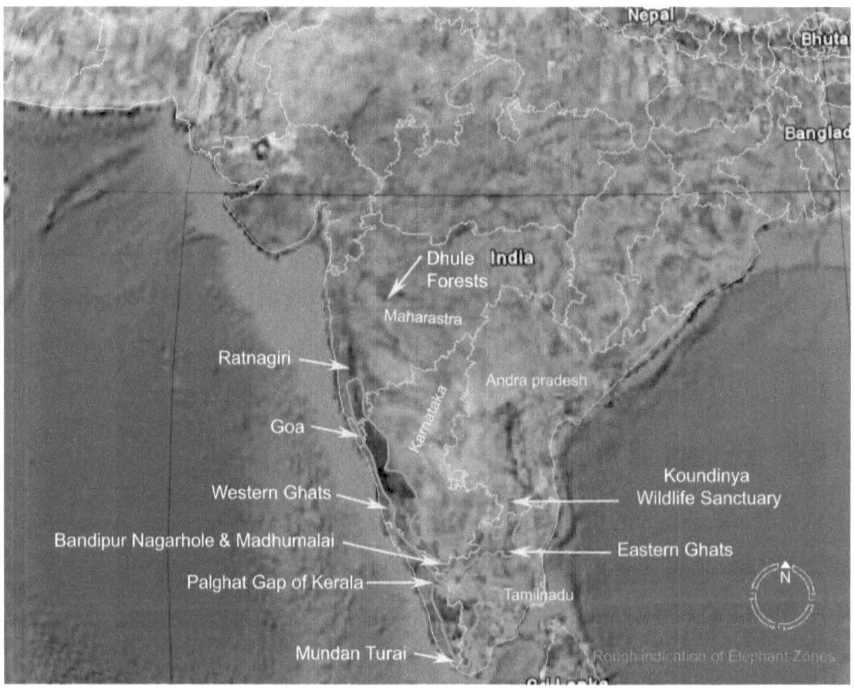

Interconnectivity of elephant reserves by insular corridors for southern India-proposed.

8.20.1 PAs to South of Palakkad Gap of Western Ghats

The Western Ghats (Sahyadris) region is the richest in biological diversity and recognised as one of the 34 "global hot spots" of species complexity. To the south of the Palakkad (Palghat) gap, there lay chain of great mountain ranges that inhabit large population of elephants. The region includes: the Parambikulam, Eravikulam, Chinnur, Rajamalai, Devikulam wildlife reserves of Kerala and the Anamalai tiger reserve, of Tamilnadu. There are 800-1000 elephants that roam in this region. From the high range mountains, including Anai Mudi, the highest mountain (2695 m) in south India, extending down to Periyar plateau, Tenamala hill ranges of Kerala are the famous protected areas for elephant populations. Towards eastern parts of the above cluster of hill ranges, such as Palani hills and newly formed Meghamalai wildlife sanctuary extending further down to Kalakkad-Mundanthurai tiger reserve of Tamilnadu also are known for elephant populations. The estimated elephant population of 150-200 drift from place to place in this region. Rubber and Tea plantations are the man-made barricades, coming in the way of interconnecting the above elephant ranges. In all, there are reported to be 1,650-2,100 elephants roam freely in the regions of south of Palakkad gap. These elephant populations require an estimated 6000-7,500 km^2 forest expanse for their free ranging movements. The ecologically viable forests/private holdings adjoining to the existing elephant reserves are needed to be identified, demarcated and blue print prepared, so as to promulgate them as insulated corridors for the elephants to socialise with distant herds.

8.20.2   PAs North of Palakkad Gap of Western Ghats

This region extends over, Silent Valley, newly constituted New Amarambalam sanctuary, Wayanad sanctuary of Kerala, connecting the elephant reserves of Deccan plateau, such as, Mukurti and Madumalai national parks of Nilgiri Biosphere Reserve of Tamilnadu, connecting Western Ghats with Eastern Ghats. There are estimated to be 500-800 elephants roaming in this region.

8.20.3   Regional Elephant Net-working – Deccan Plateau

The Nilgiri Biosphere Reserve (NBR), comprising of Nagarahole and Bandipur national parks of Karnataka State, Madumalai and Mukurti national parks of Tamilnadu state, Wayanad (north and south) sanctuaries of Kerala, ranging over 5020 km^2, if extended further by connecting

Biligirirangan Hills Tiger reserve and Kavery (Malai Mahadeswara Hills) Elephant Sanctuary, including Bannerghatta national park, towards the east of Bandipur. If this region is connected with Sathyamangalam, Anchetti, Denkinkotta and Palamner forest ranges of Tamilnadu state; further north it is connected with Koundinya Elephant Sanctuary of Andhra Pradesh. In the year 1984, some seven elephants from Tamilnadu had crossed over into Andhra Pradesh. Over the decades few elephant herds have colonised the forests of AP state.

Brahmagiri Hills Sanctuary in the western parts of Nagarahole if connected by proposed corridor after acquiring a stretch of coffee estates, a mega elephant habitat could be carved out. Further on, the Brahmagiri hills sanctuary gets connected with the rest of the Sahyadri hills region. Further north lay the Pushpagiri hills, Kuduremukh national park, Bhadra tiger reserve, Sharavathi Valley Biodiversity reserve, Dandeli-Anshi tiger reserve of Uttara Kannada district, with elephant populations of 350-400. Small herd of elephants numbering 3-10 cross over to Molen and Mahavir sanctuary of Goa and over to Radhanagari sanctuary of Ratnagiri district in Maharashtra.

The elephant populations of Bhadra Tiger Reserve numbering about 300 elephants are reported to be safe. Elephants around Kuduremukh National Park with 20 elephants and a small population of elephants are found getting killed by electrocution in island like forest near Alur of Hassan district that move about aimlessly, killing people and damaging crops, coffee estates and property. The fate of these isolated and fragmented herds is gradually narrowing down to threshold of extinction.

The Sahyadri region of Maharashtra with Chandoli national park (318 km^2) and Koyna wildlife sanctuary (424 km^2), is also potentially rich with biodiversity to sustain elephant populations, including tigers and leopards. This region needs to be interconnected from Goa and Karnataka reserves by insular corridors. The proposal to declare the entire region as "Sahyadri Biosphere Reserve" is on the anvil. This will be a step in the right direction in the making of a mega elephant conservation corridor. There are estimated to be 35 to 50 elephants criss-a-crossing this region.

8.21 Regional Elephant Reserves Networking (RERN) – Central India

The bulk of the elephant population is found in this region, comprising of Orissa, Jharkhand, Chhattisgarh states and southern parts of West Bengal. This region is inhabited by an estimated elephant population of about 2000, ranging over 20,000 km^2 expanse. These forests are spread over 21 forest divisions, including Simlipal Tiger Reserve of Orissa, Singhbhum, and Dalbhum forests divisions of Jharkhand state. An isolated population of about 40 elephants are in Palmau National Park of Jharkhand ranging over 1000 km^2. Badalkhod-Tamaorpingla, a combined reserve over the two districts of Sarguja and Jashpur and Lemru in Korba district of Chhattisgarh are the potential habitats for elephants. The Lemru, in particular, is characterised by dense cover, perennial water sources and moist riverine forests that form most suitable habitat for elephants. The added advantage is that this proposed reserve comprises of 400-500 sq km wilderness, free from human habitation. The only threat facing this area is mining of mineral-rich for coal. The highly broken chain of elephant habitats need be interconnected by insular corridors for the use of elephants during their annual migration. Detail survey to identify the potential elephant reserves and corridors need to be undertaken by respective state governments.

8.22 Regional Elephant Reserves Networking – North-Western India

Along the foothills of Himalayas, the region of Uttarakhand, has an isolated population of about 500 elephants, ranging over forest divisions of West and East Deharadun reserve forests, Siwaliks, Lansdowne, Bijnor, Kalagarh and the Haily national park, which was renamed as Jim Corbett national park in

1956, Ramanagar Tarai-Bhabar and Haldwani need to be interconnected. To the east, some of these elephants cross over to the international borders of Nepal. Another herd of about 25 elephants, which are isolated have been reported from Dudhwa National Park. Rajaji national park, which was set up in 1983, by joining three wildlife sanctuaries, namely the Rajaji, Motichur and Chilla – plays host to fairly large population of elephants. Ramaganga reservoir, Rishikesh-Chilla power channel and a paper mills pose a threat to these elephant populations. About 525 elephants in the region need 1500-2600 km^2 of forests for their free movements. These highly fragmented ranges need to be interconnected by insular corridors. The survey work for identification, and demarcation followed by preparation of blue prints of ecologically potential areas shall have to done by respective states.

8.23 Regional Elephant Reserves Networking (RERN) – North-East India

North-east India comprises of northern parts of West Bengal, southern parts of Sikkim, Assam, southern parts of Arunachal Pradesh, Meghalaya, Nagaland, Mizoram and Manipur, touching the international borders of Bhutan in the north and Myanmar in the east. Elephant population in north-east region of India are quite large, numbering more than 8,900. Such a large population to sustain with their seasonal movements, they need to be provided safe habitats extending over 26,000-45,000 km^2. Attempts are needed to prevent large scale denudation of forests that took place threesome four years ago, apart from interconnecting existing elephant reserves by ecologically potential corridors. It would be prudent for the respective state governments to initiate action to acquire large chunks of private tea estates with the financial support of the government of India.

8.24 Networking of Elephant Reserves – Anticipated Benefits

The following products, information or service benefits anticipated to accrue are:

i. Consolidation and development of existing elephant reserves with enlarged ranges of distribution. Expansion of elephant reserves inter connectivity by insular corridors would prevent over crowding of elephants and help spill over and socialise with distant island-like populations, thus help maintain healthy gene pool.

ii. Improved food and water supply for a longer duration of the season that help prevent over use of habitats and over crowding in squeezed locales, thus, help reduce crop raiding proclivity.

iii. To regain some of the lost ancient elephant corridors of bygone era and to return their lost home ranges for the elephants to rebuild their steady populations, that was affected due to human invasion over centuries.

iv. Use of remote sensing technology that helps obtain outputs of regional data with speed and accuracy, as against physical survey and demarcation.

v. By conserving the elephant – the National Heritage Animal, the country would regain her lost glory of biodiversity that helps keep the earth green and clean, thus help remedy the climate crisis.

vi. In the final analysis it would help to mitigate human-elephant conflict, a step forward in formulating conservation management blue-print.

8.25   In Conclusion

The successful implementation of such a mega project of Regional Elephant Reserves Networking (RERN) is a challenging task. It calls for coordinated and action driven efforts of respective state governments, led by the government of India. The strong political will of the Central Government, including those of state governments concerned, will help achieve this stupendous task. Of course, public participation plays a prominent role in achieving such a mega projects of national interest. Perseverance of officials heading the task is another important step in making the project a success. It goes a long way in involving national and local green warriors, such as WWF-India and NGOs of national and international repute, who shall assist push through this mega project. The programme entails participation of number of state governments that need to work with nature, but never against it, so as to justify the top-notch status granted to the elephant, the "National Heritage Animal".

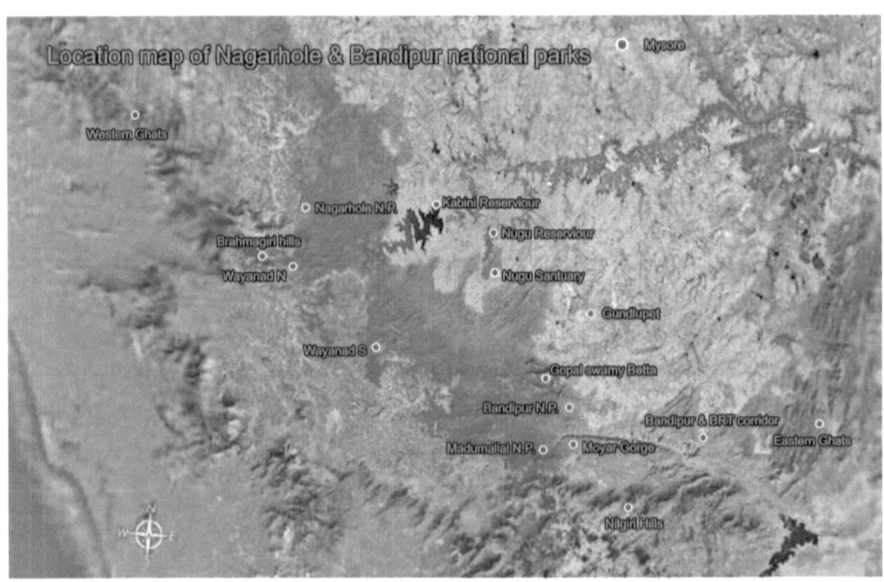

Distribution of elephants in Karnataka

Chapter IX

The Indian Elephant beyond 21st Century

Elephant – human relationship had been extremely good in most parts of India, since ancient times, due to unlimited human compassion and tolerance towards this magnificent pachyderm. Ancient people considered elephants as "Gaja lakshmi", the animal showering great wealth. Even during modern times, when the depredation by elephants often resulted in the loss of crops, property and human life, local people, by and large, do not have any wrath against the marauders and often find justification by blaming themselves for their sins and wrong doings, which may have brought forth wickedness by Ganesha the elephant headed God. There are occasions, when people attribute all good omens and even onset of good monsoons to the presence of this 'flagship animal' in their neighbourhood. They consider them as animals of fertility and good fortune. This excellent elephant-human relationship should not be allowed to be frittered away, just because few belligerent youngsters, occasionally, stray out into farmers' fields during their seasonal movements. The miseries of the people be redressed at the earliest and mitigation action taken expeditiously, while we are managing to conserving elephant, the National Heritage Animal of India. Let elephant-human conflict not be a great stumbling block to a plethora of elephant's glory.

The year 1984 provided a bumper harvest for the farmers of surrounding villages of Bandipur tiger reserve. All solitary male elephants, whether or not true lone bulls were generally, misconceived as 'rogues'. Some of them were belligerent towards men, some were not. It has often been said that of all the wild animals, forest-dwelling tribes are very much afraid of elephants and this is quite understandable, because of the unpredictable nature of the beasts, when chance-encountered. However, few seem to realise that the aggression in elephants towards men in areas, where they have invaded elephant country, is almost invariably meted out by human hostility initially or that the shooting of elephants is something that has to be done expertly, if it has to be done, at all and that wounding of animals may only lead to further trouble. This has been the song of miseries meted out to elephant tribe, ever since man learnt growing food crops. Almost invariably a proscribed 'rogue' that had killed a man or a few men, carried gunshot wounds, probably received in the course of raiding crops, which have suddenly sprung up in what used to be primeval forest and their original home range. For some reason, gunshot wounds do not heal easily in elephants, though some animals recover from them. As the days roll by they become festering sores, usually maggot-ridden and cause considerable pain and irritation. The wounds handicap the animal and they persist for years. The proscribed rogue that was reported, I had observed in the Madumalai Sanctuary, carried unhealed bullet wounds, when he was shot dead by the park Vet. We come across innumerable evidences in the annals of human history over conflicting factors between man and elephant. We need to have integrated approach to mitigate ever increasing confrontations. They are:

9.1 Man – an Invader in Elephants' Paradise

The impact of human invasion on elephants' habitat has deleterious and irreversible. Most other diurnal animals retreat to their hide-outs before human invades the depths of forest or else, turn into fugitive creatures of the night, hiding by day in cover, because men are active in the forests then. The elephants, on the contrary, are not entirely diurnal in their activities. . But they are both diurnal and nocturnal in their habits. It is the only wild animal feeding by day and by night with a brief respite of about four hours, any time either during the night or the day. In forests, where they are little disturbed, the normal reaction of elephants to near human presence is flight. A big herd of elephants, I was following at a distance on foot during my morning trekking along the outskirts of the reserve, turned around suddenly and came towards me at their fastest pace, running in single file, over uneven open ground. What had alarmed them came into view, a while later, was a small boy herding about a dozen buffaloes. On another occasion, a tusker about to emerge from thorny bush turned back and retreated into the dense cover on hearing the sound of a wood cutter in the eastern sector of the reserve. Many such instances of the natural tendency of wild elephants to give wide berth and even bolt-away from near presence of men are on record. They are even able to associate cattle with men and usually flee away from cattle herd, unless they are sure that there is no herdsman accompanying them.

During my trekking expeditions through the forests of the reserve, I wanted the elephants to make way for my onward march. If they were in the open, like road sides or view lines, I went and stood at a safe distance, not crossing line of critical (LoC) danger, so as to be clearly seen by the elephants. On seeing my presence, they reciprocated to my respect shown to them and slowly entered the thicket. I then continued my sojourn. At times, when I encountered them across the beaten path in a thick jungle, I tapped the near by tree trunk with *matchu*, the cutting hand-tool or with a piece of wood or bamboo, which could produce sound akin to wood-cutting; elephants associate such a sound to the presence of wood-cutter. But one must be always on alert, looking around and keeping eyes and ears wide open. While you wait for elephants in the open, keep an eye on possible sub-adult male from behind or from some other corners.

Where elephants have been much disturbed and harried by men, their reactions to humans undergo a sea-change in their perception. Flight is still the commonest reaction, but they may become more assertive and indulge in demonstration and even frontal attack. Interesting responses, I had observed in elephants, who wanted to cross the road or wanted to stay close to a water hole for a drink or feed peacefully without being disturbed. Once, on hearing the sound of my approaching vehicle, a bachelor group resorted to pull down a few culms of big bamboo from a roadside clump. On other occasion, a sapling was way-laid across the track just to constitute a road-blockade. Yet another time, I was travelling in the van for inspection on Wesley road at midday in Bandipur reserve. A matriarch accompanied by another cow emerged from the thicket and stood blocking the road, on hearing the noise of our approaching vehicle. Next time, a big bull, which I was photographing for the last half-an-hour or so, pushed down a Teak tree across the road as a blockade. It exhibited his audaciousness and started feeding peacefully on the bark and twigs. This time it was not to way-lay across the road, but to feed on Teak bark and twigs comfortably.

In assessing these responses and aggressiveness towards men, it should be remembered that elephants are long-lived animals with a clear topographical comprehension of their stamping grounds and that their resentment of intrusions such as man-made structures into their domain and their proclivity to destroy such structures is something that can be anticipated. It is said that on occasions, their hostility takes the form of flinging stones/mud at human intruders, a less wildly improbable response than it might seem to those not intimately familiar with elephants.

The usual manifestation of resentment against human intrusion is a demonstration or a mock-charge. However, even an area like Begur forests of the Bandipur reserve, for long known as a favourite haunting place of wild elephants, has been invaded by irrigation project like Kabini followed by human settlements, agriculture and plantations. Here, human population has increased enormously and hundreds and thousands of cattle are herded everyday inside the reserve. What is pitiably astonishing is, not the occasional aggression of the wild elephants but their acceptance of man-made intrusions and their tolerance of herds of humanity. Almost every year a few people are killed by elephants in and around Bandipur reserve, but the kills occur in the course of chance encounters between men and elephants outside the forests and not at human settlements. Incidentally, cows and even sub-adults are responsible for many of these attacks. Adult bulls, occasionally, cause human death by panic rather than deliberate hostility. It is possible that men in drunken state while travelling from hamlet to hamlet through the forests may bump onto bulls feeding on the road sides or a herd waiting at the periphery of the forests to raid crops. A deaf man passing through the forest at dusk had bumped on to a loner, only to be smashed when he failed to respond to the warning calls. Similarly, a villager with a poor eye sight returning from a nearby weekly shandy had fallen victim to a cow accompanied by its calf at the outskirts of Muliyur of Bandipur reserve.

9.2 Elephantine Problems – Man's Exhilarated Use of Forest Land

As a consequence of an invasion of elephants' domain by humans their range of distribution is much reduced considerably. The constant disturbance from villagers and their herds of livestock to their habitats, elephant herds are forced to move nearer to human settlements, especially, when seasonal conditions are unfavourable. Growing palatable crops by farmers in the immediate vicinity of forest boundaries attract elephants' attention. According to a maxim, 'old habits die hard', elephants tend to freely stray out in those areas that once belonged them. The methods to scare them away against such crop-raiders are primitive, such as bursting of crackers, digging of elephant – proof ditches around the fields and electric fence. There is urgent need to use of barricades of steel rails along the reserve borders, which are working effectively to keep elephants confined from straying out. Of course, use of firearms in inexpert hands usually result in elephants getting hurt and turning hostile towards men. Even men involved in killing elephants are not punished adequately.

However, as each year rolls by, compression of the elephants' range continues unabated with exponential human population growth. Looking at the sequences of things that go on at present, an established fact is that human-elephant clash seems here to stay. In fact, the very existence of elephants is now being threatened inside the protected areas by growing demands for land grabbing, livestock grazing, timber harvesting and poaching fuel wood and for flesh. It is unrealistic to contemplate any significant reduction in the growth rate of the human population of India before the turn of the next century and beyond and it would seem realistic to propose that if elephants are to survive in India, they and all other wildlife species must be integrated into our land use planning. It is important and urgent for India to plan restructuring the land use planning?

What then in store for the future? I am firmly of the opinion that all conservation organisations, scientists and wildlife managers must have the courage to adopt a long term perspective and come out with new technology that help contain elephants within the borders of protected areas (PAs), rather than attempting to tackle minor issues such as the translocation or reintroduction of locally endangered species by foreign origin. Such ill-conceived ventures rarely succeed, particularly, when attempted against the nature. It is the in *situ* conservation efforts that lead to a success, rather than attempting *ex situ* protection.

I was always wondering where the cause of aggression did lay by elephants. Of late, I realised, it was within us, the humans. Elephants including all other wild animals have one enemy in common, it is human. He has, with his greed for personal benefit, has pushed flora and fauna to a brink of extinction. Species extinction is looming large in every corner of the country. Extinction of species, as we understand, is not an event but a process. We can't stop it, nor is it possible to turn the clock back, but we can only slow down the process. Man is the greatest threat to their existence and he alone is the hope of their survival. The future survival of elephants, therefore, depends mainly on man's love for nature and compassion towards the beasts.

9.3 Who Needs Elephants after All?

It is a fair question to mull over, if all the land on earth is needed to support the exploding human population, why the elephants need be conserved? Why the forests those provide them food and shelter be protected? Why the tigers and their prey species be saved?

And the answer has both environmental and emotional dimensions. The very essence of conservation of elephant, the flagship species of the Indian jungles is the expression of biodiversity conservation, on which survival of human society depends. In support of this rational conclusion is the protection of tiger, the charismatic species of the biome. While the elephant plays its role in maintaining the eco-biological health, the tiger at the apex of biological pyramid, plays a pivotal role in maintaining equilibrium of biodiversity. On the emotional side, the elephant has long held a special place in the heart of Indians, a symbol of wisdom, strength and gentleness. Ganesha, the elephant-headed god, is Hindu's most universally accepted deity, believed to remove obstacles, bestow success and fulfil desires.

On the strictly practical side, an anonymous Burmese author writes: "Many people are bound to be surprised, if told that there is available in Burma an extremely versatile, multipurpose, self-generating heavy duty machine of great strength and the delicate sensitiveness of a ballet dancer, which is readily adaptable to all kinds of terrain and work conditions, including the capability of working in four feet of water, requires a minimum of maintenance, is able to work efficiently on all grades of limitless fuel that grows on trees, forest floor and has a phenomenal built-in memory. And the beauty of it is that it does not cost us any foreign exchange. That living-machine is, of course, the elephant"!

9.4 Role of Protected Areas in Elephant Conservation

Elephant management as practiced today often seems like a firemen rushing around, trying to control a rash of bush fires, putting out one fire only, but to have another appear nearby. In attempting to snuff-out 'conflicting factors' between man and elephant arising each day at a different sites, what is needed is a strategic and comprehensive approach to elephant management, which should take into consideration the needs of the elephants and the needs of local people. Recognizing the importance of Asian elephants, the International Union for Conservation of Nature and Natural Resources (IUCN) formed an Asian Elephant Specialist Group (AESG) under its Species Survival Commission (SSC), with the objective of surveying the whole spectrum of man, elephant and habitat interactions; so that the information needed to manage elephant populations and their habitat status could be obtained. Incidentally, Asian elephant is also included in the list of 'endangered' animals under Species Survival Plan (SSP) under the IUCN's Red Data Book of Endangered Species. The elephant is, therefore, required to be managed on hard realities and optimism.

The AESG, whose members were elephant experts from within the tropical Asia, developed the concept of 'Managed Elephant Ranges', where healthy elephant populations would be managed. In its basic form, an elephant range is centred on a national park system or protected areas, managed, as at present, but with an extensive buffer zone concept, where certain restricted human uses are allowed.

9.5 Wilderness – Its Usefulness

One may ask how long the governments can keep vast areas of land 'remote from the people' in the form of National Parks and Protected areas. The question is prompted by the belief that all land, especially wilderness is 'useless' if it does not yield an obvious economic returns or visible advantages. Logically speaking, the governments have to maintain many departments, institutions or services which are 'remote from the people'. Universities are inaccessible to the majority of poor students; Armed Forces and Defence Production Establishments are totally unproductive; some of the government departments are wasteful. Yet in the long run even pure research, the results of which have no practical application, or beneficial to the community, are of wasteful expenditure. Despite all these, in our lamentably unsafe world, army 'produces', an atmosphere of security and peace or at least the illusion of it, which serves the purpose almost as well, without which the country's other social, political and economic activities could not be properly performed.

In the case of wilderness areas, the benefits accrued are far from being illusory. They are real. The wilderness areas of the world are the most efficient recycling and neutralising agencies of our wastes and emissions, in particular, carbon dioxide and other poisonous gasses in the atmosphere. They regulate our climate and water regime, even help in reducing the effect of climate change, due to 'global warming', all without any running or maintenance cost. The wisest investment any community or the nation can possibly make is, not to attempt to derive any other, more direct or visible revenue from them. In overexploited and ecologically devastated country, we have to spend lot more money, in order to mend damages to forests and to keep them free from pollution and environmental degradation. A sufficiently large proportion of wilderness, if exists in the country, it would help save us from avoidable climate change and human diseases.

Climatologists have been cautioning about the perceptible increase in the emissions of 'greenhouse gases', such as Carbon dioxide, Methane and Nitrous oxide, since 1980s. According to the report of the 'State of Climate', presented at Kyoto Summit, held during first week of December 1997, the rapidly increasing of burning of fossil fuel like coal, oil and gasoline at alarming levels, continued deforestation and burning of tropical forests around the globe, are leading to belching out of large quantities of Carbon dioxide and other greenhouse gases into the atmosphere. These gases continue to remain in the atmosphere for long and trap the reflected heat from the surface of the earth planet. The consequences shall be disastrous, including rise in sea level. The popular belief in the folklore is, "solution for pollution is dilution". The process of dilution is achieved by tropical forests, which act as absorbents of pollutants. Scientists assert that a hector of tropical forest can absorb 10 tonnes of Carbon dioxide. For too long, conservationists have been extolling the biodiversity conservation, as the 'national heritage', to be preserved for the benefit of future generations. But we are curiously blind to the incalculably vast, direct economic values of wilderness *per se*.

It is often argued that the poor/under developed nations can not afford to leave wilderness intact. In fact, even the so-called rich/developed countries can not afford to over exploit/destroy it. Wilderness/biodiversity rich areas are the economically soundest investment any country can make for the benefit of its citizens and the world community at large.

Moreover, large wilderness areas on either side of international borders could protect peace and tranquillity and prevent un-authorised entrance more effectively than barbed wire, watch towers, mines and all the rest of that expensive junk ever could; and it would be a lot cheaper!

Today, more than half the world's ten billion people live in conditions of near hopeless poverty and squalor. Millions are seeking escape by migrating to cities and even to other countries, where the same problems reign. At the same time, people in affluent countries consume up to 50 times or more of natural resources than the average inhabitant of a developing country.

9.6 Conserving Tropical Treasure

Today, plants and animals are in danger of extinction, wherever we look in corners of the world. But it is not necessarily a coincidence that they are suffering, while man attempts to improve his grip over the world – as natural resources are exploited and waste products (including e-waste) dumped into the sea, into the air and on the land causing pollutions.

Conservationists fight tooth and nail to halt reckless destruction of nature, where it can be highlighted as unnecessary, harmful to man himself. Their successes have been numerous and yet a mood of pessimism prevails. Campaigns are fought on scientific, technological, moral, emotional, social and aesthetic and on political grounds, but still the destruction continues by unscrupulous few. What the conservationists are up against, the thing, they cannot define, is the 'human nature' that is embedded in each one of us. We are presently witnessing a climax in evolution as we know it. There have been massive extinctions in the past. Can we ever forget the sudden disappearance of the dinosaurs from the face of the earth planet some 75 million years ago? "Extinct carnivorous mammals shrank in size and new species that evolved to half the size of their ancestors during a global warming event that occurred 55 million years ago", says a new scientific study. We know that the present day mammals are reported to be the siblings of prehistoric animals. Plant-eating mammals got smaller during the earliest Eocene (epoch) when global warming occurred, possibly associated with elevated levels of carbon dioxide. It is easy to acknowledge that the natural catastrophes will happen any time, any where, without warning again in the future. What about the present, but?

It is, today that concerns us, the events that take place, while we are alive and struggling as individuals to improve on our own positions in the world. It has to be admitted that for billions of humans, the earth planet is not a happy place to live in. How can those craving to find their niche, food and groping to earn money or those tossed between the political whims of major powers be expected to make significant contributions to the modern conservation movement, which has its origin in the wealthiest regions of the globe?

9.7 Need for Further Legislations

Should we not, therefore, attempt to solve the human problem before moving on to the safety of wild animals and plants around us, so that we can all work with equal weight, equal conviction and equal reward? In theory; yes, it is said than done. But we all know that it would be difficult to create a level ground or the world in which all humans live with equal rights. Perhaps, not all the problems are insurmountable.

So, we have to do the best we could, for the cause of wildlife under the prevailing conditions. These are not the best, but at least legislation has the advantage of slowing down the process of destruction, so that we can buy more time to gauge the next steps to be put in place. With each year that passes by, these steps become a bit more desperate, because it is not when an animal population reaches zero that it becomes extinct, but it happens much before, when numbers fall below a critical level from which a species can never recover. That is why, it is said that in 50 years' time there will be no more tigers and no more gorillas, simply because present and seemingly, unalterable trends indicate that their numbers will soon fall below a recovery threshold.

In case, the situation in India gets further aggravated, it may call for a legislation declaring elephant killing a 'heinous crime'. This would help enforce the law of the land and strengthen the hands of the Foresters, wild-lifers and the Police to deal with this malady firmly. In India, powerful laws against elephant poaching and other nefarious activities do exist. But the authorities are required to be ever vigilant to exercise powers vested with great zeal, if our elephants are to survive. Inevitably, conservation in India is over-shadowed by over 121 crore (1210 million) people. We must, however, keep in mind, in case things do not improve, a situation may arise to declare some of our wild animals, such as elephant and tiger and plants, such as sandalwood, as "national heritage animals and plants" respectively, while our national parks and protected reserves, as "national living monuments", in order to make conservation meaningful. All said and done, it is always the local communities including tribal people who matter the most in the success of conservation and they need to be addressed. We must help them to improve their quality of life and educate them in creating environmental awareness.

9.8 Highlights For Elephant Conservation

The elephant, that was listed as an endangered species in Southeast Asia, found to be fast approaching to threshold of extinction. It is easy to ask a hypothetical question, as to how many elephants may remain alive at the end of twenty first century? But it is not enough to set aside certain acreage of wilderness, unless their survival is ensured by implementing effective conservation measures with the support of local communities and political will. With all the good-will of world's NGOs and pouring in of tourist-money and even considering the earning potential of the reserve, if the population dynamics of the species concerned is not thoroughly understood by the park manager, the very survival of the species becomes difficult. There is urgent need for a well documented management plan using latest scientific and technological inputs for each of the protected areas, as specified elsewhere in the book.

It was not until the mid – 1960s that the first serious and scientific study of elephant's social life was under-taken in Africa. That was when Ian Douglas – Hamilton and Oria began studies at Lake Manyara in Tanzania of African continent, which earned them world wide acclaim, because of their basic contribution to the understanding of elephant's social life. Admittedly, their findings related specifically to one large group of wild elephants living in one particular place, but the principles of social system hold good for wild elephants covering a much wider areas of African Countries. They endorsed many of the tentative suggestions that had been formulated from preliminary studies elsewhere, particularly in Uganda. Similarly, many of my field studies, documented at Bandipur reserve, over more than five years, as to the social system of Indian elephants are almost akin to the ones enumerated by Ian Douglas-Hamilton and Oria on African elephants. However, behaviour pattern may vary, depending on local climatic conditions and vegetative landscapes and local anthropic pressures.

Above all, it is an endorsed fact that elephant protection was not enough in its own right and that once the wildlife reserves had been created, the problems were only just beginning. The ultimate cause for such a change was obviously that human-wildlife reserves are artificial by definition – with the elephants seen as on-the-spot villains of the peace. For others, it seemed a logical consequence of allowing elephants to breed within defined areas from which they could not move without risk of being shot at. The elephants seemed to be intelligent enough to know exactly where they could remain safe, with the result that not only did they remain within the reserve's limits but also others moved in from outside to join them.

However, the policy was to become one of non-interference in the hope that the elephants would regulate themselves and establish some sort of natural equilibrium with their surrounding landscapes. Perhaps, they would die younger or breed later and keep their numbers down to an ecologically acceptable level, under the law of nature!

9.9 What is in Store for Future of Asian Elephants?

Anti-elephant communities, in recent years, have threatened to decimate the elephant to near extinction by waging warfare for ivory, the white gold. Nevertheless, no one knows exactly just how many elephants are left in the Indian jungles. The overall situation has been confused by the presence of large concentrations of elephants in some regions, while they have disappeared from others.

To establish a true picture of the elephant situation about Asian and African elephants and to work out conservation strategies, the WWF and the IUCN had launched a three year project some years ago. The New York Zoological Society was actively associated with the programme. The results indicated the existence of about 40,000 Asian elephants as against 400,000 African during 1997. Presently, the population of Indian elephants alone ranges between 27,600 and 30,000.

The Asian elephant which is of a different genus (by no means Asian elephant is related to African) than that of the African, is found from China, India through continental south-east Asia and on the islands of Sri Lanka and Sumatra. Future of Asian elephant hinges in balance and its survival is to be every body's concern. The choice is ours; the need for conservation of elephants is for our own survival. So let us plan conservation strategy as the final line of defence.

The Asian elephant is also listed in Appendix-I of the 1973 Convention for International Trade in Endangered Species of Wild Fauna and Flora

(CITES) and therefore, any trade in it or its products is subject to strict regulations by ratifying nations; any trade primarily for commercial purposes is banned. The elephant is protected by law in most of the countries within their range of distribution and such a protection is often a long historical standing.

While the overall picture is one of rapid decline, a paradoxical situation has developed in many national parks and protected areas, where elephant numbers have swollen. The vegetation there may be destroyed resulting in malnutrition apart from changing the local ecology, affecting a wide range of other animal species. This could even result in the elephant becoming virtually extinct in areas, set aside for their conservation. In such an eventuality, habitat restorative measures demand topmost priority. Habitat restorative measure include: development of habitats by rewilding, rain water harvesting, creation of more grasslands, eradication of obnoxious weeds, regulation of livestock grazing, creating more water holes, restricted eco-tourism within the tourism zone, uprooting of tourist outfits from elephant corridors and interconnecting island – like elephant habitats with add on PAs.

Eco-development programmes around the parks and reserves apart from environment education to school children and their teachers, should be a part of conservation strategies.

9.10 Exhilarated Use of Forest Land for Human Elephant Conflict

The problem of depredation has three major facets: (a) loss of human life (b) killing of elephants (c) loss of property. The loss of property can be viewed into: (i) loss of food crops (ii) loss of commercial plantations and (iii) damage to houses and other structures.

9.10.1 Loss of Human Life

The annual toll of human life taken by wild elephants has risen in northern Bengal from about 30 per year in the 1970s to 90 in 2020s. In 1989, elephants killed 52 people in Assam. During 2019, straying herds killed 84 people in Bihar. Herds of elephants started straying into Andhra Pradesh from adjoining Tamilnadu in 1984. Since that time, about 200 people have been killed in Andhra Pradesh. Estimates suggest that about 150 people are killed by wild elephants annually in southern India. On an average 400 people are reported killed every year in the country.

9.10.2   Killing of Elephants by Man

At least 150 tuskers are poached for ivory each year, while another 300 elephants die of human-induced causes, such as shooting by crop protection guns, electrocution and poisoning in the country.

9.10.3   Loss of Crops and Property

Crop raiding proclivity in elephants is mainly due to the cultivated plants being more palatable to elephants than wild vegetation, which may be plentiful. Food crops have a higher nutritional value for elephants and they may feed on them as a matter of preference. Further, the damage done by trampling by the herd or unattached males, perhaps, due to confusion is much more. According to an estimate 1000-1500 sq km of crop-areas and 12,000-16,000 houses/properties are damaged in the country each year. Governments spend Rs. 200-300 million every year on measures of controlling depredation and payment of ex-gratia to the farmers.

9.11   Keeping Wild Elephants at Bay from Sugarcane Fields?

We have to accept the maxim that "elephants and human settlements are incompatible", within an ecosystem. African elephant conservation policy is based on this assumption. Contrary to the above concept depredation is a way of life in south-east Asian countries. Here humans have to make way in favour of the elephants by uprooting themselves from the elephant inhabited country. Otherwise, farmers have to compromise and learn to live with elephants. Incidentally, the problem in our management is not how to stop it altogether, but how to mitigate/control it, under a given situation of emotional, socioeconomic and political settings. I am sure latest use of steel railing across the borders of elephant reserves might yield to desired results of stoppage of elephants from straying out.

Elephant depredation has been increasing in recent years, the chief reason being the loss of habitat, leading to increasing man-elephant confrontation. Since time immemorial, the Asian elephant has been a friend of man and yet wild elephants and human settlements can not co-exist without some conflicts. This was also recognised in the *Arthashastra*, an account of Indian political and governmental strategy compiled between 300 B.C. and A.D. 300. (Attributed to Koutilya, Chief Minister to Chandragupta, the founder of the Mauryan Empire in India). At present, elephant depredation has become one of the major management problems in many protected areas and outside them as well. Steel railing in recent times along the periphery has been fairly effective and that would help keep off elephants from sugarcane fields.

9.12 Strategy to Mitigate Human Elephant Conflict

There are, however, two kinds of combat measures: firstly, the preventive; those which are designed to prevent elephants from raiding crops and secondly, the combat measures; those which deal against elephants actually raiding crops. Preventive measures can be categorised into two: deterrents, the measures such as erecting barriers, like elephant proof trench (EPT) or Solar energised fence or steel railings, which physically prevent elephants from raiding crops and b) repellents, such as lights, organics or chemicals, like tiger urine or loud music or producing sound as the wood cutter does, which though not actual physical barriers, but discourage/ repel elephants from raiding crops. Loud music or wood cutting sounds disguise the presence of humans. One must remember translocation of troublesome elephants to safer areas is no solution; experiences in Sri Lanka and Karnataka have shown that such animals invariably tend to return to the original places of capture. The better option would be to attempt in *situ* conservation than *ex situ* rehabilitation. In addition, the following combat measures could be tried, as a package to preempt elephant menace:

9.12.1 Preventive Measures

Firstly, there is need for change in the land use pattern. Farmers around the PAs, particularly, where elephants and wild pigs inhabit, should be asked not to grow food crops in their holdings. They should only grow non-palatable crops, such as cotton, castor, oil palm, rape, etc.

Secondly, physical barriers of many forms need to be tried out depending on local conditions. Some of them have been tried with varying degree of success, including solar fencing, elephant-proof trenches, dry-rubble walls, or boulders held together by galvanized wire netting, spikes embedded in concrete slabs, steel railings and continuous protective wall. They are:

i. **Solar Electrified Fence is undoubtedly, the cheapest and the most effective form of all physical barriers. The success or otherwise of the fence depends, largely on adherence to proper design and strictly on regular maintenance. Once the elephants learn to respect the fence, they avoid it by sending message of warning through ultra sounds amongst their tribe. However, it is not easy to fool the elephants; they use their tusks or nails or the soles of their front foot, which are poor conductors of current to break the fence wires. Some elephants even push trees over the fence to snap the wires and enter fields.**

ii. **Elephant – Proof Trench (EPT): A permanent remedy against depredation by elephants has been found quite effective around the reserve of Bandipur and elsewhere. Excavating elephant proof trench along the periphery of the reserve or abutting the farmers' holdings helps the aggressors confined within park boundaries. A trapezium shaped trench, with dimensions – 2.5 to 3.0 m. width at the top, 2.0 m. depth and 0.5-1.0 m. width at the bottom, serves as effective. Length of** the trench being 4 m. with intermittent breaks in between, so as to retain rain water or it may be continuous. The trench also helps as a barrier against stray cattle entering the forests in addition to serve as permanent demarcation line between forests and private holdings, thus help solve the problem of encroachments. Regular upkeep of the trench is most essential, if it has to serve its purpose.

iii. Sprinkling tiger urine as repellent (Caotin) along field boundaries in the eco-fragile buffer: Though elephants and tigers share the same niche, our observation is that they do not partake in the same feeding ground. They are the staunch adversaries of the natural ecosystem, where each tries to keep the other at bay, because of lurking danger to young ones of the other species. The tiger urine can serve as a repellent for the elephant. Tiger urine is sprinkled to keep away persistent crop raiding elephants. When attempts towards this had been made by collecting tiger urine from the Mysore zoo and sprinkling it along the boundaries of a sugarcane field adjacent to Bandipur Park, the elephants did not venture to raid these crops, where as, in the neighbouring fields there were reports of raids. The experiment could not be repeated because of certain limitations and practical difficulties, such as procuring tiger urine fairly in good quantity. According to Sanyal, former Field Director, Sunderbans Tiger Reserve (2002, prsnl. comn.), who also tried this method in West Bengal forests, the smell of tiger urine sprinkled on the boundary of the field had forced the elephants to retreat. The problem of collecting tiger urine can be overcome, if synthetic analogues of the ingredients of the tiger urine can be invented as spray.

iv. Lakshmana *Rekha* to keep off crop raiding elephants by use of red chilli (Capsicum) powder/paste: A recent experiment in drawing a line, Lakshmana *rekha*, by sprinkling red chilli powder along the boundaries of agricultural fields has been tried by the farmers living around Kakum National Park in Ghana, in collaboration with "Conservation International", a voluntary organization. It is assumed that a strong pungent smell of red chilli powder drives away the elephants from the sugarcane fields. The technique involved is that two strands of rope are run through bamboo/wooden poles fixed along the boundaries of the field. Gunny cloth pieces, pasted by mixture of chilli powder and grease/waste engine oil are hung in between strands of rope at regular intervals. This technique being simple and cheap is proposed to be practiced by farmers in Ghana and Zimbabwe. This method appears to be better than the other traditional methods, such as bon fire, beating drum, bursting *Aane pathaka* – locally made crackers, etc., But it is to be seen, whether elephants continue to respect chilli powder, as a scaring device in the long run, when they are likely to get used to the pungent smell. Other problem is that the chilli powder may lose its inherent pungent qualities due to prolonged exposure to the sun and rains. Crop raiding proclivity in elephants being prevalent only for a brief period of 2-3 moths, particularly, during flowering to harvest stage of the crop husbandry, periodical renewal of application of chilli powder may help overcome this shortcomings. Simultaneously, it is to be seen, if this technique can work against other habitual crop raiders, like wild pigs and monkeys. This ingredient, however needs to be replicated in collaboration with chilli merchants, where crop raiding problems are prevalent.

In Zambia an experiment to keep off elephants from farm lands using "pepper powder" was reported to be found successful. Like that of chilli powder, the pepper powder also works as scary ingredient to elephants. Pepper powder mixed in engine oil is smeared to gunny bags or mats and hung along the fence at regular intervals. It is also smeared to fence – posts. Pepper powder also can be mixed with cow dung and bricks/cakes prepared.

The dried bricks are burnt during night to smoke the surroundings or possible entry points. The pungent smell of pepper powder helps scare away crop raiding elephants. This easy method needs to be popularized among agrarian community by the forest departments in collaboration with NGOs/Spice Board of India.

9.12.2 Combat Measures

Various measures have been found effective with varying degrees. Elephants take to their heel at the powerful beams of spot lights, music, wood cutting sound drum beating and bon-fire. Occasional belligerent adult males may get used to repeated attempts of above tactics and may refuse to respect. A package with the following methods may work with success in keeping the crop raiders at bay. They are:

i. **Crackers and Rockets with loud bang are effective, particularly, with family groups of elephants until they become familiar to them.**

ii. ***Aane Phataka*** **(elephant cracker) – The farmers, presently, protect their crops by bursting fire-crackers to scare them away. Using hand-made bombs that are locally prepared for the purpose, called** *Aane Phataka.* **This is an improvised scaring device. Here, two strands of hard galvanized parallel wires are drawn over erected bamboo sticks of 2 to 3 ft. in height, anchored at a distance of about 10-15 ft. At** *ad hoc* **interval the wire strands are tied to small sticks laid horizontally over the frame of 4 bamboo sticks. A stone is hung to the frame below which a locally made** *Aane Phataka* **is hung with the help of a hook. The moment wire strands are pulled apart by intruding elephants/wild pigs while attempting to cross over into the field, the stone under which cracker is hung drops automatically, on another stone kept below flat on the ground. The cracker explodes with loud bang. The trespassers get scared and take to their heel. The technique is simple, economical** and quite effective. But raiders are, increasingly, getting bolder and some times are not deterred by sound barrages. In fact, some ill-tempered elephants are known to have attacked the farmers guarding their fields and have killed them.

iii. Gas Cannon: It is an equipment, which serves as police-eying over aggressors and shooting out a thundering sound, while in view, comparable to the sounds of cannon. Elephants or any animal appearing in the vicinity of its range fires automatically, producing enormous sound which drives away the intruders. Gas Cannons could conveniently, be used as a modern scaring device against wild animals of depredation. This simple technology could either be developed, indigenously or imported.

iv. Do the Way Wood-cutter Does: Wood cutting sound in and outside the forest boundary is, particularly associated with the presence of human beings. Naturally, such spots are avoided by elephants. Farmers, whose fields are likely to be raided, should only tap the tree or a branch of a tree with an axe or *matchu*, the bill hook to produce sound. This 'wood-cutting'sound drives the intruders away. This task is done sitting safely on a tree or a *machan*. While doing so, do not get excited or panicky on seeing elephants in the middle of the field. Be cool. No shouting or bursting of crackers are resorted to, lest the elephants get enraged and do more damage to the crops by trampling in an utter confusion; they may even attempt to attack humans.

v. Playing Music by Radio/Mobile Phones: A recent discovery by the farmers is to use their Radio/Mobile Phones for playing music, against wild pigs. Farmers of Gulbarga and neighbouring districts have, since been successful in keeping wild pigs at bay from their fields. It is worthwhile to play music by using Radio/Mobile phones to play music against elephants.

9.13   Conservation Must be Participative

The vital key to survival of elephants, for which we Foresters/Wild-lifers still search is, how to confine them effectively within the arbitrary boundaries of the national parks. The correct answers will depend on whether or not parks are spacious enough for seasonal cycles to work without the risk of extinction. In times, we may know, but in groping for the details, we run the risk of forgetting an even more serious aspect, that it is only man's fragile act of tolerance that allows elephants to live at all in the modern world. Temperament of elephants changes because poachers and farmers, by their constant hostility against them, have created psycho-fear in them. Lot of people get into trouble with elephants when they don't respect law of the jungle.

The most important key factor of survival strategy for elephants is, therefore, to gain the sympathy of the people with whom the elephants share the land and the politicians who represent people. This can only be done by awakening their latent interest and aesthetic awareness through the spoken and printed words, non-formal methods of environment education, films and television. From the enthusiastic response of local tribes and villagers taken around on free trips in the park, I have seen encouraging results. The park's neighbours need be provided greater economic benefits, so as to improve their living conditions. These activities need an extension organisation, within the park establishment, so that the park-ideas reach the doors steps of villagers.

Past experiences have shown that committed conservation staffs were treated with 'complete indifference'. Ill-equipped frontline staff are penalised against poaching and smuggling. The political will and administrative skill are lacking right from the top in addressing the issues concerning conservation management. Without a political leadership, India's elephants, rhinos, tigers together with many less visible species, will disappear within the next few decades. Trade in wildlife skins, fur, rhino horns including ivory, has gone out of control in India, since the last five decades. Tuskers have been so heavily poached for ivory, that in some parks the ratio of males to females is a staggering 1:200. It is emphasized that the crucial survival factor for the elephant is the safe habitat, with enough food and water. Only then, the frontiers of conservation hold light in the future safety of elephants.

Ironically, the immediate apprehension among the naturalists is that the national parks and wildlife reserves can no longer be seen as totally protected areas, since globalization and economic liberalization in the country have opened up all areas to development, like infrastructure, metros, express highways, etc., putting increasing pressure on natural resources. The wildlife habitats across the country are being encroached extensively, destroyed and even polluted by industrialization. With this sort of attitude towards wilderness, which actually represents invaluable and irreplaceable national assets, it is not likely that any one will bother much about the fate of the wild elephants/tigers. It is only a matter of time, when country's biodiversity would face threshold of extinction, unless some thing is done to address the grievances of the farmers, whose crops are raided and innocent people are killed by elephants. Make sure that elephants don't antagonise the farm lobby, which is a formidable power in the country and can play a decisive role in elections. Alas, "I wish the elephants have had voting rights!"

Paradoxically, human society enjoys the priority over elephant society; man on the street may ask who is to live, man or elephants? It is not the question of human priority over the latter, but essence of man's survival is to have healthy environment and clean air. To achieve these basic needs of human survival, the conservation of biodiversity in which elephant, the flagship species plays a pivotal role. The elephant conservation, therefore assumes global significance.

9.14 Aesthetic Significance

Elephants stand next to human beings in respect of intelligence and some of their behavioural attributes. They live in a society of which individuals behave with exceptional tolerance to their own tribe and even in times of distress or threat, hold on to their ground. As such, they deserve care in the same way that human society demands. This is why, shooting/ killing this magically majestic elephant with its dazzling personality poses moral responsibility and the same cannot be undertaken lightly. In the art of survival, if only, they had built-in speed and agility, it is said; the earth planet would have been ruled by elephants.

In trying to discover our own biological origin, it is of great significance to see how elephants started from an entirely different beginning of life form, evolved their own social structure, fitted to cope with harsh seasonal conditions, the society which braces powerful enemies and shows many parallels with ours, that are most relevant in the study of our own social basics.

Other important consideration is that the wilderness, where the elephants live, being a very beautiful landscapes and only expanse aiding healthy environment for human beings to survive, it is a sheer vandalism to annihilate anything of beauty and deprive others of the opportunity of enjoying it. Elephants have lived side by side with humans in India and other south-east Asian countries, since the dawn of human history and are an integral part of our mythology, folklore, art and culture. And their disappearance would, therefore, emotionally diminish the cultural environment of peoples of respective country.

Aesthetic and cultural factors are important, but it is my conviction that the sustainable economic development and ecological consideration also will determine the survival of many of the famous elephant reserves.

9.15 Economic View Point

It would, however be quite unrealistic in assessing the elephant's worth in today's world to confine purely to ethical, scientific, aesthetic, psychological or cultural considerations. The economic argument too has its merit.

Elephants are a great tourist attraction and earn large amounts of foreign currency. Their ivory, trophies, pelt and meat are supposed to fetch a high price. Economic value is only one aspect of human ecology and though this approach is no less rational than the other, if adapted alone, it will turn to be an impoverished philosophy which takes no account of the pleasure and interest, which man can derive from elephants. It is like judging the artistic merit of the 'Monalisa' by its current market value.

I believe that peoples of India and elsewhere in the south-east Asian countries will, even though, some sacrifice may be involved, show the non-materialistic side of their nature by protecting their natural heritages, which are richer. In view of the belief, 'best things are hard to come by' and in the final line of defence, "it is every body's concern to boost hopes of survival of elephant – emotionally noble, strikingly powerful, elegantly graceful, highly intelligent and spiritedly social animal".

9.16 Ecological Importance

It follows that if elephants to move on to stay alive and their habitats to survive in the Indian sub-continent including the Asian continent and hold on its own against increasing demands of peoples, they must all become part of a multi-disciplinary form of land use and be subjected to 'wise-use'. In other words, we must justify our desire to conserve elephants along with other wildlife, and make sure that the terms are compatible with the very demanding needs of developing countries.

Gradually, the ecological value of wildlife resources is gaining acceptance in India and this could be the single most important contributing factor, guaranteeing the promotion and implementation of realistic conservation policies. While encouraging eco-tourism hundreds of local people and tribal communities are employed by associated hotels and travel industries, which promise immense potential in preservation of natural heritage. While developing eco-tourism, we must see that part of the revenue collected as gate money, would trickle down to the welfare of the local communities. Then only we can enlist their participation in the conservation programme.

Hard statistics might make good sense, but they will not have universal appeal. The opposite point of view may also be true. To sum up, it is difficult to make, certain people understand that there is a wide spread public revulsion against the concept that the surviving stocks of wildlife must be treated as a 'consumable natural resource'. We have consumed too much of the world's resources already, in fact, more in the last 75 years of independence, than during the rest of man's occupation of this planet! I can understand this point of view, but faced with all the problems associated with the realities of human exponential population growth, have we any alternative but to produce a 'wise-use' conservation policy in contrast to the inflexible 'preservationists'?

While the economic values of wildlife are now widely accepted in a developing nation like India, I believe that the ecological values of wildlife are probably even more important as a justification for conservation. But, as the benefits are very often indirect and as they have no immediate economic values reaching the communities, they receive little publicity and are poorly understood.

What then, is the ecological value of elephant, rather including other wildlife? By wildlife, I am referring to every single living organism in the plant and animal kingdoms, with the exception of the domesticated species and this includes many thousands of species that live outside the boundaries of wildlife reserves. The value of these organisms form their essential and active participation in their immense and complex ecological systems, such as water, carbon dioxide, oxygen and nitrogen cycles, are very much considerable. It is often not acknowledged that man and his domestic plants and animals are utterly dependent for their existence on the efficient functioning of these complex cycles. For example, we depend on them for such vital functions as the preservation of the atmosphere, the disposal of our waste material and the recycling of the nutrients that are used by our food plants. Soils, in general and forest soils, in particular, (one of the many things we take for granted and are so guilty of mismanaging) are the product of the interaction of a great variety of invertebrates, living organisms (micro and macro), beneath our feet with inorganic and organic amalgamation.

Equally important is the role of elephant and other wildlife species in maintaining ecological stability and nature's equilibrium. Erosion and floods are reduced in areas with well developed natural plant communities and there is no doubt that the elimination of these communities has given rise to serious loss of soil, in far too many parts of India. There is every indication that this trend is accelerating as each day passes by.

All too often we tend to overlook these essential inter relationships that exist in forest ecosystems. I quote an example: the important role played by herbivores in seed germination in several forests of India. The seeds are greatly favoured by some herbivores including elephants and when the seeds pass through the animal's digestive system; the gastric juices soften the seeds and encourage rapid and successful germination. Experiments have shown that some dry seed pods fail to germinate, when they are directly sown.

Elephants also play their part in this complexity of interaction. Like the sambar, they are vital in the role of seed dispersal. Indeed, it is common to see the seedlings growing out of elephant dung. The dung consists of great deal of partially digested fibrous vegetable material which forms an ideal germination medium for seeds that escape crushing by mastication and then passes undigested, through the elephant's alimentary canal. In fact, there is evidence that this passage greatly facilitates germination. Elephants distribute nutrients in their dung as well, which are in turn carried below ground by termites and dung beetles, thus enriching the forest soils.

9.17 Need of Political Patronage

The Indian Tiger was rescued from the threshold of extinction, because Indian politicians led by Indira Gandhi, former Prime Minister, recognized that future generations would forever blame us, if the tiger 'burning bright' was snuffed out from the face of the earth. In fact, laws set forth to protect country's biodiversity – flora and fauna and the environment are strong enough, but their non-enforcement and flagrant abuse have placed conservation proclivity at the back seat. Political will to save wildlife and their ecosystems evaporated with the assassinations of Indira Gandhi. Abuse of power and political corruption increased and demoralisation started even among committed field personnel. Political insurgency started to use forests as their haven to consolidate them against the Indian Government. The legal system in the country crippled, resulting in attacks on citizens, even butchering of wildlife. Once the famous protected areas were thrown open to all kinds of nefarious activities keeping all protection staff out of the park boundaries. Insurrectionary also resorted to large scale poaching sandalwood, timber, including tigers, lions and leopards in many parks of the country. While elephants are killed on mass scale for ivory, the lions, tigers and leopards are slaughtered for fur, penis and bones. Even herbivores in the forest became targets for meat of insurrectionary. Guns boomed regularly in the depths of forests of Karnataka and elsewhere in the country. According to a confession made by forest brigand Veerappan, who was killed in a gun battle, had been responsible in killing more than 200 tuskers in the forests of Karnataka and Tamilnadu. Equal numbers of tuskers were killed by other poachers in the disguise of Veerappan. It is feared if hostility continued with the devastating fire power of modern weapons by forest brigands like Naxalites, Bodos, Ultras and Militants and other Extremist outfits, the fate of elephants would be sealed. The tuskers would be exterminated within a few years. These are only tips of the iceberg. Even in the recent past the massive scale of killings of elephants are reported from different parts of the country. Recently, High Court of Tamilnadu ordred the Central Bureu of Investigations to investigate series of elephant killings in the state!

The international community must do everything under their command to stop illegal trade in ivory and other wildlife products, in an effort to support the cause of conservation. India should do its best to help and reward suitably the forest and wildlife personnel, who risk or loose their lives, while attempting to put an end to poaching and smuggling.

Forests and wildlife being state subjects, the Chief Ministers of concerned states are impressed to evince more interest and spare some of his valuable time in conservation programmes, so as to bless with political patronage. We have realised that without the political blessings, there is no effective conservation of nature and natural history

Indian and International green outfits, who air their concern on important environmental issues, are fighting apathy by the authorities concerned. There has been an outcry from many greens against the inactions by the official machinery in the implementation of conservation programmes and lethargic attitude in providing timely relief to victims involved in human-elephant confrontation. Present day print media and electronic media including public are of demanding type. They need quick action and transparency on each issue from the concerned officials of the departments. This is really commendable.

9.18   What Does it Mean to be an Elephant?

I was quick to appreciate the advantages of discussing the relevance and significance of my own observations on elephant's social life with people from different disciplines, who visited Bandipur reserve. I used to sit down all alone on a rocky out crop or underneath a shady tree or near a water body, asking myself some searching questions, about the challenges faced by Indian elephants throughout their range of distribution.

That a tusker falls target to poachers' bullets each day has come to be accepted even by the reluctant wildlife managers under whose charge such elephants are supposed to be safe. This was evidenced from the reports of rampant smuggling out of the country, the huge quantities of ivory, tiger and leopard pelts with their bones. On the borders of Tibet-China, Taipei and Thailand, trading of these products is going on unabated. Even today, we come across poaching of tuskers and tigers in most of the national parks and tiger reserves. But another, equally serious loss that has somehow escaped the public eye is, "we are currently loosing a tusker a day to poachers"!

Meanwhile, I had come to appreciate that in the evolution of complex biodiversity of Bandipur reserve, some dynamic changes had occurred. Ever since, the 'Operation Tiger' was put in place, the strict conservation measures adapted there had evolved the composition, distribution and status of most of the plant and animal species, in that,

1. **The survival of an elephant is a matter of grave concern to all of us in India. These wild creatures amidst wilderness they inhabit, are not only important as a source of wonder and inspiration to all of us, but are an integral part of country's natural history and of our future livelihood and well-being.**

2. **In accepting the trusteeship of our wildlife, we solemnly declare that we will do everything in our power to make sure that our children's grand children will be able to enjoy India's rich and precious natural inheritance.**

3. **The conservation of elephants and the places inhabited by them, calls for specialist knowledge, trained man power with personal involvement. It is time; we stopped looking for external aid from international organisations and developed countries. In the ultimate analysis, it was my conviction, if we look after our elephants and their habitats; they take care of themselves, thus helping to maintain nature's balance.**

9.19 India's Developing Economy Can Now Foot the Bill of Environment Conservation

One may ask, with poverty, hunger, lack of educational and health facilities and land hunger, urban land grabbing, rampant corruption still facing the country, can we expect the developing country, like India to allocate a large share of her budgetary allocation to the 'preservation' of our elephant, "the national heritage animal" in our national parks and wild-life reserves? Yes, it was the situation some two decades ago. Now things are changed for the better. Indian economy has, since taken off and comfortably improved, food position is comfortable, foreign exchange reserves are growing and agricultural sector is doing extremely well in increased food production. Globalization and economic development have set Indian economy prospering. Being the third developing economy in the world, the country is in a position to spend required money on conservation of nature and natural resources. Of course, international bodies may also come forward in aiding such of the ventures, because saving the Asian elephant has become the global issue. Saving the elephant is synonym to biodiversity conservation that is responsible in the reduction of greenhouse gases, principal cause for global warming and climate change.

The ecological problem is fundamentally one of balancing resources against human needs, both in the short term and in the long term considerations. It must thus be related to a proper evaluation of human needs and must be based on resource conservation and judicious use including optimum land use and sustainable development of the habitats? The situation has reached, I am convinced that it is impossible to prevent or stop spatial and temporal progression of our country or is it possible to reclaim the lost land of pachyderms. Can we not, at least, attempt to protect the existing elephant habitats, in addition to creating insulated corridors where essential to interconnect country's fragmented elephant ranges and island like potential forests?

In view of the nuclear arms race in the sub-continent, when Pakistan tested 6 nuclear bombs on May 28th 1998 and on a subsequent date, in reply to India's test firing of 5 nuclear bombs on May 11th and 13th, a serious threat to environmental degradation and poverty that are directly linked, have resurfaced. Experiences in the past have shown that nuclear tests gave no genuine sense of security to the people of the sub-continent and continued tension in the region, likely to jeopardise sustainable environmental development. Apart from finding a lasting political solution of more than eight-decade old issue, like Kashmir and border disputes with China, we need to redefine the country's biodiversity wealth within the ecological frame work. India has entered world's elite club of GSLV launchers and landing on moon. Hence, the nation is in a position to foot its environment conservation bill.

9.20 Conservation Management Approach

A package of "Ten Commandments" to help conserve elephants is as under: i) Integrated land use planning, ii) Rainwater harvesting and moisture conservation, iii) Reappraisal of the present system of Environmental Conservation Education, iv) Eco-development programme (the Green Heart), v) Controlled eco-tourism, vi) Research and In-house training, Fighting poaching, viii) Fighting encroachments and wild fires, ix) Interconnecting of Elephant Reserves by Corridors, x) International support. The above dynamics are highlighted in brief here under:

9.20.1 Integrated Land Use Planning

A completely new approach to land use planning is paramount, for, the magnitude of the problem requires immediate attention in the whole of India. As just an example, there is an urgent need to slow down the accelerating downward spiral of land degradation associated with the unplanned settlement of people on lands that are totally unsuited even to primitive subsistence agriculture. All too often, these people live next to national parks and wildlife reserves and once their land has been degraded to the point of no return, they inevitably turn their attention to eco-sensitive areas adjoining to wildlife sanctuaries and start demanding to have *patta* for this extra piece of fertile land. In short, unplanned subsistence agriculture is not a sustainable development, as we project and is at best, as short term expediency.

Every state government in India aims at high food production target, as its priority sustenance and accordingly, land with high agricultural potential will have to be used. Land with low agricultural potential can then be assessed for other possible uses such as for raising tree cover, livestock grazing, constituting wilderness areas or a host of multiple land use purposes. Faced with these problems, India requires a positive rural land use strategy which recognises the prime importance of food production, but at the same time safeguards soil fertility, habitat improvement and wildlife protection.

Purist might be alarmed by these concepts, for, some existing wildlife sanctuaries would almost certainly face de-proclamation due to the prevailing conditions there. Such a proposal is accepted, provided double the extent of the above area, as add on sanctuaries are created or expanded elsewhere on the basis of the objectives of land capability classification.

9.20.2   Rainwater Harvesting and Moisture Conservation

"Rain is grace; rain is the sky condescending to the earth; without rain, there would be no life", said American writer, John Updike. Rainwater harvesting enriches ground water that helps ecosystems to remain greener. Rainwater harvesting also helps prevent run off and soil erosion, leading to increase in the level of water table. Elephants and other herbivores can feed on green pastures over a longer period of the season and maintain good health. Creation of more water bodies, well distributed over an ecosystem help elephants and other wildlife uniformly distributed, thus preventing an overuse of a particular areas of the reserve.

9.20.3   Reappraisal of the present System of Environment Conservation Education

"Catch them young and teach them the values of conservation of nature and natural history", should be our motto. Educating school children in the neighbourhoods of the reserves on the values and their importance is an effective strategy for getting broad-based and long-term support from local communities in conservation programmes. School children and teachers are brought to reserves to provide them in *situ* experience and understanding the role of protected areas for human survival. Additionally so, the conservation message be carried to the classrooms, so as to provoke the concept of "Green heart".

Involving children in these programmes is important for two reasons: firstly, many children in the remote rural areas do not attend school, so an alternative environment education programme, outside the class room is necessary to reach them; secondly, children's concerns and activities always evoke greater participation on the part of teachers, parents and gradually local leaders. Children and teachers can also be trained as communicators and made to talk to the rural folk in their villages and at organised local gatherings. It is also believed that law of the land becomes stronger when children start caring for nature and environment around them. Environmental education must also invade every class room through every textbook. Children are the powerful force behind the conservation programmes. It is they, who can put pressure on Governments to implemrnt "Green Agenda".

"Rural women are heart and soul of the country", it is said. Educating them through environment awareness programmes would be more effective in organic farming and livestock management. They, in turn, teach their children and motivate their men folk. Rural youths and tribal communities also should form an important segment of human society for being considered in creating an awareness in the conservation of nature.

9.20.4   Eco-Development – Creating Lungspace and Green Hearts

The eco-development strategy aims at conserving the biodiversity by the participation of local people, living around the protected areas. Eco-development, programme has two main thrusts: (a) sustainable development of the reserve by involvement of local people (b) in doing so, it seeks to improve capacity building of the local communities, who in turn participate in the conservation efforts.

Eco-development is the programme for the people and of the people living around the reserves. Local people are provided with certain incentives thereby they can improve their living conditions, through organic farming and rain water harvesting. They are also assisted to generate alternatives in their backyards to prevent wanton destruction of natural resources in the neighbouring forests. Governments with the assistance of international, national or local Greens provide the above incentives and alternatives with the principal objective of weaning local communities away from dependency on forest resources. Conceptual approach of this exercise is that satisfied communities rely least on forest resources and extend support in the conservation efforts. Eco-development also addresses the issues concerning welfare of local people and their improved behavioural attributes and finally, integrates their concerns into management planning.

Good public relations, followed by people's movements are the cornerstone of park management policy. It becomes hard to convince villagers on the importance of wild life conservation, when they suffer depredation from those marauders. Every year we see some sensational and unpublished incidents, such as, some agriculturists crushed to death by a herd of elephants, while asleep in their threshing yard; a bachelor group of elephants rampaged the suburbs of Bengaluru; a farm labour was gored by a tusker; a woman was mauled by leopard on the village road and so on. It becomes a Herculean task for the park officials to calm down their feelings and to console them when a bread earner of the family gets killed, followed by untold miseries they undergo. It becomes the responsibility of the government to compensate the victim's family members, while the protective squads to drive away the offending animals from the scene.

Making peace between farmers and elephants/tigers is challenging. Creating an awareness through environment education and eco-development approach are, by far, the most important and effective tools in the conservation efforts. In other words, the objectives of conservation and social reforms are the two sides of the same coin.

Experiences world over have shown, where human needs are given due attention, conservation efforts have been successful. Elsewhere in the country, attempts of conservation without considering even primary needs of local people have often failed.

People living around the reserve forests have been enjoying benefits for a long time. If we are to prevent their entry in the name of conservation of biodiversity, we must provide them with alternatives to meet their daily requirements, should be made available to them next door, either in their backyards, in their fields, village common lands or waste lands, so that their dependency on neighbouring forests, is gradually minimised.

The daily needs, such as health care, drinking water, social welfare and child care, primary education are their fundamental rights, which should be addressed by the government under 'eco-development' programme. This programme also envisages supply of alternate energy sources, like *gober*-gas plant, bio-gas plants, solar heaters and solar cookers, improved *chulah* and even cheap electricity or LPG so that, pressure for fuel wood from forests is reduced. Stall-feeding of their cattle by switching over to improved breeds of cows and buffaloes, combined with poultry, sericulture, fish-culture, sheep breeding and other cottage industries, be encouraged involving rural banking network. Encouraging use of alternate raw material, like agricultural waste in place of wood also helps save our forests. The above programmes under generate tremendous employment potential and create conditions for self-reliance. Rural communities, so motivated serve as partners in the development of nature and natural resources. While implementing any of the conservation programmes, sustainable development and short term exploitation should be the policy of eco-development.

9.20.5 Controlled Practice of Eco-Tourism

India's beaches, bushes and beasts are the natural treasure. India can offer these treasure-troves to tourists apart from its great castles, palaces, historic monuments, art and culture. The Tourism Policy of India is to ensure the integrated development of infrastructure and to focus on 'cultural and eco-tourism' in a big way. The tourism industry has an immense scope in providing employment and earning valuable foreign exchange, besides facilitating sustainable development of backward and rural areas. It is the third largest foreign exchange earner for the country, fetching more than

`100,000 million (US$3000 million). It also provides direct employment for some nine to ten million people accounting for about 2.4 % of the total labour force in the country.

National parks and wildlife reserves are the paradise of biodiversity, with rich forests and wildlife. The declared policy of eco-tourism is, essentially, to have conservation of biodiversity at the prime place and the wildlife tourism, only in the status of an incidental benefit, keeping in mind to pass on certain benefits to local communities.

It is, however, important for visitors to the parks to note, the reserves should be respected and maintained as biodiversity friendly, rather than tourist friendly, littered with plastics, food wastes and liquor cans and bottles.

9.20.6   Research and In-house Training

In order to achieve the objectives of biodiversity conservation and management, a better understanding of the relevant issues is necessary. Since attempts of research by the park authorities in the past have often been unsuccessful, wisdom of authorities should prevail on entrusting the responsibility to Universities, Educational Institutions and Research Organisations. National research institutions have national level mandates and have to shift their research focus topically and geographically when required. It is, therefore, inevitable that much of the research must be carried out in coordination with the Forest/Wildlife Departments of respective states. This would help build up research interest and support informal groups of scientists who are working in a particular reserve. Veterinary care against wildlife diseases, interaction between vegetation and ungulates, prey-predator relation, habitat management, impact of eco-tourism, participative challenges of local communities, are few of the general topics that need considered attention under the programme of applied research.

Wildlife management is a multifaceted and specialised science, comprising number of pure sciences, such as botany, zoology, sociology, biology including forestry. Wildlife management being dynamic, apart from basic training, it is essential for personnel to keep abreast with latest scientific and technological developments. So periodical in-house training for working personnel of different rungs would help manage wildlife better.

9.20.7 Fight Poaching on Warfooting

Poachers know many dubious hunting methods for elephant ivory and its big meat. Ivory poaching as in India and other Asian countries is restricted to male elephants only, as the females do not carry tusks. Unlike in African countries, this selective poaching of males may not affect population growth. But it shall certainly have an impact on population dynamics. Southern India, for example, had the highest rate of ivory poaching during 1980s, 1990s and subsequent decades, such as 2000 2010 and even 2020s. Consequently, the legislation passed by the Indian Parliament in favour of complete ban on trade in ivory of Asian elephants is certainly a ray of hope of their survival. The speed, with which the international community moved in imposing a total ban on the trade of ivory, has choked the international traders, but illegal domestic trade goes on unabated. The survival of the Asian elephants also depends on the extent of safe habitats they can secure. The rich cultural association between the elephants and humans can appeal powerfully, in favour of its conservation. This intelligent gentle giant and flagship animal of the Indian jungles, deserves to be respected by the citizens of the world, more so, by ivory traders and poachers. The Indian elephant also has the potential of serving as keystone species of the jungle and that it entails global efforts to save it.

9.20.8 Fighting Against Encroachments & Wild Fires

The Supreme Court's directive to the Government of Karnataka issued on May 5, 1998, to take stern action against those who have encroached the Reserve Forests in Western Ghats, has come as a bang in he history of the country. The concern and anxiety of the apex court of the country could be gauged by the fact that it had warned the Government that it would be forced to appoint a receiver for the entire coffee belt of Chikmaglur

District of Karnataka, if it failed to evict the encroachers. Interestingly, courts have become effective weapons of defence (judicial activism) for those seeking to protect India's environmental health. The judges remarked with displeasure, for every right thinking Indian, while accusing, "what can you expect of a government, which has given permission to 3000 saw mills and says that it has banned the felling of trees? And politicians are found to abuse forest land by encroaching them at, will".

In a landmark judgement on Tathkola forest encroachments of Chikmaglur, the apex court of the country, on 30th October, 2002, ordered a recovery of fine of Rs.500,000 from each of the 148 offenders, if they failed to vacate within 3 months. It has become all the more important for green activists and wild-lifers to bury their hatchets and create a solid bridge as defenders (Green warriors) of the natural heritage of the country. Such unlawful activities will continue to repeat all over again if authorities concerned fail to take timely action against the offenders. Of late, increasingly large scale encroachments are reportedly taking place around the borders of Bandipur reserve and elsewhere in the country. This is again a wrong signal coming in the way of conservation efforts. The effective and possible solution to on going human-biodiversity confrontation is to concentrate in educating the rural mass around the reserve and see that economic benefits accrued from eco-tourism are shared for their welfare.

9.20.9   International Support

Ruthless destructions of elephant habitats are the serious challenges, the country at large, is facing today. Anti-biodiversity communities spread over the country are taking heavy toll of our forest resources. Strict enforcement of law of the land, banning the trade in ivory and ivory products was expected to bring positive results. But, poaching of male elephants for ivory is still rampant, apart from killing crop raiders by poisoning, shooting and electrocution. The need of the hour is to protect breeding bulls from poachers and trigger happy and anti-elephant people. Forest Departments of various states have to come out with actual number of cases of poaching for ivory, so as to make out a strong case for international support in fighting biological terrorism.

In an earnest effort to stop illegal killing of elephants for ivory, Kenya had banned all big game hunting and trading/export of wild animal products. But black marketers were still thriving with penalties too small and the rewards too great. Former President, Daniel Arap Moi of Kenya had shown his government's commitment to the preservation of elephants by setting fire to nearly 12 tonnes (2,000 nos) ivory worth $ 100,000 millions on 18ᵗʰ July 1989. Moi's dramatic action was part of a sustained campaign by conservationists, which caught the hearts of many across the world, focussing on the savage decimation of elephants hunted out for their valuable tusks. In eight brief years, from 1981-1989 the elephant population in Africa had dwindled by half and given the trend then, it was estimated that the elephant could be extinct within just 20 years.

This paved way for other nations to follow suit in initiating environmentally sound policy decisions.

World concern reached a feverish pitch. Britain offered Kenya the services of SAS, its highly advanced anti-terrorist elite regiment to fight poachers. Steinway, the world famous piano manufacturer, received hate mail and abusive telephone calls accusing them of elephant murderer because they used ivory to make keyboards. Western conservationists gave the clarion call, "Only elephants should wear ivory". The campaign culminated in a worldwide ban on trade in ivory in October 1989 and the elephant was declared safe.

In the meantime, significant shifts in environmental politics and philosophies surfaced. During June 1997 the Convention on International Trade in Endangered Species (CITES), held in Zimbabwe decided through secret ballot to allow resumption of strictly controlled trade in elephant ivory. This meant, opening of a flood-gates for indiscriminate killing of tuskers in Indian jungles. Behind the demands for secret balloting lied accusations that some western environmental groups and governments used 'aid' as a weapon to force poorer countries to vote the way they wanted them to.

Interestingly, Kenya which fought and pushed for the ban then seemed to be having second thought, as it faced a problem of elephant over-breeding. Kenya's Warden in Chief, who was beating the loudest trumpet in favour of the ivory ban, started saying, "Kenya could never support 65,000 elephants, the population of which was 15 years ago and 20,000 elephants in other places is too much. With the elephant in danger of becoming a massive pest for the local population, Kenya started considering the ludicrous birth control by using contraceptive loops to the prosaic culling the elephants.

9.21 American Legislation Aiding Elephant Conservation

Alarmed at the fast dwindling number of Asian elephants, the US House of Representatives passed a bill in the year 1995 for setting up a mega fund to save the Asian elephants – the endangered species. The bill also approved US$ 5 million a year for the next five years, ending with 1999-2000. This urgent measure warranted the US Government, since there remained only 40,000 elephants in 13 South-east Asian countries, as against 400,000 elephants in African countries. Elephant having been reckoned as the 'keystone species' plays a critical role in the protection and regeneration of the biodiversity in an ecosystem, where it inhabits. Biodiversity conservation, in turn serves as an antidote to global warming and climate change, which is the frontrunner in recent times. The world scientific community, as a whole is seized with the resolving problems of climate crisis. The elephant being an important component of the biodiversity, has since, attained a global significance. It became, therefore, obligatory to the US Government – the leading economy of the world to assist in the conservation efforts of highly endangered Asian elephants.

It is true, world's leaders have a duty to seek solutions to these burning issues. What is imperative is that they do not choose ways, which can only exacerbate existing problems or create new ones. When capital resources such as climate change leading to global warming, depletion of forests and wildlife, pollution of fertile lands, rivers, oceans, scarcity of clean drinking water and over-exploitation or senseless destruction of other natural resources, such as, coal, iron ore, etc., it calls for world leaders to step in and take unanimous decisions, preceded by dialogues.

It is appreciable of the US Government to continue its gesture at an interval of every five years, but it is not known how and where the money is spent by which organisations? I have not seen any significant contributory factors showing visible benefits in elephant conservation! Such events needed vigilant watch....?

9.22   Abridged Census Data to Publicity Media

An incidental consequence of the human invasion and occupation of elephant country is the news either based on official reports or rumours, published from time to time in popular print media to the effect that there is an alarming increase in the number of elephants and that this has been noticed by forest and wildlife officials, who during their census operation had seen huge tuskers and increasing calves in the herds, which were formerly not seen. Naturally, more elephants are seen by field staff and officials with their penetration into the depth of a forest. Presumably, these were also seen during earlier counting. But the crux of the issue is of the news published through media that there is an increase in the population of elephants, in particular, male to female ratio. The sudden appearance of the news about the ratios of males (tuskers) to females and calves to mothers alert the anti-elephant communities, like poachers and ivory traders. The park authorities concerned should take necessary precautions not to announce before the media reporters, the actual numbers or even male to female or calves to mother ratios. Instead, just indicate the increase or decrease, in terms of density: say X – numbers of animals per sq km and that the growth healthy/poor. The actual data is maintained in the registers for official use only. The actual data could, however be freely used for research and documentation. Thus, release of abridged data of elephants/

tigers may help to mitigate poaching activities. This should be taken as a word of caution by the authorities concerned.

9.23 Elephant – the Super Conservationist of the Indian Jungles

The living elephant that represents India's glorious past and the promise of embodiment of the "Super Conservationist" of the earth planet is also reckoned as the "National Heritage Animal", so as to insure its future, for the benefit of coming generations. Elephant tribes have withstood the tests of time in Asian jungles. They have passed through ice-age, stone-age, iron-age, apart from climate change due to global warming, continental drifts, upheaval of earth's surface, natural disasters, like floods, earthquakes and tsunami in Sri Lanka and so on. All wildlife and birds, in particular Elephants have inbult system in them of forewarning against upcoming natural disasters. Social structure, coordinated group defence among elephant clans have been the key of their survival, for hundreds of thousands of years against a multitude of adversaries and enemies. Man, the master predator, arrogantly attempted to rewrite 'law of the jungle', that is as old as the sky, to suite his greed, while adversaries like tigers learnt to live amicably sharing the same niche. Man with gun and plough seemed to have determined to upset the balance of nature. But, with all its better level of intelligence, the elephant is under the mercy of humans – the notorious poachers and disgruntled farmers. Today, elephant problem is more alive than ever before; as a matter of fact, it is on the increase as modern human demands are exploding.

The range of elephants' distribution is now confined to islands like fragmented habitats, lapped by seas of humanity. Not only are they prevented from wandering far and wide, but their numbers have swelled by the invasion of countless refugees fleeing from neighbouring areas and due to mounting human persecution. This is likely to cause wholesale destruction of woodland habitats in future. In that case, should there be a change in the perceptions of role in the national parks system? And can we safely hand over these habitats along with elephants, the 'super conservationist' of the world, to the future generations? There is no such a thing, as large coffee and small beer. As a final line of defence, we as nation's citizens with overwhelming passion for nature must conserve our forests, which are the heart and the soul of healthy environment. We must make firm commitment in tackling the problems to ensure survival of elephant, an animal that can play a big part globally. Because elephants are now protected as the national heritage animal, may well see a century, even next millennium. Let us be optimistic, the vanishing giant gets a fair chance of survival under ecologically sustainable development.

9.24 Elephant – the National Heritage Animal

The Indian elephant is since, declared as the "National Heritage Animal" in a bid to give its share of conservation, the same momentum of the national pride, "save the tiger" campaign evokes. This must be accompanied by a "substantial enhancement in the budgetary outlay". This should pave way for increasing the number of elephant reserves in the country; monitoring elephant populations; curbing poaching and mitigating human-elephant conflicts and protecting elephant corridors by regulating livestock grazing, relocating tribal populations and last but not the least the sustainable development. Apart from 30,000 or so wild ones in the country, nearly 3500 captive elephants must also be protected.

Elephant, the keystone species of the Indian jungles needs more freedom to roam about within its home range. There are millions of people in India, who love elephant as the gift of nature, bringing good rains and fortune; if we all speak in one voice, "Save The Elephant", I'm sure it will be heard by the concerned authorities to help conserve the elephant for posterity. Yes, together we can do it!

"Long live elephant; long live its tribe!!"